The Mystery of Death
A Catholic Perspective

Janie Gustafson, Ph.D.

BROWN-ROA

A Division of Wm. C. Brown Communications, Inc.
Dubuque, Iowa

Book Team

Publisher
Ernest T. Nedder

Managing Editor
Mary Jo Graham

Project Coordinator
Phil Niles

Art Direction and Design
Cathy Frantz

Production Services Manager
Marilyn Rothenberger

Marketing Manager
Ginny Schumacher

Acknowledgments are on page 231.

ISBN 0-697-17757-2

10   9   8   7   6   5   4   3   2   1

Contents

Dedication

In loving memory of my grandparents,
Lloyd and Esther Schull,
who taught me the secret of being happy.

Preface

In our modern-day society, it is almost impossible to go an entire day without hearing about or experiencing death—violent, sudden, accidental, or otherwise. Sometimes death strikes in foreign lands; sometimes it occurs in our own neighborhoods and homes. Consider, for example, the eighteen American soldiers who died in Mogadishu, Somalia, as a result of a battle there in October 1993. Or the thirty-four passengers who were killed when a US Air Boeing 737 collided in early 1991 with a Sky West commuter plane in Los Angeles. Or the seven astronauts who died when the space shuttle *Challenger* exploded shortly after launch. Or the growing numbers of young people who die each year from gunshot wounds or gang-related violence. Death, in one way or another, affects everyone nearly every day.

The topic of death arouses as many diverse reactions as there are individual people. Some people seek to deny death as a fact of life; others fear it or those who are dead. Some people defy death by engaging in high-risk activities. Some who philosophically believe that death means personal extinction advocate living life to the full. Others seek all possible means to prolong their lives indefinitely. Christians, on the other hand, look at death with the eyes of religious faith. To those of us who believe in the Paschal Mystery— Jesus' passing from death to life—death is the beginning of a new kind of living, a glorified eternal existence.

This book examines the many facets of death and death as the passage to new life. When you begin to look at the topic of death, it soon becomes clear that death reaches into all aspects of life: philosophical, historical, cultural, psychological, social, financial/ legal, moral, and religious. This book examines these aspects of death from a specifically Catholic perspective. This perspective takes into account both meanings of the word *catholic*. First, it considers the universal dimension of each aspect of death. And second, it considers the specific viewpoint of the Catholic Church.

A basic premise of this book is the Christian belief that death is the beginning of the fullness of new life with the resurrected Christ. Each chapter reflects this faith stance. Thus within the context of the resurrection, you will learn about the stages of dying, grief reactions, death customs, financial considerations, and moral issues related to dying. You will also see how this belief has affected Catholic teaching and practice: for example, the works of mercy, devotion to the saints, the saying of certain prayers, the feast days of All Saints and All Souls, the Sacraments of Baptism,

Reconciliation, and Anointing of the Sick, the celebration of the Easter Triduum, and the *Order of Christian Funerals.*

The topic of death can seem overwhelming; yet I believe that examining it is essential to a life that is well lived. What you do with this book will be up to you. Hopefully, this brief look at a variety of death-related topics will spur you to continued independent exploration and personal reflection. I pray that as you pause for introspection throughout these pages, you may come to understand more fully the meaning of Jesus' words, "Amen, amen, I say to you, whoever hears my word and believes in the one who sent me has eternal life and will not come to condemnation, but has passed from death to life" (John 5:24).

Janie Gustafson

Memorial Day

Part One: Philosophical Aspects

There is an appointed time for everything, . . .
A time to be born, and a time to die.
　　　　　　　　　—Ecclesiastes 3:1–2

1 The Denial of Death

A fact of life

Whenever people talk about the "facts of life," they usually mean sexual intercourse and procreation. As exciting and interesting as these facts may be, some adults still have a tough time discussing them with one another or with their children. And with good reason. It's difficult to be objective about something so highly personal, so charged with emotions, and so laden with values. It's more comfortable to pretend that sex doesn't exist. And it's certainly easier to let someone else do all the teaching.

In this respect, sex and death are closely related. Death is also a fact of life, even more than sex is. After all, it's possible to get through life without having sexual intercourse, but no one can get through life without dying. And yet many people in today's society refuse to talk or think about death. They think that death is something far removed from them and their children—something that will happen only after they grow old. Often it takes a tragedy such as the death of a child or the death of a loved one to make them face the real fact of life—death—and, in so doing, to discover that death and faith are connected.

This is what happened to me. I am a cradle Catholic who attended Catholic schools through college, and later went on to complete a Ph.D. in theology. At one point in my life, I even entered a convent. For most of my adult life, I have worked as an editor and writer of religion books for Catholic elementary and secondary schools. There was no doubt in anyone's mind—including my own—that the Catholic faith ran strong in me. Truly, I thought I was a believer.

But then in 1990, the grandparents who had helped raise me both died. Their deaths hit me hard. I found myself asking painful questions about the meaning of life, as well as taking a new look at my Catholic faith. I needed to get beyond the catechism formulas to the real "meat" behind the Church's teachings on death and eternal life. Like Jacob who wrestled with an angel at Peniel, I too needed to grapple one-on-one with the mystery of death. I had to know, not just WHAT the Church said about this topic, but WHY it said it and WHY I should choose to believe it.

What I discovered in my struggle has become the basis for this book. I now see that talking about death is morbid only if it has no other point. This book is not intended to be morbid. Rather, it is intended to portray death as an important part of life and as an essential starting point for mature faith. Whether you are a priest, religious, or layperson, whether you are a cradle Catholic, a returning Catholic, or someone preparing for baptism in the Catholic Church, this book can help you make sense out of the mystery of death and many related doctrines taught by the Church. This book will provide you with information that can help you approach death realistically when it happens in your own family and relationships. More important, it can provide you with a faith vision that will be your source of strength in times of sorrow. While this book will present the specific views of the Catholic Church regarding death and the afterlife, it will also take a broader, more universal, approach (another meaning of the word *catholic*).

Before proceeding, take time to reflect on your present attitudes toward and experiences with death. You may even want to start a journal. In this journal, write any thoughts, questions, and prayers that may occur to you while you are reading. In addition, write your answers to the questions at the end of each chapter.

Some basic questions

People in every century have asked questions regarding death. Among the more basic ones are these: "What is death? How do we know when someone is truly dead?" "Why do people die?" and "What does death teach us?" In beginning our study of death, let's take a closer look at each of these questions.

What is death?

How do we know when someone is truly dead?

Until recently, it was difficult to tell if a person was dead or in a coma or shock. The techniques used to determine whether a person was dead were quite primitive. In ancient Rome, for example, the family called the person's name three times to "make sure" he or she was really dead. The Jews at the time of Jesus laid the "dead" person in an open sepulcher for three days. If there were no signs of life during that time, the body was buried. In the early part of the twentieth century, people held a mirror to the person's lips. If no beads of moisture formed on the mirror, the person was pronounced dead.

Only recently, with the advances of medical science, do we have a more accurate understanding of what death is. Today we do not consider someone dead until (1) total brain function, (2) spontaneous function of the respiratory system, and (3) spontaneous function of the circulatory system cease permanently.

After a person dies, the body undergoes certain changes. These changes, used by doctors and coroners to determine the time of death, include the following:

- Cooling (*algor mortis*). The temperature of the body drops. The amount of cooling depends upon environmental temperature, type of clothing, and amount of body fat.
- Rigidity (*rigor mortis*). Five to ten hours after death, the muscles usually stiffen. Jaw muscles often stiffen first. The muscles again relax after three or four days.
- Blood clotting. The blood clots shortly after death; sometimes clotting occurs before the heart stops.[1]
- Staining (*livor mortis*). Gravity draws unclotted blood downward. This may result in reddish-blue discoloration on portions of the body.
- Cell breakdown. This occurs after death due to a lack of blood supply.
- Putrefaction. After death, decomposing bacteria and fungi start to work, producing gases, greenish discoloration of the tissues, and a foul smell.[2]

These signs, along with machines that measure brain waves and heartbeat, rule out the possibility of mistaken death pronouncements today.

Why do people die?

In ancient times, people in many different cultures told stories to explain why people die. Many of these myths connected the origin of death with snakes, which were thought to live forever since they could shed their skins. Here are two tales, one from Melanesia and the other from Vietnam, that "explain" why people die.

Melanesian tale: In the beginning, people lived forever. They were like snakes; when they got older, they shed their skins and became young again. One day, an old woman went down to the stream to peel off her wrinkled skin. When she returned, looking

---

1. The Cathedral of Naples has two vials of blood from St. Januarius, who was beheaded in 304. Many times each year, especially around September 29 (the anniversary of the saint's death), the blood liquefies. This "defiance" of the signs of death may have been explained by Italian chemists who recently created a dark brown gel that looks like blood and turns to liquid when disturbed.

2. In medieval times, a pleasant smell emitting from a dead body was considered evidence of sanctity. For nine months after the death of St. Teresa of Avila, a fragrant perfume arose from her grave. This contributed to the term "odor of sanctity."

young and beautiful, her young daughter no longer recognized her and began to cry. No matter what the woman did, her daughter would not let her come near. So the woman went back to the stream and put on her old skin. The daughter recognized her mother immediately and went to her. Ever since then, people have not had the ability to shed their skins and to live forever.

Vietnamese tale: *God hated snakes and loved people. God wanted snakes to die and people to live forever. So God sent a messenger to earth to explain these wishes. When the snakes heard the message, they threatened to bite the messenger if he did not change the message. Fearing for his own life, the messenger said, "When snakes are old, they will shed their skins and live; when humans grow old, they will die." And that is how death entered the world.*

What does death teach us?

Because death is a fact of life, it can teach us some important lessons about life and what it means truly to be alive.

First, death can motivate us to make sense out of life and the meaning of being human. We are not immortal; we are not gods. And yet we are the highest form of life on this planet. As the psalmist writes: "You have made him little less than the angels, / and crowned him with glory and honor" (Psalm 8:6). Death forces us to reflect on our identity and destiny. Death challenges us to approach life with faith and trust that God's wisdom is greater than our own. Because death surrounds us, the prophet Jeremiah states,

> *Let not the sage boast of wisdom,*
> *nor the valiant of valour,*
> *nor the wealthy of riches!*
> *But let anyone who wants to boast, boast of this:*
> *of understanding and knowing me.*
> *—Jeremiah 9:22–23*

God can make sense out of death; God can give true and lasting meaning to our lives.

Second, the inevitability of death can lead us to prepare wisely for death. People naturally prepare for important events in their lives—a vacation, the birth of a child, a wedding, a college entrance exam. And yet many people do not prepare for death. In many instances, we are stunned and unprepared when death strikes. We react with disbelief and shock.

Maybe we are afraid that if we prepare for death, death will actually come. We think that by not preparing, we can somehow fend off death or keep it at a distance. As Jesus himself tells us, such thinking is not logical.

Be sure of this: if the master of the house had known the hour when the thief was coming, he would not have let his house be broken into. You also must be prepared, for at an hour you do not expect, the Son of Man will come.

—*Luke 12:39–40*

Third, death can provide us with insights about dealing with the little deaths that happen all through life—experiences of loss, failure, and rejection. These types of death are familiar to everyone. No one in our society could live to be an adult without some experience of loss: moving to a new town, changing jobs, illness, rejection, the divorce of parents, broken relationships, failing, having something stolen or broken, separation from friends, low self-esteem, or the death of a pet. The finality of death can help us to keep these smaller deaths in perspective. The reality of death can help us survive these losses with hope and courage.

Lastly, death can teach us the importance of living fully. Just ask anyone who has had a close brush with death. He or she will tell you that life is short; that each moment should be cherished. There is no better time than the present to explore, search for knowledge, and love others. Indeed, we may not have a tomorrow in which to do these things.

Coming to grips with death can itself be a source of spiritual insight and creativity. As the poet Kahlil Gibran writes,

If you would indeed behold the spirit of death, open your heart wide unto the body of life.

For life and death are one, even as the river and the sea are one. . . .

Only when you drink from the river of silence shall you indeed sing.

And when you have reached the mountaintop, then shall you begin to climb.

And when the earth shall claim your limbs, then shall you truly dance.[3]

Many poems, plays, novels, paintings, statues, and musical compositions deal with the theme of death. Just as death has inspired their creation, so they continue to inspire us to "have life and have it more abundantly" (John 10:10).

Why we deny death

Though we have many questions about death, we tend to shy away from it. In fact, most people tend to talk around death, rather than talk about it straight on. We speak gingerly about the "deceased," the "decedent," or our "dearly departed," rather than the dead person. We use phrases such as "passed away" or "expired" instead of saying that someone died. These euphemisms are meant to soften the blow of death. In reality, they contribute to an elaborate conspiracy of silence. Death makes us uncomfortable because we have no control over it, so we continually strive to deny its reality.

Possibly the greatest example of the denial of death in our modern society is the cryonics movement. Some people actually believe that if their bodies (or heads, in some cases) are frozen immediately after death, they will be kept in a state of suspended animation indefinitely. These people hope that sometime in the future, when science has discovered a cure for whatever disease they died of, their bodies will be revived and the disease cured. Theoretically, a person kept alive by these means could live forever.

There are many reasons we as North Americans tend to deny death. Here are just a few of them:

1. Since the Civil War, North Americans have not had firsthand experience of wide-scale death. No war has been fought on our home soil. This is true not only for the United States, but also for Canada and Mexico. The news media may run stories on war casualties and "the human cost" of war, but these statistics are quickly hushed up after victory.[4] Politicians, generally, do not want to mention death because it is a sign of failure.

2. In former times, executions of criminals were public events. In the Wild West, trees or constructed gallows were used to hang outlaws as many looked on. Today public executions have been banned. Capital punishment is a theoretical subject to debate, not something for general audiences.

3. Medicine and better nutrition have prolonged life. Fewer women die in childbirth; fewer children die in infancy. In 1789 New England, a woman could expect to live 36.5 years; a man's life expectancy was 34.5 years. In 1900, the average life

---

4. Two hundred and twelve United States men and women lost their lives in the 1991 Persian Gulf War against Iraq. If the same number of people had died in an airplane crash, the event would have been treated as a major tragedy. Instead, the news media reported the deaths as only "relatively few."

life expectancy in the United States was still only 47.3 years. By 1925, the average had risen to 59 years. It was not until 1965 that Americans could expect to live more than 70 years.

In 1991, the average life span of whites in the United States was 75.2 years; the average life span of blacks was 69.2 years. White males could expect to live 72.7 years; white females could expect to live 79.6 years. Black males, on the other hand, had an average life expectancy of 64.9 years; African-American females could expect to live 73.5 years.

4. Death has been removed from mainstream living. New church buildings usually do not have their own adjacent cemeteries. People are not buried in the floor of the church, as in traditional European churches. In the past, people died at home. Now they die in hospitals or nursing homes. Death is treated as a sickness, rather than as a normal part of life.

Removing death from mainstream living also affects the way our society treats the elderly. Instead of living with their children and grandchildren, elderly people are sent to live in leisure villages, retirement homes, nursing homes, and convalescent homes. Entire communities in Florida and Arizona have been developed solely for those who are elderly and retired. Only recently have gerontology and thanatology become recognized fields of science.

5. Our society tends to glorify youth. Youth is big business. Just think of the millions of dollars people spend each year on cosmetics, hair dye, anti-wrinkle creams, health food, plastic surgery, and exercise equipment. Despite laws to the contrary, businesses still discriminate against people who are "too old." Such discrimination was seen in the 1980s when certain female news broadcasters were fired for being "over the hill." Age discrimination also surfaced when Ronald Reagan first ran for president in 1980 at age 69. His opponents argued that he was "too old" for the job.

The fear of death

There are many fears associated with death. First, we fear the loss of life itself. We don't want to be separated from loved ones; we have so much more we want to accomplish. Second, we fear the process of dying. We are afraid of losing control over our lives and bodily functions. We shy away from pain and indignity; we don't want to be a burden to others. Third, we fear death itself. Maybe we are afraid of the unknown or personal annihilation; maybe we are afraid of eternal punishment. Fourth, we fear those who are dead. Just think of the movies you have seen or the books you have read about ghosts, goblins, zombies, and evil spirits.

Fear of death cuts across every age and culture. Primitive peoples believed that dead spirits envied the living and would thus bring sickness, sterility, weakness, and bodily harm to them. Most feared were the ghosts of powerful men who died in their prime, women who died in childbirth, and those who committed suicide or died by means of violence.

The ancient Mesopotamians believed that some souls (those who had drowned, those whose bodies remained unburied, and those who had no one to carry out the prescribed funeral duties) never found rest in the abode of the dead. These restless souls roamed the earth, bringing sickness, misfortune, and other ills. Because people feared these souls, they tried to placate the spirits through magic, conjuration, and necromancy. In Babylon, a special class of priests was in charge of spiritualism.[5]

Anglo-Saxons used to remove a tile or cut a hole in the roof to "let out" the spirit after someone died. They so feared the dead that they cut off the feet of corpses to prevent them from walking back home. They also drove stakes through the bodies of people who had committed suicide, in order to "keep them down." Until recently, people in Europe turned the mirrors toward the wall when someone died in the home so the mirrors wouldn't catch the dead soul and keep it present.

People in other cultures were also worried about getting the spirit out of the house for good. In Russia, people were afraid to take a corpse out through the regular door. Instead, they took the dead out through a window and then hurriedly shut the panes. In old Italy and Denmark, people built special doors for the dead. In Thailand, pallbearers rushed the dead person around the house three times in order to make the spirit dizzy and thus to disorient it. Koreans put blinders on corpses so they couldn't find the way back from the cemetery.

---

5. Jewish law forbade Necromancy (cf. Leviticus 19:31; Deuteronomy 18:11). Nevertheless, the Israelites seem to have practiced it (cf. Leviticus 20:6, 27; 1 Samuel 28:3, 7, 9; 4 Kings 21:6; 23:24; Isaiah 8:19; 29:4). Other Old Testament practices give evidence of fear of the dead: Rending garments, wearing sackcloth, imposing ashes, pulling out one's hair, self-mutilation, and covering one's face and beard with a veil were supposedly ways to make oneself unrecognizable to the spirits. Other customs based on fear included burial of executed criminals before evening (cf. Deuteronomy 21:22–23) and heaping stones on the tomb (cf. Joshua 7:26; 8:29; 2 Samuel 18:17).

Cemeteries themselves were sometimes built in such a way as to keep contained the spirits of those buried within them. The ancient Minoans of Crete built tombs shaped as a maze or labyrinth so that the ghosts couldn't find their way out. After burial, the mourners might cover their footprints as they walked back home so the ghost could not follow them. Because they believed that ghosts could not cross water, the Etruscans in Italy always put their cemeteries on the other side of a river. They also made sure the tombs had plenty of food in them so the ghosts wouldn't get hungry and come home looking for food.

Some modern-day customs concerning death also reflect ancient fears. Closing the eyes of a person soon after death was originally done so that the ghost couldn't "see" the living and then haunt them. Covering the face of a dead person with a cloth or sheet was done for the same reason. The customs of loud wailing, funeral bells, and gunshots were based on the belief that ghosts can't stand loud noises. Tombstones, in addition to marking who was in the grave, were intended to weigh down the dead and keep them in the ground.

Our present-day custom of trick-or-treating on Halloween has its roots in an old European festival of the dead, when the spirits were invited inside to eat with the living. Bonfires and candles were lit to show the way for the spirits (perhaps the origin of our lighted jack-o'-lanterns). After the "meal," people put on gruesome masks and costumes to frighten the spirits back into their graves.

The communion of saints

The early Christians did not deny the fact of death; nor did they fear those who were dead. On the contrary, they saw death as a passage through which those who had been faithful to the teaching of Jesus would be united with him in heaven. The faithful dead were regarded as good spirits who cared about the Christians still on earth. When the Christians gathered for Eucharist, they celebrated it as a time to be united not only with Christ and with one another, but also with all the faithful who had died, both those in heaven and in purgatory. For this reason, the earliest prayers, hymns, and canon of the Mass contained references to the saints and to the dead.

By the fifth century, this belief in the solidarity of all the faithful—living and dead—found its way into the Apostles' Creed with the expression, "I believe . . . in the communion of saints." Because the early Christians believed that all the faithful formed the one Body of Christ, each part of that Body had a responsibility to help the other parts. The living on earth could affect the well-being of those in purgatory by praying for them. Likewise, the saints in heaven could intercede with God on behalf of the needs of the living.

Quite early in the Church's history, the martyrs were remembered and honored at Eucharistic gatherings, especially on the anniversaries of their deaths. Gradually these death anniversaries were recognized as the saints' feast days. These days eventually formed the sanctoral cycle of the Church's liturgical year. In the sanctoral cycle, the feast day of a saint (as a general rule) is observed on the day of death. Some exceptions include the feast of St. John the Baptist, who is honored on June 24, the day of his birth, and joint feasts, such as Saints Basil the Great and Gregory Nazianzen and Saints Cyril and Methodius.

At first, the Church celebrated each saint's day separately. As more and more Christians died and were revered as saints, the need arose for a common celebration of all known and unknown saints. This celebration became known as All Saints' Day, which is a holy day of obligation for Catholics in the United States and in many other countries.

It seems that All Saints' Day was originally celebrated on May 13, perhaps to offset *Lemuria*, a Roman festival of the dead observed on May 9, 11, and 13 by people who were polytheists. According to one historian, Pope Gregory IV (827–844) moved the feast to November 1 one year because provisions were inadequate that May for the many pilgrims coming to Rome for the feast. Another historian states that the Irish originated the feast on November 1 because that day was the beginning of the Celtic winter and because they had a custom of assigning the first day of the month to important feasts.

In A.D. 988, St. Odilo of Cluny established a second feast to pray for all the faithful departed. This day, known as All Souls' Day, quickly became an established custom in many churches. It was added to the Roman calendar in the thirteenth century. Today, the Catholic Church celebrates All Souls' Day on November 2, unless that day falls on a Sunday. Then the feast is transferred to November 3.[6]

---

6. Each priest is allowed to celebrate three Masses on All Souls' Day: (1) for particular people who have died; (2) for all the faithful departed; and (3) for the intentions of the pope.

In some parts of Europe, All Souls' Day is a day of the dead. People visit cemeteries and put flowers and candles on family graves, much as the ancient Romans did. On the eve of All Souls' Day, children used to beg from house to house for doughnuts called "soul cakes." (The circle made by the hole in the center of the doughnut represented eternity, with no beginning or end.) The soul cakes were eaten in remembrance of the dead or were put on relatives' graves. In return, the children were obligated to pray both for the dead and for a good harvest.

Today, in addition to celebrating All Saints' Day and All Souls' Day, the Catholic Church sets aside the entire month of November as a time to remember the dead. Parishes are encouraged to make available a book near the entrance of the church, the baptistery, or some other convenient location, in which people can write the names of their deceased loved ones. These dead are then remembered in prayer throughout the month.

How long will you live?

Doctors, scientists, and sociologists now know that many factors work together to determine how long people live. Genetic factors—such as gender, race, and the tendency toward high blood pressure, heart disease, strokes, or certain forms of cancer—and medical history (for example, a personal history of asthma) can directly affect the length of your life. Likewise, your life-style (drug use, amount of exercise, cigarette smoking, weight, willingness to take risks, and so on) can lengthen or shorten your life.[7]

Where you live in the United States also seems to make a difference in how long you will live. People who live in Hawaii have the longest average life span; those living in Louisiana tend to have the shortest. Those living in Montana, Missouri, Indiana, and Wyoming can expect to live to the national average. People who live in urban areas with a population of more than two million tend to die sooner than those who live in small towns or rural areas.

You have no control over the genetic factors you have inherited or your family's medical history. But you do have choices about the kind of life you lead and the risks you take. Environment, stress, and general behavior can add or subtract years from your life. The earlier you start to take care of yourself, the more you can expect to make a difference in the length and quality of your life.

---

7. According to the 1990 *Guinness Book of World Records*, Shigechiyo Izumi of Asan, Tukonoshima Island, Japan, lived to the oldest authenticated age ever. He was born on June 29, 1865, and died on February 21, 1986, at the age of 120 years and 237 days.

For your journal

1. Have you had any personal experience of death? If so, who died? (relative, parent, neighbor, child, pet, and so on)
2. When did you first learn about death? How did you react?
3. What are your present feelings about death?
4. Why do you think people die? Write your own story to explain the origin of death.
5. What is your biggest fear about death? Why?

Discussion questions

1. Have you had a close brush with death? What happened? How did you feel about life after that experience?
2. Would you like to know the exact time when or the manner in which you are going to die? Why or why not?
3. What would you do if you knew you only had three months left to live?
4. When you were a child, did your family ever talk about death? If so, what was said? If not, why not?
5. Would you really want to live forever? What would the world be like if no one ever died?
6. Would you like to have your body frozen after death with the hope of being restored to life in some future time?
7. When is the feast day of your patron saint? What do you know about the life and death of this saint?
8. Does your family have any customs surrounding All Saints' Day or All Souls' Day? Explain.
9. Why do you think women tend to live longer than men?
10. What are possible reasons that blacks have a shorter life expectancy than whites? What might be done to increase the life expectancy of blacks?

2 Responses to Death

Staring death in the face

Over the past thirty years, TV has brought us blow-by-blow accounts of death: the assassination of John F. Kennedy, the killing of his assassin by Jack Ruby, the murder of Martin Luther King, Jr.; the slaying of Robert F. Kennedy; the attempted killings of Pope John Paul II and President Ronald Reagan; the murder of musician John Lennon; the Persian Gulf war. On the nightly news, we now see the victims of car accidents, murders, wars, and natural disasters. In addition to real-life scenarios, numerous TV shows portray death-defying stunts and spectacularly faked deaths.

Instead of making us more responsive to death, such media overexposure can numb us. Because death, Hollywood style, is not real, it is hard not to view real-life death as fiction. Because death, Hollywood style, is so commonplace, many people look for more sensational ways to overcome their boredom both with TV and with their own lives. Thus ordinary people turn to high-risk activities, such as bungee jumping, taking drugs, and motorcycle racing.

Just think of the professional death-defiers you have seen: high-wire circus acts, stunt persons, magicians, high divers. What motivates a David Copperfield to go over Niagara Falls tied to a flaming raft, or a Harry Houdini to try to get out of a locked coffin submerged in water, or an Evel Knievel to attempt to jump over the Grand Canyon on a motorcycle? Certainly, money is one motivation. Another motivation involves the thrill of looking death in the face and living to tell about it.

In the last chapter, you read about the denial of death and fears regarding death. In this chapter, you will explore four other responses to death. You will also learn about individual people who have looked death in the face.

Response one: death as final

What people believe often determines how they respond to death. In this section, you will look at the views of some philosophers who believed that death is final, that there is no life after death. Some of these philosophers believed in God; others were atheists.

Socrates (470–399 b.c.)

Socrates was sentenced to death by the Greek government for presumably corrupting the youth of Athens with his teaching. He spent considerable time in prison prior to his death, describing his feelings and attitudes during the final days of his life. Although he could have escaped from prison and lived out his days in peace, Socrates chose to abide by the decision of the State. In the end, he administered his own death by drinking hemlock. Because Socrates approached death with dignity and courage, many people have considered him a role model of *Ars Moriendi*, the art of dying.

Because Socrates himself left no written records of his philosophy, it is difficult to sort out his thoughts about life and death from those of Plato, his biographer. According to Plato's report, Socrates wanted to convince his followers that death is not to be feared. Socrates himself was unclear about whether the soul lived on after death. In Plato's *Apology*, Socrates is presented as not believing in immortality. Later, in the *Phaedo*, Plato has Socrates giving many arguments for immortality. In short, Socrates did not pretend to know what, if anything, exists after death. Yet his belief in God's goodness and justice led him to overcome all fears regarding death. "Since there is God, no evil can happen to a good man, either in life or after death," Socrates argued. "Death is an unspeakable gain, perhaps a journey to another place. What can be greater than this? . . . It is always better to die than to do evil."

Martin Heidegger (1889–1976)

According to Martin Heidegger, a German philosopher, dying is one thing no one can do for another; we all must die our own death. Because we die alone, the reality of death gives us a sense of individuality and uniqueness. We define who we are and what our lives are to be only in the light of death.

Indeed, Heidegger saw all of life from the standpoint of death. "As soon as we are born, we are old enough to die," he wrote. For him, the important thing was to face death as final and to take possession of it. We are to "advance" resolutely toward death, taking charge of our lives and seizing each moment as an opportunity to fulfill ourselves as much as possible. Just as no one else can die for us, so no one else can live our lives for us. We are ultimately responsible for finding meaning and purpose in our own lives.

Jean-Paul Sartre (1905–1980)

For Jean-Paul Sartre, a French philosopher, death is absurd. The soul is not immortal; after death, there is only nonbeing. Death is something we can never understand or control. It prevents our completion and wholeness; it deprives us of our full potential.

Faced with his finiteness, Sartre discovered a sense of personal freedom. "I am free to make meaning out of my life, despite my mortality," he wrote. What we make of ourselves, what we accomplish in life, is entirely our own responsibility. We must make sense out of life while we have it. We must celebrate our days while we possess them; we must engage in a daily effort to find meaning in life.

Karl Jaspers (1883–1973)

Karl Jaspers, another German philosopher, parted from Heidegger by defining death as the fulfillment of human life. According to Jaspers, death is entirely natural and in keeping with human identity. Human life belongs to a larger cycle of birth, growth, decline, and death. We are part of a cosmic process. Just as we had no control over our own birth, so we have no control over death. When we remember that life itself is a gift and that we did not create ourselves, then we can approach death with a leap of faith. This faith is not based on belief in God or an afterlife, but rather on an understanding of the nature of the material universe.

Response two: death as a way out

Some people look death in the face and see it as an end to their suffering. They embrace death as a way out of their problems; they end up committing suicide. In the traditions of some cultures, suicide has been considered an honorable way to die. For example, in ancient Rome a soldier was expected to fall upon his sword in certain adverse circumstances. The Japanese respected the practice of hari kari (ritual self-disembowelment). In Polynesia, if a man thought he was being unjustly treated, the respectable thing for him to do was to swim out to sea until he drowned.

These examples are exceptions. Almost universally, suicide has been considered wrong. Although the Old Testament contains several examples of suicide (Saul, who fell on his own sword when the enemy surrounded him in battle; Ahithophel, who hung himself after betraying King David; and Razis, who disemboweled himself instead of being taken by enemy soldiers), the Jews considered this type of death to be a violation of the Fifth Commandment, "You shall not kill" (Exodus 20:13). The early Christians also regarded suicide as a serious moral evil. Although the Gospel of Matthew records that Judas Iscariot hung himself after betraying Jesus, the Acts of the Apostles leaves open the possibility that his death may have been accidental. During the Middle Ages, St. Thomas Aquinas refined the Church's thinking on suicide, saying that it is wrong for three reasons: (1) it violates the instinct to love oneself and to preserve one's own life; (2) it is an offense against society, since it deprives the community of one of its rightful members; and (3) it is a crime against God, who alone has power to give and to take away life.[1]

The social dimension of suicide may be seen in numerous civil laws. English law once listed attempted suicide as a crime. Even today, California state law says that aiding and abetting someone to commit suicide is a felony.

In the United States, over thirty thousand people committed suicide in 1988. This meant that roughly thirteen out of every 100,000 people saw death as a way out of their problems. Eighty percent of these people were male; 20 percent were female. Native Americans had the highest suicide rate among any race. One sixth of all suicides occurred among the 10–24 age group. Surprisingly, the suicide rate among doctors and dentists is twice the rate of the public.

Teen suicide is a growing problem in our society. Indeed, it is among the top three killers of teens today. Statistics tell us that a teenager commits suicide every ninety minutes. While more girls than boys attempt suicide, more boys are actually successful in completing the act. Television shows that portray suicide and lyrics (sometimes subliminal) of heavy metal music may have some influence on these statistics. A significant number of suicides among teenagers occur in clusters or are "copycat" actions of earlier suicides seen on TV or committed by friends and family members.

The reasons people choose suicide are varied. Romeo and Juliet, for example, felt they couldn't live without one another. Marilyn Monroe and Judy Garland felt they couldn't live without more and more of the drugs that the doctors had prescribed for them. Mitch Snyder, nationally known advocate of the homeless, committed

---

1. Because suicide was regarded as a mortal sin, the Church for many centuries forbade those who had committed suicide from having a Catholic funeral or from being buried in a Catholic cemetery. The 1983 revised Code of Canon Law does not mention those who have committed suicide among those who are to be forbidden Church funeral rites.

suicide supposedly because of a botched love affair. These people undoubtedly felt what most people who attempt suicide feel: desolate loneliness, alienation from others, despair, hopelessness, guilt, rejection, low self-esteem, and self-hatred. These negative feelings feed upon themselves and become so dominant that life no longer seems worth living. Death appears to be the only way out of pain and misery.

Many of the stereotypes about suicide are wrong. Because suicide affects so many people in today's society, you need to know these stereotypes and what really is the truth.

Stereotype 1: Only the very rich or the very poor commit suicide.

Fact: People of every economic and racial group can and do commit suicide.

Stereotype 2: Suicide tends to run in families. The desire to commit suicide is inherited.

Fact: Although there is no known gene for suicide, people who have had a family member commit suicide are more likely to commit suicide themselves. The reasons may include the survivor's feelings of guilt ("What did I do wrong?" "If only I had done this. . ."), similar problems facing members of the same family, and inherited chemical imbalances that lead to depression.

Stereotype 3: People who commit suicide are mentally ill.

Fact: In the majority of cases, the suicide victim is not mentally ill, but is extremely unhappy due to prolonged depression or emotional upset.

Stereotype 4: Most suicides occur around or after Christmas.

Fact: Even though most suicides occur in February, there also seems to be a correlation to the person's birthday. One study has found that half the people who commit suicide do so within ninety days of their last birthday and that nearly eight in ten suicides occur within the first six months after a person's birthday. Few people kill themselves in the three months before their birthdays.

Stereotype 5: Suicidal people want to die and there is little that can be done about it.

Fact: Most persons who threaten suicide don't know if they want to live or die. They gamble with death in the hope that others will save them.

Stereotype 6: People who talk about suicide will not commit it.

Fact: Eight out of ten people who give definite warnings about killing themselves will do so. The warning signs include one or more of the following:

- mood swings, emotional outbursts, aggressive behavior
- ongoing depression, loss of interest or involvement in social activities, withdrawal from family and friends
- drop in grades or work performance
- change in eating habits and weight (either up or down)
- change in sleeping patterns (either insomnia or sleeping all the time)
- increased use of alcohol and other drugs
- less concern for personal safety
- saying things such as "I wish I were dead" or "Maybe people will appreciate me once I'm gone" or giving similar hints about suicide
- giving important things away, or making out a will
- obsession with death, heaven, hell, and death drawings

These warnings should be taken seriously.

In times of severe depression, a person's outer strengths (connections to others) and inner strengths (religious convictions) can be real lifesavers.[2]

Response three: death as self-sacrifice

For some people, death is the ultimate expression of love—a way to express belief in a noble cause or ideal, a way of sacrificing oneself for others. Death that is motivated by the love of God and others is known as altruistic death.

Every century has known such deaths involving faith, courage, and love. In the Old Testament, Samson gave up his own life in fighting his people's enemies. In the New Testament, Jesus died on the cross rather than compromise the message of God's love that he lived and preached. Many Christians in the early days of the Church gave up their lives rather than disavow their allegiance to

---

2. There are more than two hundred suicide prevention centers throughout the United States, and most major cities have a suicide prevention hot line that is listed in the telephone directory. For more information about suicide prevention centers near you, write to the American Association of Suicidology, at 2459 S. Ash St., Denver, CO 80222 or call (303) 792-0985.

Christ. The Church has honored such people as martyrs, a word that means "witness." In dying, such people gave witness to their values and beliefs. They sacrificed their lives for what they held to be important.

Modern-day society has had many examples of people who have risked and sometimes given up their lives for others. During World War II, for example, Japanese kamikaze pilots deliberately plunged their aircraft (and themselves) into U.S. warships for the sake of their country. Each day across the United States, fire fighters, police officers, and paramedics risk their lives to save others.

Before his own death, Jesus told his disciples that giving up one's life for one's friends is the greatest possible expression of love (cf. John 15:12–13). Here are the stories of two modern-day people who gave up their lives as expressions of love.

Maximillian Kolbe (1894–1941)

"Welcome back to Poland, Father!" the young priest said enthusiastically. "Or should I call you Doctor? Or perhaps General?"

Maximillian laughed and embraced his brother Franciscan. After a long time in Japan, he was at last returning home to his own country and to *Militia Immaculatae,* the Army of Mary Immaculate, a religious community he had founded. "How about calling me Editor?" Maximillian quipped. "It's time I got back to work doing what I like best."

The young priest frowned. "Since the Germans took over Poland, we have been forbidden to publish the newspaper," he said. "They consider it subversive of their political viewpoint."

"And rightly so," Maximillian remarked.

That very afternoon, he began work on the next edition of the paper. Soon after the newspaper was released, the Nazis came and arrested him. He was taken to the concentration camp at Auschwitz.

The place was a death camp. Those who could not work were exterminated immediately. Those who could work were worked to death. In any event, the Nazis intended for there to be no survivors.

One day a desperate prisoner successfully escaped from the barracks where Father Kolbe lived. The Nazi commander lined up all the men in the barracks and told them that, in retaliation for the escape, he would choose ten of them to die.

Maximillian waited in fear as the Nazi commander made his selection. He felt sad for those chosen and helpless, but he also felt relieved at not being among them.

Suddenly Francis Gajowniczek, one of the condemned men, broke down and cried. "I have a wife and small baby," he pleaded. "I can't die. They need me."

Maximillian's heart went out to the prisoner. In an act of supreme courage and selflessness, he found himself stepping forward. "Take me instead," he told the Nazi guard. "I'll die for Mr. Gajowniczek."

And so it was done. Maximillian and the other nine men were taken to Cell Block 11 to be starved to death. As the horrible days passed and death began to claim them one by one, Father Kolbe continued to lead the surviving prisoners in prayers and hymns. Finally, when there were only four of the original ten remaining, the soldiers killed Maximillian with a lethal injection of carbolic acid. News of his death spread quickly throughout the camp. And everywhere the prisoners began to speak of him as "the saint" who gave his life for others.[3]

Jean Donovan (1953–1980)

"Surprise!" the voices called out in unison in the Connecticut parish hall.

Jean smiled with happiness to see all her old friends. She had just returned from a year as a lay missionary in El Salvador, and she really had missed everyone. Jean went around the room, laughing, hugging, and exchanging stories with her friends.

After a festive meal and boisterous singing, the crowd began to thin out. Eventually only Jean and her closest friends remained.

"You're not thinking about going back to El Salvador again, are you?" one of them asked.

Jean looked around the room. "As a matter of fact, I am."

"But you can't," another friend warned. "It's too dangerous. If they could kill Archbishop Romero, they'd easily kill you."[4]

---

3. Maximillian Kolbe was declared a saint by Pope John Paul II, in 1982. His feast day is August 14.

4. Archbishop Oscar Romero (1917–1980) was gunned down while he celebrated Mass in the oratory of the *Divina Providencia* cancer hospital on March 24, 1980.

Jean laughed to ease the tension in the group. "Believe me, blue-eyed blondes are safe there. We're easily identified as Americans, and no matter what, the Salvadoran army doesn't shoot Americans."

"Father Crowley told us about the death threats you'd gotten before you left," a third friend said. "Be smart, and don't go back."

Jean sighed. "Sometimes you can't make choices by your head," she explained. "You have to follow your heart. My heart is with the poor in El Salvador. They're hungry and homeless, and I promised them that I would come back."

Despite the warnings, Jean returned to El Salvador in the fall. On December 2, she, Ursuline Sister Dorothy Kazel, and Maryknoll Sisters Maura Clarke and Ita Ford were kidnapped a few miles from the San Salvador airport. The next day their fire-gutted van was found on a deserted road. The following day their bodies were found in a shallow grave in a cow pasture. Each had been shot in the head; at least two of them had been raped.

Over a decade later, Jean's murderers still had not been identified or brought to trial.

Response four: death as the beginning of the fullness of new life

Seeing death as the beginning of the fullness of new life marks one of the radical differences between Christianity and traditional Judaism. Usually, authors of the Hebrew Scriptures viewed death as final. When people died, their spirit left them. The deceased continued to exist for a time in Sheol, but they were incapable of any vital activity, even the worship of God. Thus death was a terrible evil, something to be avoided at all costs.

As the Israelites grew in their understanding of God as good and all-powerful, they also grew in the realization that God must have power over the forces of evil. The Messiah that God promised to send would therefore have power over the evil of sin and the evil of death. The Messiah would not only free the people from their sins; he would free them, once and for all, from death. The Messiah himself would not die; his kingdom would last forever.

This is the background with which the apostles approached Jesus. As they grew in their belief that he was the Messiah, they also grew in the expectation that he would live forever and that he would include them in his eternal kingdom on earth. Many actions of Jesus supported their viewpoint. He cured the sick, restored sight to the blind, made those unable to speak talk again, calmed the wind and the sea, and even revived people who had died.

It is no wonder that Peter protested ferociously when Jesus predicted his own death. Nor is it surprising that James and John would fight over the best positions in Jesus' kingdom. In some ways, it is even understandable how Judas could have told the Jewish officials where Jesus was, in exchange for silver. None of the apostles ever expected Jesus to die.

If you can put yourself in the apostles' frame of mind, then you can see why the crucifixion of Jesus was so horrible. It wasn't just that it was a painful, humiliating way to die; it was that everything the apostles had hoped for also died with Jesus. They thought they had believed in him in vain. How disappointed and disillusioned they must have felt.

These were precisely the feelings that a story in the Gospel of Luke says two disciples were discussing on their way to Emmaus three days after the death of Jesus. Then they met up with a stranger who explained to them why it was necessary for the Messiah to die in order to conquer death. Only when that same stranger later broke bread with them did they recognize him. Then the truth hit them: Jesus had risen from the dead.

The resurrection of Jesus is the cornerstone of the Catholic faith. Jesus overcame death by his own death and resurrection. Because he deprived death of its power, we too shall pass through death to new life. We no longer need to be afraid of death. Death is not final. Seen with the eyes of faith, death takes on new meaning: "Unless a grain of wheat falls to the earth and dies, it remains just a grain of wheat; but if it dies, it produces much fruit" (John 12:24); "I am the living bread that came down from heaven; whoever eats this bread will live forever. . ." (John 6:51); "I am the resurrection and the life: whoever believes in me, even if he [she] dies, will live, and everyone who lives and believes in me will never die" (John 11:25–26).

Through baptism, we enter fully into the Paschal Mystery. We are baptized into the death of Jesus so that we can rise with him to a new life. As St. Paul wrote to the Romans:

> *Are you unaware that we who were baptized into Christ Jesus were baptized into his death? We were indeed buried with him through baptism into death, so that, just as Christ was raised from the dead by the glory of the Father, we too might live in newness of life. . . .*
>
> *We know that Christ, raised from the dead, dies no more; death no longer has power over him. As to his death, he died to sin once and*

for all; as to his life, he lives for God. Consequently, you too must think of yourselves as dead to sin and living for God in Christ Jesus.
                                                    —*Romans 6:3–4, 9–11*

Because of the resurrection, death has no more power over us. For those who have faith in Jesus, it is merely a passage to everlasting life and to the fullness of the new life they have already begun to experience here.

Where you stand

Where do you stand in response to death? How much do you really value life? Do you unnecessarily put your life in danger? Are you at risk regarding suicide?

To answer these questions, reflect on the items in the questionnaire that follows. Quietly reflect and pray over each item. After you have finished, write a short paragraph in your notebook about your philosophy of life. Do you value life highly, or are there areas at which you may need to take a closer look?

Have you ever . . .

1. Used illegal drugs?
2. Driven a car above the speed limit?
3. Raced a car, boat, or motorcycle?
4. Driven a car while drunk?
5. Ridden in a car with a drunk driver?
6. Played Russian Roulette?
7. Carried a gun or knife?
8. Gone scuba diving?
9. Parachuted from a plane?
10. Flown a plane?
11. Raced an all-terrain vehicle?
12. Gone bungee jumping?
13. Dived off a high dive or cliff?
14. Smoked cigarettes?
15. Gotten drunk?
16. Had unprotected sex (homosexual)?
17. Had unprotected sex (heterosexual)?
18. Gone white-water rafting?
19. Climbed mountains?
20. Been on high-thrill amusement rides?

21. Lived on or near an earthquake fault?
22. Tried to copy stunts done on TV?
23. Thought about killing yourself?
24. Deliberately disobeyed traffic laws?
25. Been depressed for a long time?

If your answer is "No" to most or all of the questions, you are probably a person who values life highly. If your answer is "Yes" to most or all of the questions, you may need to take a closer look at your personal stance toward life and death.

If you or one of your friends are at high-risk regarding suicide, or if you're just depressed by the way your life is going, take time NOW to make some changes. No one needs to go through life unhappy, and no one needs to commit suicide. Here are some tips that can help you build a happier and more meaningful life:

1. **Take charge of your own emotions.** You may not be able to control everything that happens to you, but you can control how you will respond to what happens. No one can make you feel a certain way. Only you can choose how you will feel.

2. **Commit yourself to projects that help others.** Donate some time each week to give generously of yourself.

3. **Take the initiative in developing friendships.** If one person isn't interested in being your friend, move on to someone else.

4. **Don't count on only one activity or friendship.** In other words, find meaning in all sorts of relationships and activities. Don't put all your meaning in one person, or one job, or a team, or even your children. If many things give you meaning, then if something bad happens in one area, you still will find positive support in the other areas.

5. **Learn to distinguish a bad situation from feelings of self-hatred.** Just because someone rejects you doesn't mean that you are a bad person. Learn what you can from the bad situation, reaffirm your own goodness, and then move on.

6. **Develop a friendship with yourself.** Sometimes we are our own worst critics. Learn to be gentle with yourself, to affirm your positive points, and to look at any mistakes you make as an opportunity for learning.

7. **Never be afraid to get help.** People are social beings, and sometimes talking things over with someone else is the best way to make a problem manageable.

By following these tips, you will not only grow in personal happiness and have a more fulfilling life. You will also be more effective in reaching out and contributing to the happiness of others.

For your journal

1. What are your feelings when you learn about death in the nightly news?
2. Do you believe the soul lives on after death? Why or why not?
3. If you had been Socrates, would you have chosen to drink the hemlock? Explain.
4. At this point in your life, what gives you meaning? Do you think this will change in the future?
5. Suppose a friend tells you that he or she is thinking about suicide. How would you respond?
6. For what (or whom) would you be willing to give up your life?
7. What difference has the resurrection of Jesus made in your life? In your own response to death?
8. On a scale of 1 to 10 (with 10 being the highest), how happy would you say you are right now? If you are a 10, what are some things that have contributed to your happiness? If you are lower than a 10, what are some things you might do to increase your happiness?

Discussion questions

1. Think about the TV shows you have seen this past week. How was death portrayed in these shows? How many people died?
2. According to Heidegger, no one else can die for us or live our lives for us. What do you think this statement means for adults today?
3. What do you think Socrates meant when he said we should fear doing wrong more than we should fear death? Give examples.
4. In what sense does death prevent us from achieving our potential? In what sense is death a fulfillment of life?
5. How does the "faith" of Karl Jaspers differ from Christian faith?
6. It has been said that "suicide is a permanent solution to a temporary problem." Do you agree or disagree with this statement? Explain.

7. What are possible reasons Native Americans have higher suicide rates than the public?

8. Why do you think the Church changed its position about suicide victims and Church funeral rites?

9. The writer Tertullian (A.D. 197) once said, "The blood of the martyrs is the seed of the Church." What do you think this statement means? Do you think the same is true of today's martyrs? Explain.

10. What do you see as the difference between a death-defier and an altruist?

11. Is an altruist really a hero, or is this just another form of suicide?

12. The Bible tells us to "choose life, not death." How do you think these words apply to adults today? How do they apply to your own choices each day?

Part Two: Historical Aspects

Joseph died at the age of a hundred and ten. He was embalmed and laid to rest in a coffin in Egypt.

—*Genesis 50:26*

3 Customs and Beliefs, B.C.

A question of respect

Some people believe that progress means marching ever forward and forgetting about the past. Others think that we should study history to learn from it and to avoid the mistakes made by those who have gone before us. Death itself seems to be the "Great Divide" between the past, present, and future. Those who die no longer have a future on this earth, nor do they belong to our present reality. Their remains (regardless of what we believe about an afterlife) are now relegated to history.

Respect for the remains of one's loved ones may be found in most cultures throughout history. Some cultures based this respect on fear of the dead; some, on love for the person and the person's memory. Nevertheless, the concept that we should have respect for human remains continues into our century. Throughout the United States, it is a misdemeanor to vandalize a cemetery; it is a felony to dig up a grave without a permit.

Although our lives today are very different from those of ancient peoples, in some ways they are the same. Despite our modern-day technology and scientific achievements, for example, there is nothing new about the way we dispose of our dead. All our present methods of interment have their roots in the past. This is just one reason a history of funeral rites and burial customs has been included in this book. Hopefully, such knowledge also will lead you to a greater appreciation and respect for the humans who have come before us.

A practical problem

For people of every age, death was not just a topic for philosophical discussion. It was an immediate, practical problem. What, for example, should be done with the dead body? How should it be disposed of?

Archaeological evidence tells us that ancient peoples disposed of their dead in a variety of ways. The oldest form of interment was cave burial. Forty-four thousand years ago, Neanderthal peoples buried their dead in the same cave in which they lived. With the dead they buried food and flint tools. They laid out the bodies in an east-west orientation, with the feet toward the rising sun.

Before burial, Cro-Magnon peoples (35,000–10,000 years ago) covered their dead with red ocher.[1] They buried shells, necklaces, clothes, tools, and animals with the dead. Sometimes the head of the person was buried in a place separate from the body. This practice may have been meant to discourage the dead from returning.

The second form of interment was earth burial. Before 4,000 B.C., massive stone tombs were built throughout Spain, the British Isles, Scandinavia, Germany, Holland, and France. These tombs were communal graves, containing anywhere from five to one hundred bodies buried over many years. Some archaeologists have proposed that these tombs represented the womb of an earth goddess. If the dead were put inside that womb, they would be reborn.

A third method of disposing of the dead consisted of burning the body. Cremation seems to have begun in Europe during the Stone Age. Cremation did not completely dispose of the dead; often the remaining ashes and bones (cremains) were placed in ossuaries and then buried.

The simplest way of disposing of the dead was to leave the corpse exposed to the elements. The body may have been left on the ground, in trees, on rocks, or on a special platform. The ancient Persians, for example, exposed their dead to scavenger birds. The ancient Chinese left the dead in rock caves or in the jungle, protecting them only slightly with a covering of leaves or brush. Today, the Dayak of Borneo believe that it is essential to treat the body with great respect until the flesh has completely decayed. Only then will the soul detach itself from the body and go to its afterlife. When someone dies, the Dayak wash and prepare the body. Then they place it on a funeral platform near the village. The body remains there until the flesh has decayed. As people see the body decompose, they gradually become separated from the deceased.

Water burial was perhaps the second easiest way to dispose of the dead. Sometimes this consisted of disposing of the corpse in a river or lake. In some cultures that practiced water burial, the dead were wrapped to protect them from fish and then weighted with stones. Water burial was prevalent among island peoples and those who had to deal with death while at sea.[2]

---

1. The red ocher might have been intended to resemble the blood that covers a newborn baby. One theory is that the red color represented health and life, and was supposed to help the dead person be reborn in the afterlife.

2. Navy personnel who dies at sea are no longer buried at sea. The remains are frozen and brought back home for interment.

The most elaborate forms of disposal involved preservation of the entire body or parts of the body. Methods included smoke-drying, treatment of the body with mineral or vegetable preservatives, and embalming. After preservation, the body was usually placed in one or more coffins. The coffin was then laid to rest in a houselike tomb. Both the ancient Egyptians and the Aztecs of Mexico entombed deceased rulers in elaborate pyramids.

The Great Pyramid, just outside Cairo, contains 2.3 million blocks of stone, each weighing about two and one-half tons. The pyramid measures 750 feet per side and is as high as a fifty-story building. In the Mexican temple town of Teotihuacan, the tombs below the mammoth pyramids contain painted walls, realistic clay figures, flowers, fruits, and other burial gifts.

The last form of disposal of the dead was endocannibalism. This was a ritualistic eating of the dead person, usually including the brain. The eating was regarded as an act of piety toward the dead. It was thought to be a way for the living to absorb and carry on the dead person's power and personality.[3]

Sometimes an entire culture would dispose of its dead by only one of these seven methods. Some cultures used more than one method simultaneously. Still other cultures practiced one method for a while and gradually switched to another one. The method chosen by a particular society almost always reflected its belief system concerning fear of the dead or the afterlife. To get a better understanding of the connection between death customs and beliefs, we must take a closer look at specific cultures.

The Egyptians

The Egyptians thought that at death, a person's *ka* (spirit) left the body. For a person to be reborn in the afterlife, the spirit and body had to be reunited. Reunion would only take place if the spirit could recognize the body; thus it was imperative that the body be preserved from decay. If the body had decomposed, the spirit would roam forever, searching for a body that no longer existed.

Not everyone in Egyptian society, however, was destined for immortality. Only the rich "merited" preservation by an elaborate mummification procedure. The bodies of the poor were not em-

---

3. As late as the early 1960s, the female members of the Fore Tribe of Papua, New Guinea, practiced endocannibalism. Through this custom, the women unwittingly passed on a deadly nerve disease known as *kuru*. Medical doctors and Christian missionaries were able to persuade the Fore to give up endocannibalism. Since the practice stopped, no new cases of *kuru* have developed.

balmed. Instead, they were merely washed and then buried directly in the sand.

Mummification was a religious ritual that lasted seventy days. While a priest chanted, embalmers used hooks (somewhat like crochet needles) to draw out the brain, bit by bit, through the nostrils. Then the embalmers cut open the left side to remove the stomach, liver, intestines, pancreas, and genital organs. (The heart remained with the body.) They rinsed out the abdominal cavity with palm wine and filled it with myrrh and cassia. Then they shaved the body and dehydrated it in natron, a natural soda. After washing and anointing the body with scented oils, the embalmers wrapped it tightly in hundreds of yards of resin-soaked linen. Between the layers, they put amulets inscribed with magical incantations to protect the wearer during his or her journey in the afterlife. Amulets were made of different materials according to the person's station in life. The best were made of gold; others were made of bronze, stone, glass, wax, or clay, which was first baked and then enamelled.

On top of the wrappings, the embalmers then placed a stylized mask that resembled the face of the deceased and would allow the spirit to recognize its body. Such masks were commonly made of cloth covered with stucco or plaster, which was then painted. The mummy was placed in an elaborately decorated coffin. If the person was important, three coffins, fitted together each inside one another, were used.[4] These were then carried in procession to the place of burial.

The funeral procession varied, depending upon the location of the pyramid. Sometimes oxen pulled a boat carrying the coffin up the river (or a specially built canal) to the pyramid. Behind the mummy's boat came another boat with a chest containing the preserved vital organs. On other occasions, servants carried the coffin and its organ chest in a procession. Heading the procession were other servants who carried flowers and trays of food, oils, jars of water and wine, embalmed pets, furniture, swords, necklaces—indeed, everything the person would need for the afterlife. Directly in front of the coffin and organ chest came hired mourners, dressed in the blue-gray color of mourning. According to custom, they smeared their faces with dust and mud, beat their heads, and wailed loudly during the procession.

---

4. The Vatican has some similar customs. When a pope dies, his body is placed in a cypress coffin along with medals struck during his pontificate. This coffin is placed inside a second coffin made of lead, which contains the death certificate and the pope's coat of arms. Then this coffin is placed inside a third coffin, made of oak.

When the mummy arrived at the tomb, a jackal-masked priest (impersonating Anubis, the divine embalmer) held the coffin upright. He ritually opened the mouth of the dead person, thus symbolically restoring its ability to move, talk, and eat.

The mummy, along with food, furniture, and other items, was placed in a sarcophagus in a multichambered, richly decorated tomb that was tunneled underground. Next to the coffin were placed papyrus scrolls containing verses from the Egyptian Book of the Dead. These were meant to act as a road map, guiding the soul past any obstacles on its journey in quest of reunion with the *ka*, or spirit.

Usually animals were sacrificed at the tomb. Sometimes, for an important ruler, wives and favorite slaves were also killed and buried with the dead person so that his every need in the afterlife would be met. After the burial ceremonies were complete, people stayed outside the tomb and had a feast celebrating the creation of a new god.

The tomb of King Tutankhamen (1342 B.C.), a minor pharaoh who died when he was eighteen, gives us a tantalizing hint of the elaborateness of Egyptian funerary rites. Tutankhamen's embalmers wrapped each toe and finger separately. His funeral mask and one of his coffins were made of gold. Buried with him were 143 different amulets and an astonishing treasure of diadems, rings, necklaces, bracelets, and pendants.

The Chinese

The ancient Chinese consistently buried their dead. Wealthy families also buried dogs, horses, and other humans with their dead. Some emperors went to their graves with three hundred servants.[5] These customs stemmed from a belief that dead ancestors should be worshiped. Neglect of the ancestors could cause sickness or disasters to living family members.

When a member of a family died, mourners dressed in white. The coffin was elaborately decorated with gold and flowers and then placed on a litter and carried through the streets. After the burial, the family kept a memorial shrine to the dead person in the house and worshiped there daily.

---

5. A similar practice evidently occurred in ancient Central America. Below the pyramid of the Mayan temple of Palenque, archaeologists found the skeleton of a prince in a richly carved sarcophagus. The skeletons of seven men lay next to the coffin. They had been killed to provide the prince with attendants in the Land of the Dead.

The Greeks

The ancient Greeks considered earth burial important; otherwise, the dead spirits would never find peace. Around 1000 B.C., however, the Greeks began to cremate their dead. This may have been a health measure; it may also have been a way to protect the body from becoming carrion or from being desecrated as the body of Hector was dishonored by Achilles. Not all Greeks merited the "right" of cremation. Suicide victims, infants who did not yet have teeth, and persons struck by lightning (a sign of disfavor with the gods) could not be cremated. This prohibition suggests the Greeks may have thought that cremation and burial affected the dead differently.

The Etruscans

Outside Caere, Italy, the Etruscans built an elaborate City of the Dead in the fifth century B.C. Because they thought life after death was similar to life here, they constructed each tomb as a house, with rooms and elaborate wall paintings. Daily, the people brought food for the dead to eat. On special days, they sacrificed animals, letting the blood sink into the earth. This practice was based on the belief that the dead needed blood in order to live on in the afterlife. The Etruscans also staged "funeral games" to honor the dead. The losers of these chariot races, wrestling matches, discus throws, and other contests were killed in order to provide enough blood to appease the dead.

The Romans

The ancient Romans buried some of their dead and cremated others. The Laws of the Twelve Tables (mid-fifth century, B.C.) forbade both the burial and the burning of bodies within the city, showing that both customs were then practiced.

In ancient Roman burials, often a death mask resembling the deceased was placed over the face of the corpse. Such masks, made of wax, were usually fashioned right on the face to assure their likeness to the dead person. Sometimes the mask was worn by a hired actor, who accompanied the funeral procession to the site of burial. Patrician families saved the masks as ancestor portraits and displayed them on ceremonial occasions. During the last month of the Roman calendar, the people held a state funeral, known as *Parentalia*, which honored deceased ancestors. One of the rites performed on that day was repairing and decorating ancestral graves.

Romans probably received the custom of cremation from the Greeks. Virgil says that cremation was used before the founding of Rome; Ovid mentions that the body of Remus (one of the founders of Rome) was cremated. Cremation reflected Roman belief that the soul alone lived on after death. Cremation was a way to release the soul from the body. Often a bird was released as the body burned, to symbolize the upward flight of the spirit. The ashes were preserved in elaborately decorated urns. Final inurnment took place in specially built columbariums.

Sometimes the Romans disposed of their dead by a practice called *os resectum*. Before cremation, they cut off a finger from the corpse. The body was burned, but the finger was saved. Funeral rites were held for the finger, which was then buried.

The Romans held a similar belief to the Etruscans about the need to appease the dead with blood. At the funeral of Brutus in 264 B.C., three pairs of gladiators (professional combatants) competed in the amphitheater. During the time of Julius Caesar (d. 44 B.C.), the wild popularity of these funeral games swelled the ranks of the gladiators to three hundred pairs. Gladiators were chiefly slaves and criminals. Most gladiators fought with shields, armor, and swords. Some fought with short swords, lassoes, and tridents. The battles were fought on foot, on horseback, or in chariots. If a gladiator survived several funeral games, he became famous and could be discharged from further service. If a gladiator was wounded, the spectators themselves decided whether he should die or be granted mercy. As people converted to Christianity, gladiator shows began to fall into disfavor. Constantine abolished the games in A.D. 325, without much effect. They were again abolished by Honorius (393–434).

People of the Hebrew Scriptures

The Israelites regarded death as the ultimate enemy of life. Death was the climax of all earthly pain and sorrow, the final estrangement from God. Death was seen as punishment for primeval, as well as personal, sin. Thus sin was to be avoided at all costs. A person who died early was thought to have sinned. Israelites could save themselves from early death by practicing virtue, doing good deeds, and giving alms to the poor. Indeed, they believed that long life was the most tangible proof of God's favor. Based on these beliefs, important Israelite heroes—Abraham, Isaac, Jacob, and Joseph—were all depicted in Genesis as living a hundred years or longer.

Beliefs about death and the afterlife (or lack of it) were related to the Jewish understanding of the human person. A human being was thought to be an animated body, not a composition of material body and immaterial soul. As long as the body (or the bones) remained, the soul continued to exist in a land of the dead called Sheol. In Sheol, the soul continued to feel what happened to the body, but was incapable of any living response. Once the body decayed completely, the soul, too, became extinct.

These beliefs made it important for the Jews to inter the dead properly. Proper interment meant earth burial or entombment, not cremation (as was practiced by many of their neighbors, who did not believe in the same God). As a rule, the Israelites did not embalm their dead; the exceptions to this were Jacob and Joseph, who both died while the Israelites were in Egypt (cf. Genesis 50:2–3, 26).

Immediately after death, the nearest relatives closed the eyes and embraced the body. The corpse was washed and then dressed in the clothes he or she had used in life. A soldier, for example, was buried in armor, with his sword under his head and his shield under his body. The body was laid out in the best room in the house, and friends and professional mourners came to grieve with the family members.

The Jews rarely used coffins. Instead, the corpse was carried to the tomb or grave on an open bier. The corpse was placed in the grave or tomb, either drawn together in a fetal position and laid on the left side, or stretched out straight on its back. Interment took place either in burial sites outside the city walls, in tombs in family gardens, or in caves carved out of hillsides.

The oldest graves were single or connected caves. The entrance to such a cave was blocked by a stone. During the Bronze Age, people of the Hebrew Scriptures used shaft graves. Entrance to the underground cave was a perpendicular shaft or tunnel, which, after burial, would be filled with rubble. Later burial caves had burial ledges for the dead. Previous remains were swept away into a bone pit to make room for the recent dead. During the Greco-Roman period, underground tombs had several chambers provided with niches or shelves. If a niche was reused, the previous remains were put into an ossuary and labeled with the name of the dead person.

Sometimes the Jews buried their dead with articles used in life: dishes, bowls, perfume containers, lamps, weapons, and jewelry. This practice may have come from the neighboring Canaanites, who equipped their dead for the afterlife. In one tomb found by archaeologists in Canaan, a rich woman had been buried with bronze cauldrons, carnelian beads, cosmetic and perfume containers, lamps, incense boats, and drinking bowls. There is no evidence that the Jews followed this custom to express belief in an afterlife; rather, they were merely following the customs of the area in which they lived.

The Jews believed firmly that cremation was a form of sacrilege. Only animals, enemies, and criminals could be cremated. The only example of cremation in the Hebrew Scriptures is found in 1 Samuel 31. After Saul and his sons died in battle, the Philistines mutilated and displayed them. To prevent further dishonor to the bodies, the men of Jabesh-gilead burned them. Another account of the same incident (cf. 1 Chronicles 10:12), however, does not mention cremation.

The Church and cremation

The early Christians tended to dispose of their dead according to local custom. Around Jerusalem, the Christians followed the Jewish custom of earth burial or entombment. In Egypt, the Christians practiced mummification. But the Christians in Rome never adopted the practice of cremation.

There are perhaps two reasons for this. First, cremation was a practice of those with other religious beliefs. Burial, on the other hand, was a common Jewish practice and many early Christians previously had been Jews. And second, cremation was thought to show disrespect for the dead body. According to Origen, burial gave the body "due honors." From the viewpoint of Tertullian, cremation was a cruel "punishment," something the body of a Christian did not deserve.

Many people have erroneously thought that the Catholic Church opposed cremation because of its belief in the "resurrection of the body." In times of persecution, the enemies of Christianity made sure the bodies of martyrs were cremated. As Eusebius wrote about a second century persecution in Lyon:

> After torture and execution the bodies of the martyrs were guarded by soldiers, so that their friends could not bury them. Finally after some days the bodies were burned and reduced to ashes and swept into the Rhine "so that no trace of them might appear on the earth." And this they did as if able to conquer God, and prevent their new birth; "that," as they said, "they may have no hope of a resurrection."[6]

The early Christians, by and large, never believed that destruction of the body by fire would prevent resurrection.

---

6. Eusebius, *Church History*, Book V, Chapter 1, in *Select Library of Nicene and Post-Nicene Fathers*, eds. Philip Schaff and Henry Wace (New York: Charles Scribner's Sons, 1905), p. 215.

While the early Church resisted cremation as a practice of those with other beliefs, the Catholic Church of the Middle Ages and the nineteenth century opposed it because of the anticlerical and anti-ecclesiastical beliefs of some of those who practiced cremation. The Church legislated against it because cremation was thought to be a means of subverting the faithful.[7] In 1300, Pope Boniface VIII supported burial as normative Catholic practice and threatened to excommunicate anyone who did otherwise. In 1886, Pope Leo XIII forbade Catholics to join cremation societies and to request cremation for themselves or others. Catholics who violated these decrees were to be denied burial by the Church. In 1892, the Church officially excluded violators from receiving the last sacraments.

Canon 1203 of the Code of Canon Law of 1917 forbade cremation. Other pertinent canons included the following:

Canon 1240: *(1) Anyone who has requested that his body shall be cremated shall be deprived of ecclesiastical burial unless he has shown signs of repentance before death. (2) If there is any doubt in a case such as above, and time permits, the bishop should be consulted. If there is still any doubt, ecclesiastical burial should be accorded in order to prevent scandal.*

Canon 1241: *Anyone who has been deprived of ecclesiastical burial will be deprived also of a requiem mass on the anniversary of his death and of all other funeral offices.*

In 1963, the Church modified its opinion on cremation. The "Instruction with Regard to the Cremation of Bodies" (issued by The Congregation for the Doctrine of the Faith) upheld the traditional practice of Christian burial but said that cremation could be permitted for serious reasons, provided it did not involve any contempt of the Church or any attempt to deny the doctrine of the resurrection of the body. A person who was cremated could receive the Last Rites and be given ecclesiastical burial. A priest could say prayers for the dead at the crematorium, but not conduct full liturgical ceremonies there. The cremains were to be treated with respect and placed in consecrated ground. This new opinion is expressed both in Canon 1176.3 of the Revised Code of Canon Law (1983) and in the new *Order of Christian Funerals*. As Canon 1176.3 states, "The Church earnestly recommends that the pious custom of burying the bodies of the dead be observed; it does not, however, forbid cremation unless it has been chosen for reasons which are contrary to Christian teaching."

---

7. To show its disdain for the condemned heretic John Wycliffe, the Council of Constance ordered that his body be dug up (forty-four years after his death) and cremated and the ashes thrown into a river.

The temple of the Holy Spirit

Respect for a dead person's body is a logical extension of Catholic teaching that one's body is holy. The body is holy, first of all, because God created us "in the divine image" (Genesis 1:27). The body is holy for another reason as well: It is a dwelling place of God. We are filled with God's own life and presence.

For the Jewish people, the dwelling place of God on earth was the Temple in Jerusalem. Jesus used the analogy of the Temple when speaking about his own death and resurrection. "I can destroy the temple of God and within three days rebuild it" (Matthew 26:61). The same destiny awaits all followers of Jesus. As St. Paul writes, "Do you not know that you are the temple of God, and that the Spirit of God dwells in you? If anyone destroys God's temple, God will destroy that person, for the temple of God, which you are, is holy" (1 Corinthians 3:16–17).

For these reasons, the Catholic Church teaches that the human body is the temple of the Holy Spirit. So what does this teaching have to do with today's adults? Simply this: We need to treat our own body and the bodies of others with respect. This respect should not start after death, but should begin now.

Respect for the human body is an attitude. But it is also expressed through actions. In addition to dressing modestly, we have a duty to keep ourselves strong and healthy. This means eating the right food, getting enough sleep and exercise, and having regular medical checkups. It also means helping to protect the safety of others and helping them to maintain their health. In particular, four areas involving respect for the body deserve additional mention.

The first area is *eating disorders*. Many adults (especially women) dislike their bodies and try, through eating, to change them. Anorexia is a habit in which someone eats little or nothing. In essence, the person starves his or her body. Bulimia is a pattern of stuffing oneself and then vomiting in order not to gain weight. Compulsive overeating is a pattern of eating too much all the time. Yo-yo dieting is a pattern of alternate overeating and starving. All these behaviors show disrespect for one's body, and can lead to death.

The second area is *drug use*. Despite national campaigns to the contrary, more and more Americans are trying marijuana, cocaine, and other types of illegal drugs. Almost no one thinks that he or she will get "hooked," but often that is what happens. Soon the person needs higher doses to get the desired effect. The same can happen with prescribed drugs. In many cases, the dosage taken becomes lethal. Even in cases where no addiction occurs, "recreational" drug use can lead to death. Many people are killed each year in drug-related fights and shootings.

The third area is *abuse of sex*. The Catholic Church teaches that full sexual expression belongs only in marriage. Therefore, it has always opposed premarital sex, seeing it as, among other things, disrespectful of the body. But both promiscuous sex and "date rape" take disrespect a step further. In promiscuous sex, a person has sex with many different people in a short period. There's no love involved, and no consideration for the feelings of the other. In date rape, one friend forces sex on the other. There's no respect for the person's right to say "No." Both types of behavior can be deadly. Not only can they transmit the AIDS virus; they can hurt someone so much that he or she tries to commit suicide.

The fourth area is *sexual harassment*, an issue which has now come to the forefront in the business place. Adult workers are now realizing that it is wrong to treat others as sexual objects rather than as persons or to value a person's physical endowments above professional qualifications and accomplishments. Examples of sexual harassment can include anything from the display of pin-up calendars and magazine centerfolds to actual propositions for sex. Although sexual harassment most often involves female workers who are taunted, ridiculed, or propositioned by male supervisors and colleagues, it can also involve homosexual workers. In either case, the harassment is not about sex; it is about exerting power over and belittling the worker. In a very real way, it expresses disrespect for the human body.

Very often, these four areas involving respect for the body are not black-and-white issues. It is easy to fall into disrespectful behaviors without even realizing it. For this reason, respect for the human body must be a habit—a daily choice. We strengthen the habit of respect (also known as the Holy Spirit's gift of reverence) whenever we receive the sacraments and participate in the life of the Christian community. If we happen to fall or to make a mistake in any of these areas, it is important to know that God's forgiving love can help us to begin again.

For your journal

1. If you could take three things with you to the afterlife, what would you take? Why?
2. When you die, do you want to be buried in the ground, entombed in a mausoleum, or cremated? Why?
3. On a scale of 1 to 10 (with 10 as the highest), how do you feel about your body? Do you like the way you look? how much you weigh?
4. On a scale of 1 to 10, how well do you respect your own body?
5. On a scale of 1 to 10, how well do you respect the bodies of others?

Discussion questions

1. How did each method of disposition show (or not show) respect for the dead body?
2. Compare the two biblical accounts of the disposition of Saul's body (1 Samuel 31:8–13 and 1 Chronicles 10:8–14). Why do you think the accounts differ?
3. Review each of the cultures presented in this chapter. How did the burial customs of each reflect beliefs about death and the afterlife?

4 Customs and Beliefs, A.D.

Memories and keepsakes

Death often changes the value we place on things. A simple watch, a photograph of the deceased, a piece of clothing—suddenly these items become important keepsakes. While the monetary value of these items may be insignificant, their sentimental value is priceless. After all, they are mementos of our loved one who has died; they help us to hang on to the past, and to keep the dead close.

No one can study the history of Christian burial customs without noticing the importance of preserving the memory of those who have died.[1] Just think of some of the memorial customs in your own life. Perhaps your family has written the name of its dead members in a Bible. Perhaps your town library or a branch of your local hospital was built "in memory" of someone who died. Perhaps your parents have scrapbooks containing pictures of people who are no longer living. Perhaps you have a painted portrait of an ancestor, or a locket of that person's hair. In this chapter, you will see how these customs were handed down to us from the Christians of earlier centuries.

Burial customs of the earliest Christians

Much of what we know about the burial customs of the Jews in the time of Jesus comes from the Christian Scriptures. For example, after John the Baptist was beheaded, his disciples came and buried his body (cf. Matthew 14:12). When someone died, the family hired wailers and instrumentalists to gather around the deathbed (cf. Matthew 9:23). Burial took place the same day the person died (cf. Acts 5:5, 10), unless that day was the Sabbath.

The Jews had no undertakers or formal cemeteries. Family or friends would wash the body, anoint it with oils and perfumes, bandage the hands and feet, wrap the corpse in a linen shroud, and cover the face with a cloth. Entombment might be in a family garden or in one of Palestine's abundant caves. (The law said that human burial had to be at least twenty-five yards from a house and

---

1. Christians are not the only ones who memorialize the dead. The Taj Mahal outside Agra, India, is a seventeenth century mausoleum built by the Mughal emperor Shah Jahan in memory of his wife, Arjumand Banu Begam, who died in childbirth. The building, with its bulbous double dome, parapets, pinnacles, and domed kiosks, is considered one of the seven most beautiful buildings in the world.

not along a main road.) The corpse was carried to the tomb or grave on an open bier, accompanied by family members and spectators (cf. Luke 7:11–12). Inside the tomb, the person was laid on his or her back, in the posture of sleep.

The burial of Jesus followed the same customs. All four Gospels agree that Joseph of Arimathea came and took Jesus' body for burial. The Gospels of Matthew, Mark, and Luke tell us the body was merely covered with a linen cloth and placed in the tomb, which was then sealed with a stone. The women had to wait until after the Sabbath to anoint the body with spices. John's Gospel, however, tells us that Nicodemus brought a mixture of myrrh and aloes (a fragrant resin from India). Jesus' body was wrapped in the linen, along with the spices, and then laid in Joseph's tomb.[2]

Christians continued the Jewish practice of closing the dead person's eyes and mouth after death.[3] Next, they washed the body (cf. Acts 9:36–37) and anointed it with myrrh and spices to preserve it before burial. The body was wrapped in white linen (a reminder of the white garment worn at baptism) and then dressed with clothes worn during life. The outer garment was usually violet.

During the second century, a wake was sometimes held in the home of the deceased before burial. When burial occurred on the same day as death, a three-day watch took place at the grave. When burial took place the day after death, the wake took the form of a night vigil, sometimes in church. Friends consoled relatives and prayed for the deceased. The body was surrounded by candles; priests read Scripture passages dealing with death and resurrection.

In the funeral procession, the body was placed on an open bier with the head exposed. Young men, frequently relatives, acted as pallbearers. Acolytes led the procession, and deacons carrying torches escorted the corpse. Instrumental music, hired mourners, actors and buffoons were all excluded because these were the practices of those who did not believe in the Judeo-Christian God. Instead, during the procession the Christians sang psalms (most frequently Psalms 22, 31, 100, 114, and 115).

---

2. The Basilica of the Holy Sepulchre, located in the Christian quarter of Jerusalem, is visited frequently by pilgrims. Under the basilica is the tomb where Jesus was supposedly buried. Originally a cave in a small hillside, it had an outer chamber and an inner burial chamber. In the second chamber, pilgrims can see a slab covered by a piece of marble, where the body of Jesus lay.

3. In Jewish funerals, closing the eyes was the time for loud wailing. Christians curbed this practice by singing psalms. In his book *On the Care of the Dead*, Augustine mentions Psalm 100, which speaks of God's mercy and judgment.

The Eucharist was celebrated either at the grave or in the church. During the Mass, the body was anointed again (a reminder of baptismal anointing) to signify that the deceased had persevered in the faith to the end. At the grave, a funeral oration, or eulogy, was given by a relative or friend (if this had not already been done in church). The speech praised the virtues of the deceased and offered consolation to the family members.

After the eulogy, relatives approached the corpse to give it a final kiss. Then the body was wrapped in linen and placed in the grave as if sleeping. The hands were either extended alongside the body or folded across the chest. Usually the body was buried with the feet to the east, to await the Second Coming of Christ. Before leaving the cemetery, the priest offered farewell prayers, called *vivas*, that the departed might live in God and intercede for the living.

Christians made frequent visits to the graves of their loved ones, especially on the third day, seventh or ninth day, thirtieth or fortieth day after death, and on the year anniversary. The entire Christian community remembered the dead during prayer offerings at the Eucharist. Special Masses were celebrated on the annual feasts of death, in memory of the dead and for the benefit of their souls.

The catacombs

At the end of the second century, most Christians of Rome were poor; thus they tended to live in "the suburbs." The Church owned only one cemetery, called St. Callixtus. It was named after the deacon Callixtus, who was appointed head of the cemetery under Pope Zephyrinus (199–217) and who, when he himself was pope (217–222), greatly enlarged it. Eventually, the cemetery had five levels underground, spread over six miles. Nine popes were buried there.[4]

By the third century, a number of wealthy people had converted to Christianity. Their homes became *tituli*, or church centers much like parishes today, where Christians could gather to celebrate the Eucharist and the sacraments, to receive religious instruction, and to assist the needy. The wealthy Christians donated land to the Church for private burial grounds. In turn, these cemeteries were named after their benefactors: Priscilla, Domitilla, Maximus, Thraso, Commodilla, Agnes, and so forth.

---

4. The nine popes (also saints) who are buried in the catacomb of St. Callixtus are St. Pontian (230–235), St. Anterus (236), St. Fabian (236–250), St. Lucius I (253–254), St. Stephen I (254–257), St. Sixtus II (257–258), St. Dionysius (259–268), St. Felix I (269–274), and St. Eutychian (275–283).

Halfway through the third century, Pope Fabian (236–250) divided Rome into seven districts. He appointed seven deacons to supervise these districts. Among their duties was funeral organization, a task that the state did not provide. Each district was allotted a burial zone outside the walls of the city, with a certain number of cemeteries. These underground cemeteries are what we now call the catacombs.

Despite popular belief, the catacombs were not secret places built by the Christians to flee persecution. Rather, they were subterranean tunnels once used by the Romans as part of a vast network for waterworks. When the Romans abandoned the tunnels, Christians found in them a solution for the space they needed for burials. The Christians simply dug ledges or shelves, one on top of the other, along each side of the narrow walkways. Thus they were able to provide burial for the poor in great numbers.

The Christians wrapped each corpse in a sheet before placing it on a shelf, which often contained two or more members of the same family. The name of the deceased, along with date of death, was painted or sculpted on the slab that served as its door. Small terra-cotta lamps and vases for perfume were often placed above the tomb.

Periodically throughout the maze of catacomb tunnels were small rooms that the Christians used as chapels. While these rooms were much too small to accommodate an entire community, family members and friends could gather there to celebrate the Eucharist for their dead loved ones. The walls of these chapels contained painted frescoes that reminded the mourners (who, for the most part, couldn't read) of biblical stories that expressed belief in the resurrection.

Among the pictures that can still be seen today in the catacombs are Abraham's sacrifice of Isaac (Genesis 22:1–19); Moses and the spring in the desert (Exodus 17:1–7); three youths in a fiery furnace (Daniel 3:1–97); a rooster, symbol of the story of St. Peter's denial (Matthew 26:31–35, 69–75; John 21:15–23); the Good Shepherd (John 10:11–18), the miracle of the loaves and fishes (Mark 6:30–44); bread and wine or people around a table with bread and wine to show the Eucharist (1 Corinthians 11:23–34); the healing of the paralytic (Mark 2:1–12); and the baptism of Jesus (Matthew 3:13–17). Three nonbiblical symbols may be seen in catacomb art as well: (1) the dolphin, a symbol of redemption, who was thought to carry the souls of the saved "across the sea" to heaven; (2) the peacock, whose glorious tail symbolized the new and glorious life of those who die in Christ; and (3) the phoenix rising from flames, a Roman myth that symbolized the resurrection of the dead.

The fourth century brought more religious persecutions and martyrs for Christ. After more and more martyrs were buried in the catacombs, Christians sought *depositio ad sanctos*, the privilege of being buried near the graves of the martyrs. Those considered most holy—virgins, monks, and priests—were buried closest to the martyrs.

The catacombs were used as cemeteries until the early fifth century, when a new custom took over: that of burying the dead beneath the floors of cemetery basilicas. At first, Christians continued to visit the tombs of martyrs and saints in the catacombs. However, during the next four centuries, the remains of most martyrs and saints were transferred to churches within the city walls. After that, the catacombs fell into disuse; many of their entrances were covered over with buildings or vegetation. They were forgotten until the sixteenth century, when Antonio Bosio located about thirty catacombs beneath Rome.

Relics

When Bishop Polycarp was martyred in the mid-second century, the citizens of Smyrna began public veneration of his remains. Each year, on the anniversary of his martyrdom, the Christians honored his bones because of his faithfulness in following Christ. This practice of honoring the remains of the martyrs spread quickly among Christian communities as more and more of their members were martyred. By the fourth and fifth centuries, this practice had grown into a liturgical cult, known as the veneration of relics.

Under this practice, the tombs of martyrs were opened and the relics were distributed to Christians in the form of objects that had touched the actual body or bones. These objects were enclosed in little cases, called reliquaries, and hung around a person's neck. St. John Chrysostom and St. Basil of Caesarea defended the cult of relics, saying that relics reminded people of saints who could serve as Christian role models. St. Augustine also defended the cult of relics, pointing to the miracles worked by God through them and to their origin in Scripture (cf. Acts 19:12).

Eventually people developed the notion that the more extraordinary the miracles associated with the relic, the holier the person who had died. Thus, the Church began to require the working of miracles through the intercession of a dead person before that person could be canonized. One miracle had to be worked in answer to prayers to that person in order for the person to be declared "blessed," two miracles to be declared a saint. Before beatification, the person's body had to be disinterred and examined, to make sure the remains were truly those of the person and also to obtain relics.[5]

In the Eastern Church, the bodies of saints were exhumed, dismembered, and transported from place to place for the edification of the people. In the Western Church, such plundering of graves was outlawed. It was not until the eighth century that Pope Paul I and Pope Paschal I authorized the dismemberment and dispersal of the bodies of the saints. During the Middle Ages the cult of relics became so popular (and so economically profitable) that many relics were falsified.

During the Crusades, commerce in relics reached a new peak. After crusaders sacked Constantinople, Antioch, and Jerusalem, they sent back many relics to churches and cathedrals in Europe. Because so many fraudulent relics appeared in circulation at this time, the Council of Lyons (1274) prohibited the veneration of new relics without the pope's prior authentication of them.

By the late Middle Ages, most churches displayed bodies or relics of the saints close to the altar. According to Church law, an altar could not be dedicated unless it contained the sealed relics of two martyrs. The pastor of a new church had to request from Rome the relics of the saint in whose honor the church was named.

Because many superstitions arose regarding relics and because some Christians erroneously began to worship the relics themselves, theologians restated the Church's teaching. As Thomas Aquinas noted in his *Summa,* every relic is a record, or reminder, of a saint. Relics themselves have no sanctifying or miraculous powers; rather, it is God who works miracles through them. Thus God is to be the principal object of worship, not the saints or their relics.

A first-class relic is a body or body part (skin, bones, eyes, hair, etc.) of a saint. One example of a first-class relic is the body of St. Ambrose, which is preserved in a glass coffin under the altar of

---

5. On November 14, 1987, Church officials exhumed the remains of Father Juniper Serra (founder of the California missions) as a requirement for his beatification. He was buried in a grave below the stone floor of the Carmel Mission. Physicians and forensic anthropologists identified Serra's remains by comparing bone measurements with information listed on Serra's Spanish passport and from information recorded about him by fellow Franciscans. Serra was beatified by Pope John Paul II on September 25, 1988. His feast day is July 1.

St. Simpliciano's Basilica in Milan. A second-class relic includes any part of the saint's clothing, an article used by the saint, or instruments of a martyr's imprisonment or death. A third-class relic is any object touched to the body or grave of a saint.

Today, the authentication and use of relics comes under the jurisdiction of the Vatican's Congregation of Rites. According to the present Code of Canon Law, the Church may buy relics, but not sell them.

St. Peter's Basilica

Hundreds of thousands of Catholics visit St. Peter's Basilica in Rome each year to hear the pope speak and to attend liturgical celebrations. But not all of these pilgrims realize that the present church (built in the seventeenth century) lies over a first- to fourth-century burial place, once used by non-Christians and by Christians. Non-Christians called this place the *necropolis,* or "city of the dead." The Christians referred to it as the *coemeterium,* or "land of sleeping people."

The necropolis-cemetery was situated close to the Circus of Gaius and Nero where, according to tradition, the apostle Peter was martyred between A.D. 64 and 67. Non-Christian Romans used the necropolis to inter the bodies or ashes of their dead along the north side of the circus. During the first and second centuries, some Christian tombs were built on the south side. The burial place consisted of rows of mausoleums or family chapels decorated with paintings and mosaics. It contained places for the ashes of the cremated and sarcophagi for those who were buried. Christian art—the shepherd, the fisherman, the anchor, the vine, Jonah and the whale—decorated the walls.

A church was erected by Constantine and Pope Sylvester between A.D. 321–329 to preserve what was believed to be the tomb of St. Peter. In order to create a platform for the church, Constantine's workers had to bury the necropolis and dig out part of the hill to the north. They built a monument, called the Trophy of Gaius, over the supposed tomb of St. Peter. The church had various functions. It was used as a civic assembly hall, a church and place of pilgrimage, a covered cemetery, and a hall for banquet and funeral receptions. There was no fixed altar until the time of Gregory the Great, who raised the sanctuary and concealed the tomb of the apostle in the crypt below. The altar was placed directly above the supposed tomb of St. Peter.

The twentieth-century search for the tomb of Peter was by no means a simple one. Archaeologists digging beneath St. Peter's were able to find the place in the necropolis-cemetery where St. Peter was supposed to be buried. According to tradition, he was buried at the foot of the red brick wall along what the archaeologists labeled as "Camp P."

In 1953, archaeologist Margherita Guarducci spent time studying the graffiti that covered a low wall on the right of Camp P. One of these statements read, "Peter is here." Further research led her to discover the bones and fragments believed to be those of St. Peter. On the other hand, there are a number of arguments against this belief. Today, visitors to the necropolis-cemetery can see these meager remains behind a sheet of glass in a modest irregular niche.[6]

Between the ancient necropolis and the floor of the present basilica are the remaining parts of the Constantine church and later crypt built by Gregory the Great. This area, known as the Vatican Grottoes, was restored during the twentieth century and is open to visitors. Many popes are interred in the Grottoes, among them, Pius XII, Pope John XXIII, Pope Paul VI, and Pope John Paul I, who was only pontiff for thirty-three days.

Next to St. Peter's Basilica is the Vatican Museum, which houses the richest collection of Christian sarcophagi in the world. In the first centuries of Christianity, the sarcophagus represented the most luxurious form of burial. It was a rectangular- or oval-shaped casket covered by a lid, either pitched in two directions like a roof or flat, with a tablet for inscriptions in the center. Often, biblical scenes, such as the raising of Lazarus, healings performed by Jesus, and the miracle of the loaves and fishes, were sculpted on the lid and sides.

Remembering the dead today

If you walk into a Catholic church that was built before the Second Vatican Council, you are likely to find many physical mementos of the dead. The church may contain numerous statues of Jesus, Mary, Joseph, and other saints. You may see paintings or carvings of particular saints or scenes in our Lord's life. Most likely, there is some type of artistic rendering of the Stations of the Cross. Subtler forms of mementos might be stained-glass windows purchased "in the memory of" a deceased parishioner or memorial

---

6. To visit the necropolis-cemetery beneath St. Peter's, you must get advance reservations by writing to: Reverenda Fabbrica di S. Pietro, 00120 Citta del Vaticano.

plaques on the organ, pews, and pulpit, acknowledging the financial donation by or in memory of someone who died.

In revising the liturgy, the bishops of Vatican II wanted to maintain a connection to past tradition while also making sure Catholics understood the difference between *worship* and *veneration*. Only God may be worshiped; the saints and any relics pertaining to them may only be venerated. Worship refers to the respect we owe a divine being; veneration refers to the respect we owe people who are particularly wise, heroic, virtuous, and so forth. For this reason, the bishops advised the following:

> *The practice of placing sacred images in churches so that they may be venerated by the faithful is to be firmly maintained. Nevertheless, their numbers should be moderate and their relative location should reflect right order. Otherwise they may create confusion among the Christian people and promote a faulty sense of devotion.*
> —*Constitution on the Sacred Liturgy, #125*

The 1970 edition of the Roman Missal elaborated on the bishops' point by saying:

> *In accord with ancient tradition, images of Christ, Mary, and the saints are venerated in churches. They should, however, be placed so as not to distract the faithful from the actual celebration. They should not be too numerous, there should not be more than one image of the same saint, and the correct order of saints should be observed. In general, the piety of the entire community should be considered in the decoration and arrangement of the church.*
> —*General Instruction of the Roman Missal, #278*

Thus, in churches built after the Second Vatican Council, you are likely to see far fewer statues, pictures, and artistic representations of saints and martyrs.

In addition to these changes, the interiors of today's churches contain a less obvious change. As you have learned, altars in the past had to contain the sealed relics of two martyrs. As the Roman Missal now states, "It is fitting to maintain the practice of enclosing relics in the altar or of placing them under the altar. These relics need not be those of martyrs, but there must be proof that they are authentic." (General Instruction of the Roman Missal, #266). The reason for this change is explained in *The Dedication of a Church and an Altar*:

> *The entire dignity of an altar consists in this: the altar is the table of the Lord. It is not, then, the bodies of the martyrs that render the altar glorious; it is the altar that renders the burial place of the*

martyrs glorious. However, as a mark of respect for the bodies of the martyrs and other saints, and as a sign that the sacrifice of the members has its source in the sacrifice of the Head, it is fitting that altars should be constructed over their tombs, or their relics placed beneath altars. . . . .

—*Dedication of a Church and an Altar, #60*

As Canon 1239.2 of the present Code of Canon Law makes clear, "No corpse may be buried beneath the altar; otherwise Mass may not be celebrated there." Only the relics of known saints and martyrs may be placed beneath an altar. The bodies of popes, cardinals, and bishops may be buried inside their churches, but not under the altar.[7]

What about you?

People today remember the dead by keeping photographs of them, articles of their clothing, or certain other items that once belonged to them. Sometimes people also remember the dead by contributing money to the parish, to the arts, to a charitable organization, or to a building fund. This memorial allows the dead to "live on" in a way that benefits the community.

What about you? When you die, how do you want others to remember you? Take some time to think about the ways you want certain people to remember you. Concentrate on intangible memories (a smile, friendship, a shared experience, a value, your personality, etc.). Then write your reflections in your notebook. Finally, write a eulogy for yourself—the way someone would remember you if you died (a) today or (b) twenty years from now.

---

7. Present Church laws dealing with the veneration of the saints, sacred images, and relics include these canons: *Canon 1186:* To foster the sanctification of the people of God the Church recommends to the particular and filial veneration of the Christian faithful the Blessed Mary ever Virgin, the Mother of God, whom Christ established as the Mother of the human race; it also promotes true and authentic devotion to the other saints by whose intercession they are sustained. *Canon 1187:* Veneration through public cult is permitted only to those servants of God who are listed in the catalog of the saints or of the blessed by the authority of the Church. *Canon 1188:* The practice of displaying sacred images in the churches for the veneration of the faithful is to remain in force; nevertheless they are to be exhibited in moderate number and in suitable order lest they bewilder the Christian people and give opportunity for questionable devotion.

For your journal

1. What items do you have that remind you of someone who has died? How do you feel when you see these items? How valuable are they to you?

2. How do you want to be remembered by each of the following: your parents? your brothers and sisters? your friends? your business associates? your children? your grandchildren? your parish? your civic community?

3. What would you like said in your eulogy?

4. If you had to summarize your life by five mementos, what would these be? What would each memento symbolize about you?

Discussion questions

1. Audio and video recordings have made it possible for us to see and hear people long after they are dead. Name some of your favorite songs by a composer or singer who is dead. Name some of your favorite movies or TV shows by a director, actor, or actress who is dead. In what way do these people "live on" after death?

2. Why do you think three, seven, nine, thirty, and forty days were important times to remember the dead? What might these numbers have symbolized?

3. Do you have any relics, or have you seen any? Describe them. What feelings do they invoke in you?

4. Why do you think Canon Law permits the Church to buy relics, but not to sell them?

5. How do the names "necropolis" and "cemetery" reflect different beliefs about death and the afterlife?

6. Have you ever visited St. Peter's in Rome? If so, what impressed you most? If not, is it a place you would like to visit someday? Why or why not?

7. How does your parish church remember the dead in visual ways? What is your favorite memento in the church?

8. How is praying to the saints different from praying to God?

9. Do you think Catholics today need visual images in church to remind them of the saints and martyrs? Why or why not?

Part Three: Cultural Aspects

. . . Break bread with the bereaved to console them in their bereavement; . . . give them the cup of consolation to drink over the death of father or mother.

—Jeremiah 16:7

5 Death Rituals around the World

Laughing at death

Mexicans celebrate the Day of the Dead on November 2. On this day, people bake special breads and cakes, which are called *Pan de Muerte*, in the shape of skulls, skeletons, coffins, tombstones, funeral wreaths, and crossbones. The people then eat these breads and cakes at the cemetery, and leave some behind for their dead relatives.[1]

The Day of the Dead is a time for Mexicans to acknowledge the fact of death and then laugh at it. Through the customs of this day, the living show their refusal to accept death as the definite end of life. Leaving food at the graves is a sign that the dead live on in the afterlife, and thus need nourishment. On the other hand, the dead continue to live on at family gatherings. They are present as part of the communion of saints. Both the dead person's character and genes live on in a very real way in the family members.

The refusal to accept death as the end of life transcends all cultures and races, and is found in death rituals around the world. For this reason, in this chapter we will be looking more closely at some of these rituals—especially those of present-day Jews, Hindus, Buddhists, and Muslims. Finally, you will look at the Eucharist as a memorial meal that transcends all cultures, a meal that unites the living with the dead and nourishes all the faithful for their spiritual journey through death to the fullness of new life.

Judaism

Over seventeen million people throughout the world are followers of Judaism, either as Conservative Jews, Reform Jews, or Orthodox Jews. Almost all Reform and Conservative Jews believe in the immortality of the soul. But only the Orthodox believe in resurrection of the body.

When a Jew is about to die, devout family members and friends gather to say good-bye and to recite the *Shema*.[2] After death, the

---

1. The custom of leaving food at the grave stemmed from fear that the spirits would grow hungry and come back to haunt the living. In Christian times, this custom was continued as an occasion to pray for the dead, decorate the graves, and clean up the cemetery.

2. The *Shema* is considered the greatest commandment in the Hebrew Scriptures. "Hear, O Israel! The Lord is our God, the Lord alone! Therefore, you shall love the Lord, your God, with all your heart, and with all your soul, and with all your strength" (Deuteronomy 6:4–5).

body is either taken to a funeral home for preparation or turned over to *Cheura Kadisha*, "holy societies" that care properly for the dead. Before preparing and washing the body, the *Cheura Kadisha* light candles and call the deceased by name. They apologize for any indignity they may unintentionally inflict upon his or her body.

Because Judaism considers everyone equal in God's eyes, Orthodox Jews forbid dressing the dead person in fancy clothes and jewelry. Instead, the body is wrapped in a simple shroud, a white garment with no pockets. Today, some Conservative and Reform Jews also use the shroud for burial. It is normally not the Jewish custom to view the body in death, except for purposes of identification.

Orthodox Jews do not encourage funerals to be held in the synagogue. Instead, the service usually takes place in a funeral home. Male mourners wear hats—yarmulkes—and female mourn- ers wear black lace caps during the service. Toward the beginning of the service, the presider slashes the clothing of the next of kin (a tradition from biblical times). Then come readings from the Psalms, eulogies, and prayers for the repose of the soul of the deceased. The service concludes with the Kaddish doxology:

> *Magnified and sanctified be God's great name in the world which He has created according to His will. May He establish His kingdom during your life, . . . even speedily and at a near time. . . . Let His great name be blessed for ever and to all eternity. . . . May there be abundant peace from heaven, and life for us and for all Israel; . . . He who makes peace in His high places, may He make peace for us and for all Israel. Amen.*

Most Jews do not embalm their dead. Burial takes place within twenty-four hours of death, often before sundown on the same day. The body is buried in a plain wooden casket held together with wooden pegs, except in Israel and other eastern lands where caskets are not ordinarily used.[3] Usually a handful of dust or earth from the Holy Land is laid in the grave or coffin. Mourners throw dirt on the grave and then stand in two rows, through which the next of kin walk out of the cemetery. As the family members walk by, the mourners offer them prayers and words of comfort.

---

3. Today in Israel when someone dies, the head of the family or the eldest son closes the eyes. A drumbeat announces the death to the village. Interment follows swiftly, the same day or the next morning. Men and women mourners walk to the cemetery in separate groups. Even the poor must hire at least two flutists and one mourner. Men take turns shouldering the bier. The next-of-kin tear their clothes. Women cry and clap in rhythm. Men beat their breasts and recall the virtues of the deceased.

From the cemetery, Jewish people return home for the *Seudat-Havraan*, or "meal of consolation." This ritual meal is prepared by neighbors and friends. It is not only a gesture of support and comfort to those who are mourning; it is also an affirmation of life. Sharing a meal with others reminds the mourners that life goes on, despite pain and sorrow.

Shiva, the immediate period of mourning after death, may last from three days for Reform Jews to eight days for Orthodox Jews. During this time, the mourners stay home and refrain from business and social contacts. Neighbors continue to bring in food or help prepare the meals. After the fourth day, friends may come to the home in the evening to console the mourners and to participate in a worship service.

Each day for a year following death, relatives recite the Kaddish. This duty is considered one of the highest tributes paid to a deceased person, since through it the mourners pledge their lives to God. Even in the midst of their mourning, they praise and glorify God.

Whenever a person visits a grave, the custom is to leave a pebble there. On the first anniversary of a death, Jews burn a memorial light (*yahrzeit*) in their homes. This light is lit on the eve of the anniversary and remains burning throughout the day until sunset. During the day, a service is held at the grave, at which time the memorial stone is unveiled. In addition to this memorial, many Jewish people have a tree planted in Israel for the deceased.

Hinduism

Hinduism, the primary religion of India, claims 705 million followers worldwide. Hindus believe that life consists of an endless cycle of birth, death, and rebirth. At death, the soul simply discards one body for another, in a process called reincarnation. What a person does in this life affects how he or she will be reincarnated. If a person is evil, he or she might come back as an animal, insect, or person of low caste. If a person is good, he or she might come back as a priest or holy person.

Hindu belief in reincarnation means that the body has little significance. Thus what happens to the body after death is not important. Usually, except for those who do not have sons, for ascetics, and for some members of the low castes, Hindus burn their dead on funeral pyres. The fire reduces the body to its basic elements of fire, water, earth, and air, while at the same time purifying the spirit in preparation for its reincarnation. In some sects, the ashes are put into the Ganges or another sacred river.[4] In other parts of India the bones are collected and buried in an urn.

When death approaches, relatives and Brahmans (priests) recite sacred texts. If possible, they have the dying person touch a cow (considered to be a sacred animal). After death, the corpse is placed in a shroud. There is a procession to the place of cremation. After prayers and ritual offerings, the fire is lit. (*Suttee*—the traditional practice whereby the widow was forced to lie down on the funeral pyre next to her dead husband and then also be cremated—was prohibited in 1829.) The ashes are then scattered in the river or put in an urn and buried.

For ten days after the funeral, the mourners are considered unclean. They are secluded from society, may not study the Veda, and may not cut their hair. Daily they must set out offerings of milk, water mixed with sesame, and rice balls to help the dead soul find a new body. At least once a year, family members make a memorial offering of food to the Brahmans for the benefit of the deceased.

Buddhism

Buddhism began in India in the sixth to fifth century B.C. as a reaction to Hindu belief in reincarnation. According to Siddhartha Gautama, the founder of Buddhism, an enlightened person is released from the endless chain of birth-death-rebirth. Such a person arrives at eternal bliss, or *nirvana*. This teaching spread from India to Central Asia, China, Korea, Japan, Tibet, Ceylon (Sri Lanka), and Southeast Asia. Today, over 303 million people profess Buddhism.

Among Buddhists, there is no one common ritual concerning death. Instead, customs vary according to geography and culture. In India, for example, most people are cremated. Afterwards, their ashes and bones are collected, and a *stupa* (a dome-shaped mound or tower) is built over them. On the other hand, earth burial is common in Sri Lanka. In Tibet, the bodies of great *lamas* are placed in rich *stupas*, while the bodies of ordinary people are left exposed for vultures and wild animals. In Japan, the Zen and Tendai Buddhists permit either burial or cremation. In Thailand, it is the

---

4. Some Hindus cast the ashes of their dead into the Ganges River because they believe it to be the holiest of rivers. Cremation ghats (temples at the summit of riverside steps) for burning the dead have been built in many places on the banks of the Ganges. When Mahatma Gandhi was killed by a Hindu fanatic in 1948, his body was burned on one of these pyres and his ashes were scattered in the Ganges.

practice to preserve the body for a time by embalming and then to cremate it with elaborate ritual. The remains of royalty are sometimes preserved in a temple for six months or a year before cremation. Families who do not have the money to purchase fuel for cremation at the time of death will bury the body and then exhume it later for cremation when they have the necessary finances.

Common to all Buddhists is the belief that a dying person's last thoughts are important. These thoughts determine whether the person reaches *nirvana* or must be reborn. For this reason, the sacred texts are read to the person before and after death. (The conscious principle is thought to remain in the body for three days after death.)

Some sects shave the washed corpse and "ordain" it a monk. During the wake and temple rituals that follow, there is the burning of incense, chanting, readings from the Book of the Dead, and prayers for the deceased. Buddhists believe that their good works and prayers achieve merit that can then be transferred to the dead person.

Buddhists in Japan believe that the spirits of the dead return to earth each year during Obon (July 12–16). So they clean family shrines and prepare tea, fruit, and various foods for the spirits. They also light lanterns in the cemeteries and sometimes make bonfires at doorways to welcome the ghostly visitors. In Hawaii, there is an Obon festival almost every weekend during summer.

Islam

Over 935 million people profess the religion of Islam. These people are sometimes called Muslims. Muslims believe that immediately after a person dies, he or she is judged by two angels named Munkar and Nakir. The "test" is whether or not the person can correctly recite answers about the faith. A second judgment will occur at the end of the world. Then all people will rise from their graves and assemble before Allah. Mohammed (the founder of Islam) will intercede on behalf of the just. They will enter a paradise of gardens and meadows, wear fine clothes, and spend eternity in sensual bliss. The unjust will be condemned and assigned to a hell of heat, smoke, hunger, and torture.

Before or immediately after death, the mourners lay the body in the direction of Mecca, the holy city, and recite the profession of faith from the Koran. Then they wash the body and stuff the orifices with cotton. After sprinkling the body with camphor and rose water, they close the eyes and tie the feet. Then they wrap the body in a shroud while saying prayers for the dead. It is customary to hold a "watch" by the corpse; during this time hired readers recite the Koran.

During the procession to the cemetery, which often takes place to the accompaniment of wailing, the open coffin is carried by men. The coffin is placed in a grave of ample size, large enough for the deceased to sit up when he or she is interrogated by the angels Munkar and Nakir. The body is laid on its right side, with the face toward Mecca. Before the coffin is closed, two "tutors" shout into the dead person's ears the correct answers for the angels' catechism test. The coffin is then closed. The chief mourner tears his or her clothes, while each bystander places three handfuls of earth on the grave and then departs.

On returning from the funeral to the house, the mourners share a meal and recite the *sabha*, a rosary of one thousand beads, for the deceased. Wailing is resumed by the women every Thursday for three weeks. On Fridays, they visit the grave and perform various rituals.

When Muslims in Pakistan bury a saint, they build the low structure that lies atop the grave slightly taller than the one they build for an ordinary deceased person. The additional height accommodates two tomb plaques. One, bearing the person's name, stands at the foot of the tomb. The other, containing blessings, stands at the head. People first pay homage at the foot of the grave and then proceed around it. Proper cemetery conduct requires the living to look sad, pray for Allah's forgiveness, and remember that one day they, too, will die.

Zoroastrianism

This pre-Islamic religion survives today in parts of Iran and among the Parsees of India, who are descendants of immigrants from Iran. Zoroastrians believe strongly in ecology and in preserving the environment. They regard the flesh of dead bodies as a form of pollution. Burial pollutes the earth; cremation pollutes the air and water. As an alternative, Zoroastrians leave their dead on top of *dakhmas*, or "towers of silence," to be devoured by birds of prey.

Zoroastrians believe that a dead body is dangerous to the living because demons of corruption, the dreaded Nasu, rush upon the dead body and take control of it. Anyone near the corpse is in danger of infection and pollution. That is why women wash the body immediately after death and cover it with a white sheet.

Another custom involves bringing a four-eyed dog (a dog with a spot above each eye) before the corpse and lighting a fire in the death room, which is kept burning until three days after the removal of the corpse. During daylight hours, *nasasalars* (corpse-bearers) carry the corpse on a bier to the towers of silence.

The towers are circles of stone, reaching about thirty feet high and almost three hundred feet around. The interior of each tower is built in three concentric circles, one each for men, women, and children. The naked corpses are left there. Within an hour or so, the vultures have completely stripped the flesh off the bones. The bones are then swept into the central well.

After the funeral, Parsees vigorously clean the room in which death occurred and all articles that had contact with the dead body. In order to purify themselves, the mourners eat only fish and vegetables for three days. The morning of the fourth day is marked by the most solemn observance in the death ritual, for it is then that the soul leaves the body and makes its journey to the Chinvat Bridge, where it is judged.

Each month after the death, the family prays for the dead soul. During the last ten days of the year, a Festival of the Dead is held to remember the dead.

African folk religions

Native tribes throughout Africa have developed their own belief systems that, in turn, influence the way they approach death. For example, in Kenya, members of the Giriama tribe have two funerals when a person dies. The first funeral lasts seven days and nights for a man, six for a woman. The corpse is wrapped in a calico shroud and then placed in a wooden coffin. After burial, relatives and friends wail collectively. Over the next three days there is dancing, drumming, sacrificing, and a great deal of eating. Close relatives and friends are expected to honor the dead person by providing ample palm wine, bullocks, and goats. The second funeral lasts between one and four months. During this time, the elders of the tribe settle any problems involving inheritance. The Giriama people also make wooden images to represent the dead. The images are first placed in the grave, and later put in the center of the village. During times of crisis, family members go to the image to ask the dead person for help.

Throughout the peoples of western Africa, proper burial rites are considered essential to ensure that the spirit will not linger about malevolently. Before a funeral is complete, several customs must be observed: preparation of the body for burial, the wake, the interment, mourning after burial, and later mourning at varying periods. Among the Tellensi of Ghana, a man's wealth is inherited by his sons. To prevent the father from becoming angry that his sons have profited from his death, the sons are expected to apologize to him during the funeral ceremonies.

Among some tribes, dances to ward off evil spirits must be performed during the funeral, after burial, and on anniversaries. The Dogon people of Mali wear masks that look like giant birds. In Fulani villages in Cameroon, the corpse is placed in a sitting position in a prominent place during the funeral. Solo and group dances are performed in the dead person's honor.

Some west African peoples decorate each grave with the personal effects (pots, pans, furniture, etc.) of the person buried there. The Yombe people of Zaire decorate their graves with wooden figurines. These decorations are thought to provide the deceased with companionship and protection in the afterlife. During a funeral of the Kuba people of Zaire, family members are given objects in the shape of human heads, animals, tools, or abstract geometric forms made of camwood paste. These reminders of the dead person become heirlooms that are passed on from generation to generation.[5]

Other peoples

The Chin people of India and Burma believe that only a few souls reach paradise after death. Everyone else goes to the "village of the dead," where life is much the same as on earth. For this reason, ancestor worship at household shrines is important. Those who die violently (suicide, homicide, death in childbirth, drowning) are buried without ceremony outside the village in a separate cemetery.

In an ordinary death, the body is washed, dressed in fine clothes and put on display in a sitting position. A few days later the funeral takes place. The deceased is "fed" and entertained with singing and dancing. After disposal (either burial or cremation), the people feast on meat, grain, and beer. When an important person dies, the funeral rites take place over many months. During this time the body is put in a temporary resting place (a grave, a vault, a special hut, an exposed platform, or a coffin in the house).

---

5. In Victorian America, everyone who attended a funeral was given a memento, or favor, as a reminder of the dead person. Often this memento was a pair of gloves. Needless to say, such favors made funerals very expensive.

The Batak people of Indonesia believe that a person dies seven times before finally becoming an ancestor spirit. Funeral rites are organized around the sacred number seven; the corpse is covered with seven cloths. For seven days after burial the grave is sprinkled with offerings of palm wine, rice, and betel. The ghost of the deceased is thought to remain close to the body during this period.

The Toradja people of Sulawesi, Indonesia, also wash and dress the corpse and then place it on a chair. Daily the corpse is "fed." At the funeral, a buffalo is slaughtered. (Only those children who kill buffaloes at their parent's funeral may inherit their possessions.) The corpse, now in a shroud, is tossed in the air several times and then buried in a north-south orientation. In some regions, the death of an important Toradja is announced to his or her cat. The cat has important status as guardian of the rice and possessions of the house. A relative stands before the cat and says, "Dear Lord Cat, your owner has died."

The funeral ceremonies of the Bororo Indians in Brazil last almost a month. Soon after death, elders appoint a male "avenger" to kill a jaguar or other carnivore on behalf of the dead. At the close of the funeral rites, the avenger is adorned with gourd whistles that symbolize the soul of the deceased. After burial, the grave is watered to hasten decomposition. Months later tribe members exhume the body, decorate the bones, and then rebury them. During this time, mourners use feather flutes, songs, and dances to evoke the memory of the dead person.

The bread of life

At least from the days of Jeremiah, celebrating a meal together was an integral part of Jewish funeral rites. The meal had two purposes—to console the mourners and to reestablish a oneness or bond with the dead. Frescoes in the catacombs tell us that the early Christians continued the practice of holding an *agape* or funeral meal near the tomb or mausoleum on the day of burial. In contrast to the pagan funeral banquets (*refrigeria*) common at that time, the meal the Christians shared was the Eucharist.

The Eucharist was established by Jesus at his Last Supper and was prefigured by the miracle of the multiplication of the loaves. The Eucharist began as a seder meal commemorating the Jewish Passover. Today the Church regards the Eucharist as a memorial that re-presents Jesus' own passing from death to new life, the bread of life that nourishes us on our own journey toward eternal life, and a sacrament that both points to and makes possible our bonds of oneness with the living and the dead. These beliefs may be seen in the communion rite at Mass, in the wording of the eucharistic prayers, and in each of the memorial acclamations:

- Christ has died; Christ is risen; Christ will come again.
- Dying you destroyed our death, rising you restored our life. Lord Jesus, come in glory.
- When we eat this bread and drink this cup, we proclaim your death, Lord Jesus, until you come in glory.
- Lord, by your cross and resurrection, you have set us free. You are the Savior of the world.

Because of these beliefs, the Catholic Church has celebrated the Eucharist as an integral part of its death rituals—the funeral itself, Masses for the Dead that are celebrated on All Souls' Day and anniversary dates, and in the practice of celebrating Viaticum with those who are dying.

When the Eucharist is celebrated as the last sacrament of Christian life, it is called *Viaticum*, which means "food for the journey." This last Eucharist is seen as nourishment that strengthens the dying person on his or her passage through death to eternal life. It is celebrated in anticipation of the heavenly banquet, and unites the participants both with one another and with Jesus' own death and resurrection.

The sacrament of Viaticum may take place within or apart from Mass, although the former is preferred. (In this case, the priest follows the Mass of the Holy Eucharist or the ritual Mass for Viaticum.) Depending on the condition of the dying person, the presiding priest (or the deacon or eucharistic minister in the case of Viaticum outside Mass) should make every effort to involve the dying person, the family, friends, and other members of the local community in the planning and celebration.

Both forms of the sacrament (within or apart from Mass) include Scripture readings, prayers, and songs. After the homily, the dying person is invited to make a profession of faith by the renewal of baptismal promises. If a priest is present, he may give an apostolic pardon for the dying at the conclusion of the penitential rite. One of the following forms may be used:

A. Through the holy mysteries of our redemption,
may almighty God release you from all punishments
in this life and in the life to come.
May he open to you the gates of paradise
and welcome you to everlasting joy.
Amen.

B. By the authority which the Apostolic See has given me,
I grant you a full pardon and the remission of all your sins
in the name of the Father, and of the Son, and of the Holy Spirit.
Amen.

—From the Roman Ritual: Pastoral Care of the Sick

During the Sign of Peace, all those present are encouraged to embrace the dying person. If possible, communion should be given under both species.

White vestments are usually worn for the celebration of Viaticum. The ritual Mass for Viaticum is not permitted during the Easter Triduum, on Christmas, Epiphany, Ascension Thursday, Pentecost, Corpus Christi, or a Holy Day of Obligation. On these days the Mass of the day is said instead. The Mass of the day must also be said on Sundays of Advent, Lent, and the Easter Season; however one reading from the ritual Mass for Viaticum may be chosen on these days.

Your last rites

Waiting until death is near is not necessarily the best time to plan and prepare a Mass for Viaticum. Take some time, right now, to think about how you would like to celebrate your last moments on earth. Decide on the people you would like to have present with you. Choose readings and songs for your last Mass with them. Then write out a menu of your favorite foods to serve at a "Last Supper" you would like to share with your family and friends.

For your journal

1. What foods remind you of someone who has died? What memories are connected to the food?
2. What is one recipe that has been handed down in your family from a dead relative? Write out the recipe, along with a brief story about the relative.
3. Why do you think Hindus believe in reincarnation?
4. What is attractive and not attractive about the idea of being reincarnated?
5. What do you think will be your last thoughts before you die?
6. What do you think hell is like?
7. If mourners at your funeral were given mementos to remind them of you, what would your want the mementos to be?

8. Have you ever attended a celebration of Viaticum? What are your memories of that event? How did the celebration express or affect your own belief in the resurrection?

9. Who are the people you would like to have present with you at your Mass for Viaticum? What are two readings you would like at that Mass? What are two songs?

10. If you gave a "Last Supper" for your family and friends, what would the menu be?

Discussion questions

1. Why is it important to be open minded when learning about the customs of other cultures?

2. Why do you think food is served at almost all social gatherings, including funerals?

3. Do you know any ethnic customs that seem to laugh at death?

4. Are there any Jewish cemeteries near you? Does the cemetery differ in any way from other cemeteries?

5. Which present-day Jewish burial customs reflect customs found in the Bible?

6. How do the burial customs of the Jews reflect belief in the immortal soul?

7. What is the purpose of the Jewish "meal of consolation"? How is this meal similar to present-day Christian death rituals?

8. How does cremation and the scattering of ashes reflect Hindu beliefs?

9. How does food play a role in Hindu death rituals?

10. Is there a Japanese community near you? If so, how does this community celebrate Obon?

11. Compare Islam's belief in the Last Judgment to Matthew 25:31–46. How are the two similar? How are they different?

12. How do you think present-day cemeteries "measure up" environmentally? Are they healthy places or are they places of pollution, as the Parsees believe?

13. Why do you think Zoroastrians bring a four-eyed dog before the corpse and light a fire in the death room?

14. Do you think Parsee death rituals are based more on fear of the dead or on respect for the living?

15. How is the ritual of Viaticum similar to the death rituals found in other religions? How is it different?

6 Americans and Death

A grave problem

Kathleen Phillips thought she and her family had moved to the greatest town in America—until she saw the city's cemetery. Weeds had grown up everywhere. In the oldest section of the graveyard, where citizens of the early nineteenth century had buried their dead, tombstone after tombstone had been toppled.

The newer section of the cemetery looked no better. Cracked markers looked as if they had been whacked by baseball bats. Others were covered with spray-can graffiti. Indeed, everything Kathleen saw made her sick.

On her next trip to the cemetery, Kathleen brought a number of her neighbors. They were as upset as she was. "But what can we do?" one of them asked.

Kathleen and her friends decided to meet again the following day, this time armed with ideas. They intended to present the ideas at the next city council meeting.

They followed through on their plan. At the council meeting, Kathleen explained the problem with the cemetery and then outlined some ideas to correct the situation.

"We'd like you to hire a landscape architect to design a 'new look' for the cemetery—perhaps turn it into a memorial park with benches and cobblestone paths. The fence needs fixing, and there should be a full-time caretaker to maintain the place. To prevent future vandalism, a security company needs to do regular patrolling at night, and someone needs to educate the town's students about the cemetery's sacredness—that it's not something to destroy."

"And how do you propose that we pay for these ideas?" a council member asked.

Kathleen proceeded to outline five ideas for raising money, including an "adopt-a-grave" program where businesses could make tax-deductible contributions. The council members were impressed. By the end of the meeting, they agreed to form a cemetery committee to pursue the suggestions.

"We've known about this problem for a long time," conceded one council member later. "But we didn't know what to do and, in frustration, turned our backs on it. Now that we've got people concerned, I think we can turn the situation around."

Places of culture

In the preceding story, the name Kathleen Phillips is fictional. The story itself, however, is true. For whatever reasons, Americans differ from the citizens of many other countries in their attitudes toward cemeteries. In some countries, such as Japan and Mexico, cemeteries are places of culture; they are festive places where people gather on certain holidays. In American culture, however, cemeteries run the gamut—from commercialized burial parks (Forest Lawn Cemetery in southern California), to acres of quiet simplicity (Arlington National Cemetery), to well-kept places of artistic and aesthetic beauty (Rock Creek Cemetery, Washington, DC), to shunned places of neglect and vandalism (the cemetery in Kathleen Phillips' fictional town).

Americans will continue to tolerate such diversity in the condition of their cemeteries until they are educated to the contrary. Part of such education includes learning about our own culture's approach to death. In this chapter, you will see how the people of colonial America handled death. You will learn the reasons behind certain customs—the tolling of bells, coffins, hearses, tombstones, and the funeral reception. And you will see how Americans traditionally celebrated civic holidays, such as Memorial Day and Decoration Day, that were associated with death.

Customs surrounding death are an important part of our American culture. Knowing about them can give people a sense of continuity with the past, as well as a sense of responsibility toward present-day cemeteries.

Death in colonial America

Death occurred more frequently in colonial America than it does today. Thus the pilgrims and early colonists tended to be matter-of-fact in the way they prepared for it. Often when a child was born, for example, he or she was not named until after the first birthday—due to the high infant mortality rate. At birth, a cask of wine was set aside for the child's future wedding and later—for his or her funeral reception. The Pennsylvania Dutch even built a *doedkammer*, or "dead room," in their houses. This room would be used for visitation during funeral wakes, for viewing the body. Doors were wider than usual, so that a casket could be easily carried through.

Funerals were social occasions in early America, but they differed from funerals today in that people had to receive an invitation in order to attend one. At first, such invitations were relayed orally. In Dutch New Amsterdam and up the Hudson to Albany, the *aanspreecker*, or "funeral inviter," rushed to the homes of relatives and friends of the deceased. He dressed in black and wore long crepe ribbons around his hat. By 1691, these inviters became public servants appointed by the mayor. The grieving families paid their salaries, according to the distance traveled and the length of time spent.

By the mid-1800s, funeral invitations were printed on white notepaper with a heavy black border. They were sent through the mail. Sometimes called a "ticket," a "card," or a "death notice," the invitation was usually straightforward: "Yourself and family are respectfully invited to attend the funeral of Miss Abigail Jaspers from her family's residence, 37 Center Street, Boston, on Monday, September 9, at 2 o'clock and then to proceed to Bunker Hill Cemetery." If a person received such an invitation, he or she was expected to attend. Personal enemies who met at a funeral were expected to be polite.

At the funeral itself, the bereaved family was expected to wear black. Proper funeral flowers (if present) were always white or shades of purple. After the funeral service and burial, guests were treated to a feast. During the nineteenth century, a person could expect stewed chicken, ham, cold meats, cheese, mashed potatoes, applesauce, red beets, pie, and coffee at a Dutch funeral meal.

The most common pie served at funeral receptions throughout Pennsylvania and New England was raisin. It was so popular on such occasions that it became known as "funeral" pie.

Embalming

The first Americans did not embalm their dead. The family washed the body, clothed it, and laid it out for a home wake. Burial, the most common method of disposing of the dead, usually took place soon after death.[1] If a person died during the winter and the ground was too frozen to dig a grave, he or she was buried in a coffin under the snow. After the spring thaw, a proper grave would be dug and the coffin buried. If a person died while on a sea voyage, he or she was buried at sea because there was no way to preserve the body.

Embalming did not become popular until the Civil War, when many families wanted the bodies of their dead soldiers returned home. Thomas Holmes, the father of modern embalming, prac-

---

1. The first crematorium was not built in America until 1876. It was constructed and used by Dr. Julius Lemoyne of Washington, Pennsylvania.

ticed his art during the Civil War, especially upon officers killed in battle.

Coffins

The first colonists were buried without coffins. The corpse was wrapped in a shroud made from cerecloth (linen dipped in wax) or wool soaked in alum or pitch. A rich person might be buried in a fine shroud of cashmere. All shrouds were rectangular cloth bags, with drawstrings at the top.

The first coffins were crude, fashioned from wood by the colony's cabinetmaker.[2] Because the coffins had to be made in a day, the woodworker usually had some planks dried and ready. The first rectangular burial boxes with perpendicular sides were made by William Smith of Meriden, Connecticut, in the second half of the nineteenth century. After that, the term "casket" came into use. Each box was custom-designed, according to the person's measurements. Ready-made coffins were not manufactured until the War of 1812. Some of them were lined with lead. After his death (1792), the naval hero John Paul Jones was buried in a lead-lined coffin; his arms and legs were wrapped in tinfoil. In 1905, his body was exhumed, still recognizable.

Hearses

The first colonists used a wooden frame to carry the corpse to the grave site. The first hearses were open wagons or sleighs provided by the livery-stable keeper and pulled by a single horse. In the country, open wagons were filled with straw to cushion the coffin. During inclement weather, waterproof covers were used.

In the cities, the first hearses had only one compartment, with open windows and a door at the back. A roller on the rear of the floor helped to ease the coffin in and out. Some hearses were decorated with woolen draperies or fringed curtains with tassels. Black hearses were used for adults who had died; white ones for children. The driver sat on a box attached to the front; he managed the horses (always black), which were draped in heavy veils of net.

As innovations in transportation took place, so did innovations in hearses. Abraham Lincoln's hearse was actually a funeral train that traveled nearly two thousand miles in twelve days. Later, funeral trolley cars came to be used in the cities. They carried the coffin, flowers, and mourners to the cemetery. In more modern

---

2. The Amish in Pennsylvania often placed a decorated baptismal certificate with the body in the coffin. The paper was considered to be a "passport" to heaven.

times, elongated station wagons have served as hearses. Limousines transport the family of the deceased, with special flower cars carrying the flowers to the grave site.

Bells

In early America, the sexton tolled the bell and dug the grave. The custom of tolling church bells originated in Europe. (At first, this was intended to frighten away evil spirits waiting to capture the soul.) The tolling bell was stationary. When struck by a heavy clapper, it produced a stately, solemn sound. In some places the bell was rung once for a child, twice for a woman, and three times for a man. In other parishes, the bell would toll the age of the person.[3]

Burial places and markers

In the earliest times, colonists camouflaged burial places so that the Native Americans would not be able to count the dead and realize how weak the colony was. In Puritan times (the seventeenth century), many churches had adjacent cemeteries. These cemeteries became places to wander around in or to have picnics between church services. Most people were buried in the ground. Some families, however, built mausoleums, or walk-in tombs, above or below ground. Some parishes allowed members to be buried under the church building. In colonial times, it was even possible to be buried under one's own pew, for an extra fee.

From the first colonial days, grave markers were used to identify the deceased. Usually these markers identified an individual person or a married couple. Sometimes, however, the markers identified a body part that had been buried separately. For example, a grave marker in Washington Village, New Hampshire, reads: "Here lies the leg of Captain Samuel Jones which was amputated July, 1807." In the cemetery in Newport, Rhode Island, a tombstone commemorates Wait and William Tripp and "His Wife's Arm, Amputated February 20th, 1786."

The first markers consisted of a board or a heap of stones. Later tombstones consisted of a single boulder, a slab of slate, schist, marble, limestone, greenstone, granite, mica stone, or red or brown sandstone. Markers placed over the deceased's head were called

---

3. The *De Profundis* bell, a solemn tolling of the bourdon bell (the lowest pitch in a carillon), marked the end of the day at 9 P.M. This was the traditional time for the common community night prayer for the faithful departed.

headstones; those placed over the feet were called footstones. Wolf stones were large flat stones that covered more than one grave and were intended to discourage marauding animals. Table stones were markers that outlined the grave and stood on four legs.

When churches were first built in America and graveyards started filling with their founders, it was not the material or the shape of the marker that was important, but the epitaph written on it. These words were meant not only to memorialize the deceased, but also to be words of warning to the living. Because many people could not read these epitaphs, tombstones were decorated with artistic symbols. These symbols were a kind of code, whose message was meant to be studied and taken seriously. Today American tombstones are gaining new respect as art forms. Many museums and art galleries have exhibited tombstones themselves, as well as their rubbings.[4]

African-American slaves and death

Because of the country's attitudes about segregation, African-American slaves were buried in separate cemeteries from whites.[5] When a slave died, his or her body was laid out by other slaves on a "cooling board." A plate of salt and ashes, intended to absorb disease, was placed beneath the board and later interred with the body.

Slaves made a coffin, placed the corpse inside, and took it via ox cart to the graveyard. The slaves walked along behind the cart, singing spirituals. One of these spirituals that has come down to us today is "Swing Low, Sweet Chariot." Based on 2 Kings 2:11, it is a song sung by a dying slave who is filled with happy expectation of being relieved of suffering, sorrow, sickness, and hard labor. For many slaves in early America, heaven was seen as the Promised Land, and death was seen as the chariot that took one home.

Slaves needed their master's permission to attend funeral services, even those of family members. And sometimes the permission was not given. Thus slave funerals were frequently held at night, when work stoppage was no problem. According to witnesses, these night funerals were impressive, solemn, and eerie

---

4. For more information about death customs in colonial America, see *Death in Early America: The History and Folklore of Customs and Superstitions of Early Medicine, Funerals, Burials, and Mourning* by Margaret Coffin (New York: Thomas Nelson, Inc., 1976).

5. Recently, a colonial-era cemetery for African Americans was discovered in lower Manhattan. More than four hundred skeletons were found, many of them children.

ceremonies. The slaves processed with pine-knot torches and sang hymns. At the cemetery, there were prayers by a slave preacher, ritual ring dancing, and drumming (at least in the Georgia Sea Islands). As Rachel Anderson, an elderly Georgia-coast resident, recalled:

> Use tuh alluz beat duh drums at fewnuls. Right attuh duh pusson die, dey beat um tuh tell duh uddahs bout duh fewnul. . . . On duh way tuh duh grabe dey beat duh drum as dey is mahchin long. Wen duh body is put in duh grabe, ebrybody shout roun duh grabe in a succle, singin an prayin.[6]

Because slaves frequently were unable to attend the funeral services of family members and friends, it was not unusual for the funeral sermon to be separated from the burial by several days, weeks, or even months. Such sermons—sometimes several at once—were usually preached on Sunday. The time lag did not bother the slaves nearly as much as if no sermon were preached at all. Regardless if the deceased was sinner or saint, the funeral sermon gave the mourners peace of mind.

Following the African custom of decorating a grave with the personal belongings of the deceased, the slaves placed cups, saucers, bottles, pipes, medicine bottles, wash basins, crockery, and other effects on the graves. Frequently the items were broken or cracked in order to free "their spirits" and thereby enable them to follow the deceased.

Another reason for placing the personal belongings of the deceased on the grave was fear of the dead. As Sarah Washington speculated: "I dohn guess yuh be bodduh much by duh spirits ef yub gib em a good fewnul an put duh tings wut belong tuh em on top uh duh grave."[7]

After her former master had died, one of the ex-slaves on Frances Butler Leigh's plantation placed a basin, water, and several towels on his grave. She gave this explanation: "If massa's spirit come, i want him see dat old Nanny not forget how he call every morning for water for wash his hands." Leigh records this incident as a mark of respect and affection shown by the slave for her old master. The remark also might be interpreted as an attempt to allay

---

6. From *Drums and Shadows* by the Georgia Writers' Project, Works Projects Administration. Reprint (Garden City, NY: Doubleday, Anchor Books, 1972), p. 133.

7. Frances Butler Leigh, *Ten Years on a Georgia Plantation Since the War* (London, 1883), p. 77.

the ghost of the former master once and for all, so that Nanny need not be bothered with him ever again.

While a fully developed cult of the ancestors did not persist in the United States, certain African funerary customs did remain. In Mississippi, for example, it was believed that the spirits of the dead roamed on Halloween. Thus the living cooked dinner for them at home or took food to their graves. Similarly in the Sea Islands, there were those who "put a dish uh food out on the poach fuh the spirit, but some of em take cooked food tuh the grave an leave it theah fuh the spirit."[8]

Today in Hilton Head, South Carolina, it is possible to see ancient slave graves with crude headstones fashioned from cement. Throughout America it is almost impossible to find tombstones commemorating slaves. If the graves were marked at all, the markers were made of wood that has since rotted. Roberta Halporn, in her book *Lessons from the Dead*, includes the example of one slave tombstone that may be seen in Attleboro, Massachusetts. The epitaph, while praising the slave whose name was Caesar, sadly reflects the racial prejudice of the times:

In memory of Caesar:

Here lies the best of slaves

Now turning into dust:

Caesar the Ethiopian craves

A place among the just.

His faithful soul has fled

To realms of heavenly light.

And by the blood that Jesus shed

Is changed from black to white.

Jan. 15 he quitted the stage

in the 77th year of his age.

1780[9]

---

8. *Drums and Shadows*, p. 184.

9. Roberta Halporn, *Lessons from the Dead*, (Brooklyn, NY: Highly Specialized Promotions, 1979), p. 26.

American civil customs

As a nation, America is a melting pot of cultures and religions. For this reason, it has developed a nonsectarian approach to the funerals of its military or public officials. Various customs have become tradition—flying the flag at half-mast, covering the casket with a flag, presenting the folded flag to the next of kin, playing "Taps," giving a gun salute.

At no time in our history were America's civil funeral rites displayed more powerfully and experienced more deeply than in the televised ceremonies for President John F. Kennedy, in 1963. Elected in November 1960, John Kennedy was the country's youngest, as well as its first Catholic, president. Three years later, this well-liked leader was assassinated in Dallas. Not only did the people of the United States mourn for him; the entire world grieved.

President Kennedy's closed coffin was placed on a catafalque, draped with an American flag, and situated in a place of honor in the Capitol Rotunda. A quarter of a million people walked past in order to pay their final respects to the slain president. Telegrams of sympathy were sent to the White House from all corners of the world.

The next day, the funeral procession set out from the Rotunda to St. Matthew's Cathedral. Four army drummers led the horse-drawn wagon that carried the president's casket. Behind the wagon came a riderless horse with a pair of gleaming boots reversed in the stirrups—a tribute to the fallen leader. Jacqueline Kennedy, the president's widow, wore a black dress and a black veil as she walked behind the casket.

After the funeral Mass, the procession continued to Arlington National Cemetery. People lined the streets in order to get one last glimpse of their president. Fifty fighter planes flew overhead as the casket was lowered into the ground. Air Force One, the presidential plane, dipped its wings as it passed overhead. Representatives of the armed forces gave a 21-gun salute. A single bugler played "Taps." Later, an eternal flame was installed at the grave site. This flame continues to burn today.

American holidays

It is customary for a business in America to close when its boss or owner dies. It is also customary for people to wear a white carnation on Mother's Day to recall and honor a deceased mother. In addition to these customs, America has developed several national or local holidays that honor the dead.

Memorial Day (last Monday in May)

This is a secular, patriotic holiday honoring the military dead. At least twenty-five places throughout the country have claimed to originate this holiday. One of the oldest claims is that of Jackson, Mississippi, where Sue Landon Vaughn, a descendant of President John Adams, decorated Confederate graves on April 26, 1865.

On Memorial Day, it is customary for people to visit the graves of their loved ones. They leave some fresh cut flowers or a plant, and tidy up around the grave. In addition, people enjoy family reunions, backyard picnics, and barbecues. Many communities have parades and church services honoring the dead.[10]

Decoration Day

In the South, Decoration Day (a local memorial holiday) is held any time from late May until early September. Its purpose is to honor the dead and to maintain the cemeteries. Decoration Day is a significant social, religious, and patriotic occasion, featuring picnics, preaching, speeches, and the homecoming of former neighbors and family members who have moved away.[11]

All Saints' Day

Funerals in the French Quarter of New Orleans are often accompanied by a jazz band and parade. Cemeteries in New Orleans are all made of vaults above the ground because of the swampy condition of the land. On All Saints' Day, the vaults are whitewashed and profusely decorated with chrysanthemums. The downtown cemeteries are particularly festive. Street vendors do a lively business selling gumbo, snowballs, pralines, peanuts, balloons, mechanical birds, and toy skeletons. Traditionally, schools and some businesses are closed on this local holiday.

---

10. The ancient Romans had a holiday known as *Lemuria* (Latin for "ghosts"), which took place in May and was intended to "put to rest" all roaming spirits. On this day, the Roman householder arose at midnight and went forth to meet his ghosts. He put nine black beans in his mouth and then spit them out in different parts of the house. The beans were a gift of food for the spirits. Then the Roman washed his hands (ghosts were afraid of water), banged two pots together (ghosts didn't like loud noises), and said, "Get you gone."

11. The ancient Roman version of Decoration Day was *Parentalia,* the Festival of Parents, held in February. On this day people honored their ancestors by leaving food for their dead and decorating family tombs with flowers.

Visiting a cemetery

The Catholic Church encourages its members to visit the graves of their deceased family members and friends, especially on All Souls' Day (November 2), Memorial Day, and on the anniversary of death or burial. The following prayer service is recommended when visiting a cemetery or when a tombstone or grave marker is erected. The service may be used immediately following Mass or apart from Mass at the cemetery. The leader may be a priest, deacon, lay minister, or family member.

Leader: The grace and peace of God our Father, who raised Jesus from the dead, be with you always.

All: And also with you.

Leader: My dear friends, we gather today to pray for our brothers and sisters whose bodies lie here in rest. They have passed from death to life in company with the Lord Jesus, who died and rose to new life, and are purified now of their faults. We pray that God may welcome them among all the saints of heaven.

Reading: 1 Thessalonians 4:13–18

Response: Psalm 25

Litany of the Saints (During this time, the graves are sprinkled with holy water.)

(Leader)	(All)
Lord, have mercy	*Lord, have mercy*
Christ, have mercy	*Christ, have mercy*
Lord, have mercy	*Lord, have mercy*
Holy Mary, Mother of God	*pray for them*
Saint Michael	*pray for them*
Saint John the Baptist	*pray for them*
Saint Joseph	*pray for them*
Saint Peter	*pray for them*
Saint Paul	*pray for them*
Saint Andrew	*pray for them*
Saint Stephen	*pray for them*
Saint Ann	*pray for them*
Saint Teresa	*pray for them*
Saint Catherine	*pray for them*
Saint Frances Cabrini	*pray for them*
Saint Elizabeth Seton	*pray for them*
All holy men and women	*pray for them*

Christ, pardon all their faults	*Lord, hear our prayer*
Christ, remember the good they have done	*Lord, hear our prayer*
Christ, receive them into eternal life	*Lord, hear our prayer*
Christ, comfort all those who mourn	*Lord, hear our prayer*
Lord, have mercy	*Lord, have mercy*
Christ, have mercy	*Christ, have mercy*
Lord, have mercy	*Lord, have mercy*

All: The Lord's Prayer

Prayer A: (For more than one person)

All-powerful God, whose mercy is never withheld from those who call upon you in hope, look kindly on your servants (N. and N.), who departed this life confessing your name, and number them among your saints in heaven. We ask this through Christ our Lord. Amen.

OR

Prayer B: (For one person)

Almighty God and Father, it is our certain faith that your Son, who died on the cross, was raised from the dead, the first fruits of all who have fallen asleep. Grant that through this mystery your servant N., who has gone to his/her rest in Christ, may share in the joy of his resurrection. We ask this through Christ our Lord. Amen.

OR

Prayer C: (Blessing of a tombstone or grave marker)

O God, by whose mercy the faithful departed find rest, bless this gravestone with which we mark the resting place of N. May he/she have everlasting life and rejoice in you with your saints for ever. We ask this through Christ our Lord. Amen.

Leader: Eternal rest grant unto them, O Lord.

All: And let perpetual light shine upon them.

Leader: May they rest in peace.

All: Amen.

Leader: May their souls and the souls of the faithful departed, through the mercy of God, rest in peace.

All: Amen.[12]

---

12. The International Commission on English in the Liturgy, "Order for Visiting a Cemetery," *Book of Blessings: Study Edition* (Collegeville, MN: The Liturgical Press, 1989), pp. 650–55.

Cemetery art

When you visit a cemetery, you will notice different types of styles represented in the cemetery art. Such art may take the form of statues, monuments, mausoleum designs, and tombstones. When you inspect such artwork more closely, you will notice that different times in history used different artistic symbols.

Symbols frequently chosen by the Pilgrims included skulls and crossbones, skeletons, and hour glasses. Eighteenth century art favored winged cherubs, angels, and realistic portraits. Nineteenth century art included wreaths, swags, urns, weeping willows, birches, elms, doves, lambs, and hands with pointing fingers, symbolic triangles, the eye of God, hearts, crosses, and crowns. Twentieth century grave markers tend to be much more simple, but sometimes have a photograph of the dead on them.

Such symbols not only praised the virtues of the deceased; they also were meant to be a message to the living. The artwork was included for people who could not read; hence, an elaborate "code" developed. Each symbol meant something specific.

Here is the picture code of the artistic symbols you will find most frequently in graveyards throughout America:

PICTURE CODE

angels	heavenly hosts leading souls to heaven
arch	death is the passageway through which the soul will travel
arrows	the dart of death
Bible	the Word through which salvation is won
bridal wreath broken by a dart	a young bride or groom
compass with a "v"	a member of the Society of Freemasons
crossbones	life's brevity
crowing cock	the soul awakening to repentance
crown	righteousness
cypress	hope
door	death is the door to heaven
dove	Christian devotion
evergreen	eternal life
gate	death is the gateway to heaven
grapes and vines	Christ
hands open with touching thumbs	member of a priestly line (only on Jewish stones)

heart	heavenly bliss
hourglass	swift passage of time
lamb on top of a stone	a child, a "lamb" of God
lamb as part of a design	the soul as lamb of God
mermaids	Jesus as half divine and half human
rising sun	resurrection
rosette	the soul
torch	resurrection
tree	Tree of Life (only on Jewish stones)
trumpet	eventual resurrection
urn	contains human remains from which the soul rises to heaven
winged skull	certainty of death
willow	mourning and sorrow
winged cherub	the eternal soul, resurrection
scallop shell	our journey through life
sheaf of wheat	the elderly
shattered urn	the elderly[13]

Common inscriptions found on tombstones include the following:

R.I.P.	*Requiescat in pace* (may he/she rest in peace)
Beatae Memoriae	"of happy or blessed memory"
Obiit	He/she died . . .
Hic iacet	Here lies . . .

If you have time this week, walk through a cemetery and observe the tombstone art. You may be surprised by the messages—obvious and hidden—left there by past generations.

---

13. A shorter version of this list may be found in *Lessons from the Dead: The Graveyard as a Classroom for the Study of the Life Cycle*, p. 29, by Roberta Halporn (Brooklyn, NY: Highly Specialized Promotions, 1979).

For your journal

1. Imagine that you live in a culture that considers it customary to place personal items on the grave. What personal belongings would you want placed on your grave?

2. How does your family celebrate Mother's Day, Memorial Day, Decoration Day, and All Saints' Day? How are the dead remembered on these days?

3. Design your own tombstone, choosing the artwork symbols mentioned in this chapter.

4. Write your own epitaph for those who will someday visit your grave.

Discussion questions

1. Have you ever visited a cemetery in your city or town? What condition was it in? How did this make you feel?

2. Has your family ever visited or taken care of the graves of relatives?

3. Who should be responsible for the upkeep of graves—especially the graves of those who have no relatives nearby to care for them?

4. Do you think paying for perpetual care should be mandated by state law?

5. Is a cemetery a sacred place? Why or why not?

6. In what ways are funerals social occasions today?

7. Do you think people should wear black to a funeral today?

8. How does the history of coffins show denial of death in our culture?

9. What do the symbols and rituals used in President Kennedy's funeral represent or mean to us as a nation today?

10. What is the origin and meaning of Veterans' Day? How does the nation remember its dead on this day?

Part Four: Psychological Aspects

My Father, if it is possible, let this cup pass from me; yet, not as I will, but as you will.

—*Matthew 26:39*

7 The Stages of Death and Dying

The diagnosis

Finding out that you have a terminal illness can be quite a shock. The following newspaper article tells about one man's encounter with his own death and dying.

Michael Landon, diagnosed Friday with inoperable cancer of the liver and pancreas, said yesterday, "I'm still hoping to beat it, but life has been good to me."

The star of three hit TV series spanning as many decades, Landon, 54, spoke to a gathering of reporters in front of his Malibu house. He said he will start mild chemotherapy later this week at a Los Angeles hospital.

He began his press conference by noting, "I turned on CNN this morning and heard that I was sick."

That comment was typical of the generally upbeat attitude he projected. . . .

"At first you just don't believe it," he said. "What I did right after I heard there was a possibility, I began doing push-ups, just to make sure I was just as strong as I was the day before. And I was, so I figured I could beat it."

A thin Landon said he had lost about six pounds recently, and now weighs 154 pounds. The actor said he will continue to write but has put his acting career on hold. "I might be very difficult to insure right now, I imagine."

Landon paid tribute to his wife and nine children, who range in age from 4 to a 42-year-old adopted son, for their support since finding out about his diagnosis on Friday. . . .

Although he said he feels "terrific," Landon said he has trouble digesting food. The original symptoms of the disease were severe cramping after meals. . . . He had to cut short a skiing vacation in Utah because of stomach pains that had begun six weeks earlier.

Landon recently got the go-ahead from CBS for a new series, "Us," about a man who, vindicated of murder after 18 years in prison, becomes a Charles Kuralt-like journalist.

However, he said yesterday that "there is no way for me to continue with that until I can determine whether the chemo will help."[1]

---

1. From the Associated Press, April 9, 1991. Used by permission. All rights reserved.

When death hits home

Up to this point, we have approached death from philosophical, historical, and cultural perspectives. Death, in a sense, has still been "out there." But what happens when death hits home, when death affects us or someone close to us? What is our "gut" reaction then? How do we feel when death focuses on us or on our loved ones?

In the 1970s, a psychiatrist named Elisabeth Kubler-Ross decided to study patients who were dying. She wanted to know what the experience of dying was like; she also wanted to know how her patients felt about the dying process. She published her findings in the book *On Death and Dying* and in several subsequent books. She concluded that people who are dying go through five different psychological stages—denial, anger, bargaining, depression, and acceptance. These stages are not necessarily sequential. Although people have different patterns in the way they go through the stages and how long they spend in each one, these reactions to death seem universal. You will be learning more about them in this chapter.

Denial

"At first you just don't believe it," Michael Landon said to reporters. Perhaps these words best sum up similar reactions of other people when they learn they are dying. "This can't be happening. God wouldn't do this to me. It's just not possible. I don't feel that sick. Maybe the doctor got my test results mixed up with someone else."

In her research, Dr. Kubler-Ross found that most people with a terminal illness initially deny the fact of their imminent death.[2] As Sigmund Freud had taught earlier, each of us subconsciously believes in his or her own immortality: Death may take another person, but I am exempt.

Even though people in this stage may not verbally express denial, they may act it out. Frequently, they look for another physician or specialist who can give them better news. Perhaps they continue their regular routine, working just as hard as before. Or, as Michael Landon did, perhaps they continue their regular regime of physical exercise, just to prove that they're not dying.

---

2. Psychologists say that denial is a defense mechanism that helps us to deal only with as much truth as we can handle at a time. Denial is sometimes needed in order to survive. But denial can also stop us from making needed changes. For example, many alcoholics and their families spend years denying that anything is wrong.

Denial can also take the form of joking. People in denial may put on a brave front to others and even to themselves. "If I don't think about it, it'll go away." "I don't need to deal with this now; I still have plenty of time to deal with it later."

Even though the warning signs of approaching death are there, a person in denial may not take care of unfinished business. He or she may not write a will, buy a cemetery plot, or plan a funeral. The person may never talk to family members about the seriousness of the illness or how he or she feels.

Denial can take another form as well—hope. At first a person hopes that nothing is seriously wrong. After the doctor's diagnosis, the person in denial clings to another hope—that of finding a cure. While this attitude shows that the person values his or her life, it can also be a form of denying death, of keeping death at bay for as long as possible.

Anger

Dr. Kubler-Ross found that once the defenses of denial weaken, the terminally ill person is likely to become very angry. "Why me? I don't deserve this. It's not fair." The anger comes from two sources: a sense of helplessness in the face of death (no longer being in control) and a righteous indignation at the injustice that is being done. "O God, how could you do this to me? Why did you let this happen?"

When we are angry, it is common to look for someone to blame. The writers of the Hebrew Scriptures blamed human sinfulness for death. The person who dies prematurely must have done something terrible; he or she is being punished. This same belief in personal liability for death or sickness is also found in the Christian Scriptures. But Jesus was quick to clarify that sickness and death are not God's way of punishing us (cf. John 9:1–7). Still, anger about approaching death may be self-directed. People who smoke two packs of cigarettes per day for twenty years may indeed be very angry at themselves when they develop lung cancer.

People who are angry very often take their anger out on others. They blame others for their condition. They may be angry at their doctor for not diagnosing the disease earlier. They may be angry at their spouse or family members for not believing them when they complained about being tired. They may be angry at God for letting this happen.

In his book *Death Shall Have No Dominion*, Reverend Alfred McBride explains what is going on in this stage of dying. Because it is impossible for the person to direct his or her anger toward the source of anguish—death itself—he or she directs it outward, toward others. He or she treats others with impatience and criticism. Nothing anyone does is right. The family either "never" comes to visit or "never" gives the person any privacy. If the person is "in a hospital or nursing home, he or she may complain about the food, the medical care, or the impersonal environment. The impotent rage that is felt by the [person] also affects his or her family. Relationships are strained and tension-filled as the persons involved struggle to cope with the conflicts thrust upon them."[3]

Bargaining

Bargaining is a natural part of surviving in the world. We bargain for the best price on a car. We negotiate a job contract. And we make trade-off deals with our friends. "If you'll do this for me, I'll do this for you." People who are dying use the same technique. "God, if you just give me one more year, I'll be a good Christian. If you just let me live to see my daughter's wedding, I'll donate my kidneys to science. If you miraculously cure me, I promise I'll never smoke again." In this stage, the person tries to buy time. He or she tries to keep death away by promising God reformed and virtuous behavior.

In the prize-winning play *The Shadow Box*, an elderly woman is about to die. Her unmarried daughter takes care of her. But what the woman wants is to see her other daughter one more time before she dies. She is determined to "hold on" until this daughter arrives. (In reality, the daughter died a few years before.) To soothe her mother, the unmarried daughter produces a fake telegram saying the second daughter is on her way from Mexico and not to worry. So the elderly woman continues to refuse to accept death.

We find another example of bargaining in a story in the Book of Genesis. According to the story, God is fed up by all the sins that are taking place in Sodom and Gomorrah. So God decides to level the town, killing everyone. Abraham knows that this means his nephew Lot, who lives in one of the towns, will die. So he tries to strike a deal. "If I find fifty innocent people, will you spare the towns?" God agrees. Abraham, however, has second thoughts about being able to find fifty such people, so he tries to get lowered the number of people he needs to find. "If I find forty-five innocent people, will you spare the towns?" And so the story goes on until

---

3. Rev. Alfred McBride, *Death Shall Have No Dominion* (Dubuque, IA: BROWN–ROA, 1984), p. 36.

the stakes are down to ten innocent people. For all his bargaining, Abraham is still unable to meet his part of the deal. In the end, God spares Lot and his family, but levels the two towns.

A notorious example of bargaining took place in twentieth-century America. The widow of Oliver Winchester believed that the ghosts of all those who were killed by the guns her husband invented were out to kill her. So she struck a bargain with them: As long as her house was unfinished, she would not die. She hired architects and construction workers to add on continuously to her house. When she finally died, the house was still unfinished. Today the Winchester Mystery House is a tourist attraction in San Jose, California.

In the bargaining stage, the person finds strength in hope. The person may still be hoping for a cure; in addition the person now hopes that his or her life will be prolonged so that certain unfinished business can be completed. As long as the business remains unfinished, death can be kept at arms' length.

Depression

Many volumes have been written on clinical depression and how to treat it. Depression, for the most part, is seen as a sickness—something abnormal. When a person has a terminal disease, depression may have chemical roots in the disease itself. But psychological depression may also be a normal response to a bad situation. Think about it: The dying person will soon leave behind everything he or she has ever known. The person needs time to "mourn" this separation.

Very often a dying person who is depressed does not want to talk or to have visitors. The person may brood a lot or start crying quietly. During this stage, death as a loss becomes real. The person acknowledges that he or she will not live to see another birthday, or the marriage of a child, or future grandchildren. Whatever life he or she had, whatever relationships have been developed, whatever jobs still need to be done—all this will soon be over.

In depression, the person begins to separate himself or herself from life. The battle against death is now seen as futile. The person stops fighting for more life and grows weaker. An interior battle, however, is raging. The person struggles between despair and a final ray of hope—that God will find him or her worthy, that his or her life has been meaningful, and that life somehow continues on past death.

This stage is a time of personal assessment. The person looks back on his or her life, on its strengths and its weaknesses. The final battle is perhaps the struggle to accept oneself with all one's imperfections. Such self-acceptance may be difficult to achieve in the midst of the indignities sometimes associated with dying—the loss of good looks, the amputation of a limb, possible bowel and bladder incontinence, and increasing helplessness.

At this time, the dying person may seek reconciliation with God, with the Church, and with others. The person may view such reconciliation as a necessary prerequisite to self-acceptance. During reconciliation, it is important for friends or family members to affirm the dying individual as worthy and lovable. The warm touch of a hand and a simple prayer can mean a great deal. They can help the depressed person to reach the final stage in the dying process.

Acceptance

Once the dying person has found reconciliation with self, God, and others, there is a final "yes." During this stage, the person accepts death and waits for it calmly and peacefully. The person may even be willing to talk about his or her life and approaching death.

This attitude of acceptance is not the same as giving up. Acceptance is a good feeling. "I have now finished my unfinished business. I've said everything I want to say. I'm ready to go." For the religious person, the desire to be united fully with God becomes more important than remaining with family and friends. Instead of looking at the past or even the present moment, the dying person looks forward to the future.

St. Ignatius of Loyola captured the essence of this final surrender of the person to God in this prayer from his *Spiritual Exercises:*

> *Take, O Lord, all my liberty. Receive in their entirety my memory, intellect, and will. And since whatever else I have or hold you have given to me, so I give everything back to you to be managed entirely according to your preference. To me give only your love and your grace, and with these I am rich enough and want nothing more.*[4]

As St. Paul explains in his first epistle to the Corinthians, at death the faithful person shall know God fully as he or she is

---

4. Lewis Delmage, trans., *The Spiritual Exercises of St. Ignatius,* no. 234, p. 122.

known. "Faith, hope, love remain, these three; but the greatest of these is love" (1 Corinthians 13:13). In this last stage, the dying person already begins to experience the surety of love, God's total and unconditional acceptance. He or she looks forward to a complete experience of this love in death. For this reason, the dying person can say with Jesus: "It is finished" (John 19:30), and "Father, into your hands I commend my spirit" (Luke 23:46).[5]

Jesus' attitude toward his own death

As Christians, we believe that we are not alone in our dying. Step by step, stage by stage, Jesus goes with us toward, and then through, death. As one who died himself and then conquered death, he is a savior who is both role model and companion to those who are dying. Jesus truly understands what death means and what the dying person goes through. For this reason, it is important to study the Gospels and to learn more about Jesus' attitude toward his own death.

The four Gospels give us different views of Jesus, depending on when they were written and the audience for whom they were intended. St. John's Gospel tends to be a theological reflection on Jesus as the Son of God. Because this Gospel presents Jesus as divine, it is very difficult to catch glimpses of Jesus' human personality or feelings. Throughout the Gospel, Jesus is not only aware of his approaching death; he is always in control of it.

The Gospels of St. Matthew, St. Mark, and St. Luke, which are known as the Synoptic Gospels, stand in contrast to John. They more clearly present Jesus as both divine and human, as someone who has human feelings as we do. In these Gospels, we find a Jesus who goes through stages, much like those presented in this chapter, before accepting his own death. What follows is a brief synopsis of these three Gospels.

Although both Matthew and Luke write about the infancy of Jesus, only Matthew prefigures Jesus' death at this time. He does this in mentioning the Magi's present of myrrh, the spice used to anoint corpses (cf. Matthew 2:11). The second prefiguring of death is found after Jesus' baptism, when he is tempted in the desert. The devil takes Jesus to Jerusalem and stands him on top of the parapet of the Temple. "If you are the Son of God, throw yourself down" (cf. Matthew 4:5–6; Luke 4:9). These same words are spoken later to

5. The Catholic Church recognizes St. Joseph as the patron of a happy death. Although the Bible says nothing about his death, tradition tells us that he died at home in the company of Jesus and Mary.

Jesus as he hangs on the cross (cf. Matthew 27:40; Luke 23:37, 39). Both temptations are the temptation to deny the reality of death. In both cases, Jesus rejects the temptation.

Early in Luke's account of Jesus' ministry is the reference to Isaiah's suffering servant (cf. Luke 4:18–19; Isaiah 61:1–2; 58:6). As you have already learned, most Jews expected the Messiah to live forever. Only the prophet Isaiah wrote about a Messiah who would have to suffer and die to save others. By including the quotation from Isaiah, Luke is telling us that Jesus already had knowledge that he would die.

Although Matthew and Mark do not quote Isaiah, they contain the same message. Not once, but three times Jesus predicts his own suffering, death, and resurrection (cf. the first prediction—Matthew 16:21, Mark 8:31, Luke 9:22; the second prediction—Matthew 17:22–23, Mark 9:31, Luke 9:44; the third prediction—Matthew 20:17–19, Mark 10:33–34, Luke 18:31–33). He tells his followers that they too must lose their lives for his sake in order to find them again (cf. Matthew 10:39; 16:25, Mark 8:35, Luke 9:24).

Midway through Luke's Gospel, the Pharisees warn Jesus that Herod wants to kill him. Despite their warnings, Jesus deliberately proceeds toward Jerusalem, where he knows that he will be killed (cf. Luke 13:31–33). As the time of death grows closer, Jesus knows that one of his disciples will betray him, yet he does nothing to stop him (cf. Matthew 26:21, Mark 14:18, Luke 22:21). At his Last Supper, Jesus again predicts that his blood will be "shed on behalf of many" (cf. Matthew 26:28, Mark 14:24, Luke 22:20).

Perhaps better than any other episode in the Gospels, the account of the Agony in the Garden shows us the psychological struggle Jesus went through to accept his own death. Both Matthew and Mark record Jesus as saying, "My soul is sorrowful unto death" (cf. Matthew 26:37, Mark 14:34). Luke elaborates further: "He was in such agony and he prayed so fervently that his sweat became like drops of blood falling on the ground" (Luke 22:44). Jesus seems to be a man going through the stage of depression.

All three Gospels say that Jesus needed his friends to pray with him at Gethsemane and that they let him down. Instead of keeping watch, they fell asleep—not once, but three times. How Jesus responds to them could be interpreted as anger (cf. Matthew 26:40, Mark 14:37, Luke 22:46).

The bargaining stage also seems to be found in the garden. "My Father, if it is possible, let this cup pass from me . . ." (cf. Matthew

26:39, 42, Mark 14:36, Luke 22:42). Finally, there is acceptance of death. "Not my will, but yours be done" (cf. Matthew 26:39, Mark 14;36, Luke 22:42). "Behold, the hour is at hand" (cf. Matthew 26:45–46, Mark 14:41).

Both Matthew and Mark record that while Jesus was dying on the cross, he said: "My God, My God, why have you forsaken me?" (Matthew 27:46, Mark 14:34). While these words may be interpreted as those of an angry or despairing person, it is important to know the Jewish custom of praying. By praying the first line of a psalm, the person was actually praying all of it. These words of Jesus are the first line of Psalm 22. Only a reading of the entire psalm will reveal what Jesus was expressing through these words.

Luke gives us a different glimpse of Jesus' frame of mind when he was on the cross. "Father, forgive them for they know not what they do" (Luke 23:34) and "Today you will be with me in Paradise" (Luke 23:43) both seem to indicate that Jesus' focus was on reconciliation. The final words of Jesus, "Into your hands I commend my spirit" (Luke 23:46), seem to be those of a man who has reached acceptance, the final stage of dying.

Meditation on the death of Jesus can affect the way we approach our own deaths.[6] Jesus did not sin, so death could not be God's way of punishing him. Instead of asking why he had to die at all or why he had to die at such a young age, Jesus approached death with faith, hope, and love. He believed in the Father's love for him, and this was enough for him. These same sentiments are found in Jesus' advice to us: "Do not worry about your life. . . . Can any of you by worrying add a single moment to your life-span? . . . Seek first the kingdom of God and his righteousness, and all these things will be given you besides" (Matthew 6:25, 27, 33).

The Sacrament of Reconciliation

St. Paul taught that by his suffering and death Jesus reconciled the world with God (cf. 2 Corinthians 5:18) as well as all things on earth with those in heaven (cf. Colossians 1:20). The Church, in turn, shares in Christ's ministry of reconciliation and forgiveness. The primary sacrament that brings about this reconciliation and

---

6. The seven last words of Jesus are sometimes the focus of reflection on Good Friday. These last words are: "Father, forgive them, they know not what they do" (Luke 23:34); "Woman behold your son. . . . Behold your Mother!" (John 19:26–27); "I thirst" (John 19:28); "Today you will be with me in Paradise" (Luke 23:43); "My God, my God, why have you forsaken me?" (Matthew 27:46; Mark 15:34); "It is finished" (John 19:30); and "Father, into your hands I commend my spirit" (Luke 23:46).

forgiveness is baptism. But because people, out of weakness, continue to sin after baptism, there is a sacrament for the pardon of sins committed after baptism (cf. John 20:21–23). We call this the Sacrament of Reconciliation.

The Church calls people to conversion and renewal throughout their lives. It encourages people to admit their sins against God and others, to feel heartfelt contrition for these sins, and to celebrate the Sacrament of Reconciliation from time to time. The Church especially encourages Catholics to celebrate the Sacrament of Reconciliation at the time when their own death is approaching. The sacrament may be celebrated during communion of the sick, during the celebration of the anointing of the sick, or during the celebration of Viaticum.

The Sacrament of Reconciliation contains four parts: (1) contrition on the part of the dying person for any sins committed against God and others, (2) confession of these sins to the priest, who acts as the representative of God and the Church, (3) acceptance of an act of penance that shows the desire to change one's life and to undue any injury that was done, and (4) the receiving of absolution, or forgiveness.

All of these parts may be seen in the following outline of the rite of reconciliation for someone who is dying.

Invitation to Trust. The priest invites the dying person to trust in God by saying one of the following:

   A. May the grace of the Holy Spirit
   fill your heart with light,
   that you may confess your sins with loving trust
   and come to know that God is merciful.
   Amen.
   B. May the Lord be in your heart
   and help you to confess your sins with true sorrow.
   Amen.
   C. The Lord does not wish the sinner to die
   but to turn back to him and live.
   Come before him with trust in his mercy.
   Amen.

Revelation of State of Life. If the dying person does not know the priest, the person gives the priest some background about himself or herself.

Confession of Sins. The dying person confesses his or her sins. The priest may then give suitable counsel.

Acceptance of Satisfaction. If appropriate, the priest suggests an act of penance, which the dying person accepts as a sign of amendment and reparation.

Penitent's Prayer of Sorrow. The dying person may say a familiar Act of Contrition[7] or one of the following:

A. *Lord Jesus,*
you opened the eyes of the blind,
healed the sick,
forgave the sinful woman,
and after Peter's denial confirmed him in your love.
Listen to my prayer, forgive all my sins,
renew your love in my heart,
help me to live in perfect unity with my fellow Christians
that I may proclaim your saving power to all the world.
B. *Father of mercy,*
like the prodigal son I return to you and say:
"I have sinned against you and am no longer worthy to be called your son/daughter."
Christ Jesus, Savior of the world,
I pray with the repentant thief to whom you promised Paradise: "Lord, remember me in your Kingdom."
Holy Spirit, fountain of love, I call on you with trust: "Purify my heart, and help me to walk as a child of light."

*Absolution.*The priest extends his hands over the head of the dying person and says:

God, the Father of mercies,
through the death and resurrection of his Son
has reconciled the world to himself
and sent the Holy Spirit among us for the forgiveness of sins; through the ministry of the Church
may God give you pardon and peace,
and I absolve you from your sins

---

7. Here is a traditional Act of Contrition: My God, I am sorry for my sins with all my heart. In choosing to do wrong and failing to do good, I have sinned against You whom I should love above all things. I firmly intend, with Your help, to do penance, to sin no more, and to avoid whatever leads me to sin. Our Savior Jesus Christ suffered and died for us. In his name, my God, have mercy.

in the name of the Father, and of the Son,
and of the Holy Spirit.
Amen.
The Lord has freed you from sin.
May he bring you safely to his kingdom in heaven.
Glory to him for ever.
Amen.[8]

Your last words

Imagine for a moment that you are dying right now and that ten of your closest friends or family members are with you. What would you want to say to each person? Write down your thoughts in your notebook.

As you know, death sometimes takes us by surprise. We don't get a chance to prepare for it or to say good-bye to those we love. Are there any reasons you cannot say your "last words" to your closest friends and family members now?

---

8. International Commission on English in the Liturgy, *The Roman Ritual: Pastoral Care of the Sick* (Collegeville, MN: The Liturgical Press, 1983).

For your journal

1. How do you think you would react if a doctor said you had inoperable cancer?
2. How do you think you would react if one of your children had inoperable cancer?
3. If you could choose how you will die, what would you choose?
4. If you could choose when you will die, what age would you choose?
5. If you knew you were going to die six months from today, what would you do with the time you have left?
6. Have you ever had a problem (a child's grades in school, your weight, a relationship, etc.) that you refused to acknowledge? What happened to make you finally face the truth?
7. What are some of the things that make you angry? Have you ever been angry because something seemed unfair?
8. How do you act toward others when you are angry?
9. What would you leave unfinished if you died right now?
10. Have you ever been depressed? What was the reason for the depression? What helped to get you out of it?
11. If you had to assess your life right now, what would you list as its strengths? its weaknesses? How would you "judge" yourself?
12. What does the Sacrament of Reconciliation mean to you? How important is it in your life?
13. If you knew you were going to die soon, with whom would you like to be reconciled?

Discussion questions

1. Reread the story about Michael Landon. What was his hope? Do you think this hope was realistic? Which of his responses showed that he was in denial? What other responses indicated that he was dealing realistically with death?
2. Why do you think some people die young, while others live to old age? Why do some people suffer more than others?
3. Do you think dying people have a "right" to be angry? Why or why not?

4. Do you think dying people have a "right" to take their anger out on others? Why or why not?

5. Do you think it is "all right" to get angry at God? Why or why not?

6. What are some healthy ways to express anger?

7. Do you know of any situations in which someone "held on" to life until after an important event? Do you think the person's mental state really affected the time of death, or was the timing just coincidental? In other words, is there a specific time when each person is destined to die, no matter what he or she does?

8. If you were told that you had cancer and would probably only live three more months, what would you bargain for?

9. Which do you think bargaining expresses most: fear of death, denial of death, or the need to remain in control of one's own destiny?

10. How is acceptance different from giving up? Try to give examples to explain what you mean.

11. Does knowing about the death of Jesus make dying any easier for a Christian?

12. What do you think Jesus meant when he said that we must lose our lives in order to find them? What do you think this means in today's world? Give examples.

13. What do you think Jesus meant when he said to seek first God's kingdom? How does this relate to the way Christians should approach death?

14. What are the ways that the Sacrament of Reconciliation may be celebrated by Catholics today? What are the advantages and disadvantages of each way? Which of these ways do you prefer? Why?

8 The Grieving Process

Types of loss

Death is the greatest and most obvious loss we can experience in life. But it is by no means the only loss that we have to deal with. There are many other types of loss as well. Look at the following list. How many of these losses have you experienced? How many are you experiencing now? What other losses could be added to the list?

Obvious loss

Death of loved one or pet
Breakup of a close relationship
Incest
Theft
Destruction of property
Losing money or a possession
Natural disaster
Failure
Being fired
Rape
Arrest
Chronic illness
Temporary illness
Injury or disability
Miscarriage
Loss of a limb

Unnoticed loss

Marriage
Birth of a child
The end of therapy
Achieving a longtime goal
Promotion
Graduation
Success
Finishing a creative project
Disillusionment with a person or ideal

Loss due to change

Divorce
Role reversals
Getting involved
Temporary separation
Moving
Buying something new
Selling something
Starting a new job
Change in pace
Change in schools
Change of teachers
Change in stress level
Changing roles
Leaving home
Retirement
Weaning
Puberty
Mid-life
Menopause

Reacting to loss

It is impossible to get through life without some experiences of loss. As you have just seen, the loss may be very obvious, as in the death of a loved one or the loss of a limb. The loss may be the result of a necessary change—the move to a new house or a transfer to a new job. The loss may also be associated with something positive—getting married or reaching a long-term goal.

No matter what the type of loss, all people respond in some way to their losses. Most of us don't like to lose anything. And so we feel an emotional reaction that most psychologists define as grief. Each person, however, experiences grief in different ways. The feeling of grief may be short lived or last for years. It may be overwhelmingly sad, or only mildly unpleasant. Whatever its pattern, grieving is a process, something that eventually ends.

In the last chapter, you looked at the psychological reactions of a person facing his or her own death. In this chapter, you will look at the reactions of those who mourn the death of a loved one. In addition to studying the grieving process, you will learn about customs and rituals that help mourners "get through" the time of death. You will also consider ways that mourners can work through their grief, as well as ways you can support them during this difficult time.

Psychological responses to death

Not all people respond to death in a negative way. If the dying has been particularly long or painful, survivors may feel a great sense of relief when death finally comes. At last, the loved one's suffering has ended. The suffering of the survivors has ended too. Their years of struggle, economic drain, and emotional worry have ended. Because of this, the survivors may receive death with quiet elation. Now they will have more time for themselves. They can spend their money in other ways. For the first time in years, they may be free to spend time with friends and develop new relationships.

Instead of being a callous or selfish response to death, such feelings may culminate years of grieving. Grief does not necessarily start when someone dies. For example, a wife whose husband has Alzheimer's disease grieves each time he has a memory loss. As his condition gradually worsens, so her grieving is gradual. Or consider the case of a husband whose wife has breast cancer. He mourns each step along the way—the removal of a breast, the chemotherapy and hair loss, further surgery, her loss of energy and increased pain. Another example would be grown children who grieve when they have to leave a parent in a nursing home.

On the other hand, sometimes death is sudden and unexpected—as in cases involving a car accident or a fatal heart attack or a stroke. One minute the person is alive and healthy; the next minute he or she is dead. In such cases survivors may feel a sudden beginning to their grief. They are shocked and stunned. They feel that what has happened is not real; they are disoriented, confused, and unable to function according to their usual patterns. Some people are so numb that they feel nothing. Others feel alienated and wrenched from their ordinary world; the loss seems overwhelming and causes them great pain.

Despite these differences in the way people grieve, several things may be said about grief. First, it is a PROCESS, not just a feeling. Grieving takes time. The amount of time and the intensity will vary with each individual. Second, grieving involves the whole person, not just the emotions. (Physical aspects of grieving may include nausea, insomnia, weakness, and headaches.) And third, grieving is hard work. The only way to get over grief is to go through it and actually grieve.

The nature of grief

Psychologists tell us that grief is the "price" we pay for living a full life and for loving others. When someone we love dies, part of us dies also. In one sense, our lives will never again be the same. Indeed, there are only two ways to avoid grief: (1) to die as a baby or young child, so that no one we know dies before us, and (2) to go through life never loving or caring for anyone else. Needless to say, neither of these alternatives is very appealing. Because love makes life meaningful, we must necessarily come to terms with the reality of grief and come to expect it.

It is important to keep remembering that grief is a process and not just a feeling. Grieving is a process, however, of recognizing feelings and then dealing with them. Grief is not just one feeling, but a mish-mash of numerous emotions: sorrow, fear, anger, and guilt, to name a few. To understand the nature of grief, we need to understand something about each of these separate components.

Sorrow

At this grief my heart was utterly darkened; and whatever I beheld was death. . . . Mine eyes sought him everywhere, but he was not granted them; and I hated all places, for . . . they had not him;

nor could they now tell me, "he is coming," as when he was alive and absent.[1]

These words were written by St. Augustine after the death of a close friend. They describe well the depression, emptiness, hopelessness, despair, and pessimism that accompany sorrow. Similar feelings are found in David's lament for his friend Jonathan: "I grieve for you, Jonathan my brother! Most dear have you been to me" (2 Samuel 1:26). Mary, the mother of Jesus, also knew such sorrow. As Simeon had once predicted, a sword pierced her heart when her son died on the cross.[2]

The sorrow that is part of grieving may be short lived, as in the case of survivors who feel relieved of a great burden when death comes. Or the sorrow may last for years. In some people, the sorrow may come in waves of intense distress and bring on bouts of hysteria. Some people respond to feelings of sorrow by losing motivation and energy. Others may have "a good cry."

Fear

During a time of grief, most people also have feelings of fear. Some of these may be unresolved fears about death, the dying process, or dead spirits. Other fears may include the following:

- Fear of facing the future alone. "How will I ever live without him or her?" "What is to become of me?"
- Fear of change and of the unknown. "Nothing will ever be the same because of this."
- Fear of future deaths and separations. "The other people I love are going to die too. Someday I myself will die."
- Fear of letting go of the past, of forgetting how much the person meant. "I can't even remember his/her face."
- Fear that we will not survive the loss. "I'm losing my mind. My heart can't take this."

---

1. Edward B. Pusey, trans., *The Confessions of St. Augustine* (New York: Washington Square Press, 1951), p. 50.

2. The Church celebrates the feast of Our Lady of Sorrows on September 15. This day recalls the sorrows in Mary's life, due to her love for Jesus: the prophecy of Simeon (Luke 2:35); the flight into Egypt (Matthew 2:13–21); losing the child Jesus (Luke 2:41–50); meeting Jesus on the way to Calvary (Church tradition); the death of Jesus (John 19:26–27); the removal of Jesus' body from the cross (Matthew 27:55); the burial of Jesus (Mark 15:47). The grief Mary felt was captured by Michelangelo in his *Pieta*, a marble statue located in St. Peter's Basilica in Rome.

- Fear that if we do survive the loss, we will be left emotionally crippled. "I'll never be able to get that close to someone else again."
- Fear that what we are feeling is abnormal. "Does anybody else feel this bad for so long? Why can't I get over this?"
- Fear of never being loved again in the same way. "I'll never find anyone to replace him/her."

Working through grief means learning not to fear it or death. It means coming to accept that both grief and death are necessary parts of life.

Anger

This feeling is the same as the anger found in the second stage of death discussed in the last chapter. In this case, however, it is the mourner who is angry. The mourner is angry at the deceased for dying, at God for letting this happen, at the doctors for not doing more, at himself or herself for not having seen this coming, at others for "going on with life as if nothing happened." With the anger is a sense of helplessness and loss of control. The mourner becomes irritable and restless, and may "fly off the handle" with friends and family members. The mourner may also bury himself or herself in a flurry of activity concerning the funeral arrangements in order to regain some sense of control and order.

Guilt

Very often grief is intermingled with feelings of guilt. "If only I had done this . . ." and similar thoughts of recrimination may plague the mourner and prolong his or her grieving. Steve, who had nursed his friend Jim for the two years that he struggled with AIDS, was absent only for a brief moment while Jim was in the hospital. During that time, however, Jim died, and now Steve cannot forgive himself.

A grown woman with husband and children of her own took in her elderly mother rather than have her go to a nursing home. Rita did everything the doctors told her to do, but one day, without warning, her mother died. Rita is convinced she should have done more and should have been able to prevent her mother from dying. Six months after the death, she still cannot forgive herself.

A young woman had an argument with her husband as he was leaving for work. She intended to call him during the day and patch things up, but she never got around to calling. On the way home, her husband was killed in an automobile accident. Now she cannot forgive herself.

The list could go on. And on. And on. Some survivors even feel guilty because they don't feel sad after someone has died. The only way to deal with feelings such as guilt, sorrow, fear, and anger is first of all to admit that you have them. The next step involves expressing the feelings, talking about them with a trusted friend, a priest, or a counselor. The saying "grief shared is grief halved" is a wise one. A sympathetic ear is good medicine for anyone who is mourning.

While psychologists differ in their theories regarding the grieving process, all of them agree that it is important for mourners to feel their feelings. Suppressing grief, trying to hold back the tears or the anger, will only make things worse in the long run. The grief will show itself later in another and more painful form—as a behavior disorder (excess drinking, using drugs, etc.), a serious illness (especially cancer), or a relationship problem.

Grief does end

Every person experiences grief differently. No single pattern fits everyone. Nevertheless, the grief process does have three major "movements" or "phases" that most people experience. These phases together are called the time of bereavement.

The first phase is that of intense grief. This occurs especially in people who begin grieving after death. During this time, which may last from a month to three months or more, the person is likely to experience a roller coaster of emotions and thus to act very unpredictably.

In this phase, the mourners themselves may withdraw emotionally from society. There have also been examples in various times and cultures when society itself separated the mourners from the clan, tribe, or village. In Australia, for example, Aborigine widows had to live in a separate hut. During the Victorian era in Europe and America, mourners had to wear special mourning clothes and were forbidden from many social activities. The socially mandated mourning period around the time of Civil War was two years for a spouse, one year for a parent or child, six months for grandparents, and three months for aunts and uncles.

The second phase in the grieving process is a time of transition. The mourners still feel their loss but are beginning to cope with it. They start to live with the fact that the deceased person is dead, and they become comfortable once more in the environment in which the deceased is missing. This is the time when most of the work of grieving is done. Society has traditionally marked this phase by allowing mourners out of their special huts, letting them put aside their mourning clothes, and permitting them to talk and visit more with their friends.

In the third phase, the mourners accept their loss and take up their lives again. They allow themselves to form new relationships and to have new experiences. Many cultures mark this stage by allowing the widow or widower to remarry.

How long it takes for someone to reach the third phase depends on each person and each circumstance surrounding the grief. For some people, the grief ends abruptly. They wake up one day and know that the pain is gone. For other people, grief ends slowly and gradually. Each day is a little better than the last. No matter what the pattern, however, the pain of grieving eventually does end.

Working through grief

Certain rituals—social and personal—help mourners work through their grief. These rituals help to relieve the pain of loss by providing socially acceptable ways of crying, talking, and acting. Although these rituals may seem contrived or artificial, they actually do help to move the mourners through the grieving process.

Social rituals

Every culture has its own social rituals regarding "proper" behavior during mourning. In a Tanala village in Madagascar, for example, the mourners burst out at once into loud lamentations that continue for some twenty minutes and then stop at a signal. In India, mourners shave their heads. Mourners in China and Korea wear white. New Guinea women cover their faces with ash and wear net headdresses. Australian aborigines cut themselves. Jews throughout the world have traditionally torn their clothes. Some Jewish men do not shave or have their hair cut for the month following the death of a close relative.

The American custom of wearing black as a sign of mourning came from Europe. It stemmed from a fear of the dead. Black was worn to make the living inconspicuous to any evil spirits that might be lingering about. Sometimes everyone attending a funeral, not just close relatives, would wear black. Males wore black armbands or hatbands; a "dandy" tied a black ribbon on his cane. Women wore black dresses and veils.[3]

---

3. Children in mourning were never dressed in black. They wore white in summer and gray in winter, both trimmed with black buttons, ruffles, belt, or bonnet.

By the nineteenth century society had definite "rules" that widows were expected to follow during the prescribed two-year bereavement period. For the first year, the widow had to wear a solid black dress with collar and cuffs of folded untrimmed crepe. She might wear a simple bonnet (not a hat) and a long black veil. If she wore gloves, they were to be made of black cotton or silk, or crocheted or knit from black thread; never was she to wear kid gloves. The rules even extended to handkerchiefs, which had to be made of the sheerest white linen with a broad black border.

During the second year of mourning, the widow might wear a lusterless silk dress with black lace on the collar and cuffs. She could then shorten her veil and make it of net. During the last six months of mourning, she was allowed to wear gray, violet, or white. Her bonnet could be trimmed with white or violet lace or flowers.

At one time in America, it was the custom for mourners to decorate their homes. Funeral wreaths, hung to let passersby know of the bereavement within, consisted of white or purple flowers or black, white, or purple ribbon streamers. The doorbell might also be covered, to notify those approaching the house to do so with quiet dignity. (A black ribbon was used when the deceased was married or elderly; a white ribbon was used when the deceased was young or unmarried.)

The rituals surrounding the funeral—the notification of friends and family members, the funeral arrangements, the wake and the viewing of the body, the funeral service, the interment, and the reception following—were all social rituals meant to help mourners express their feelings and remove any sense of guilt. At these times, the survivors were shown real support and expressions of sympathy.

Personal rituals

Most psychologists agree that the real work of grieving begins after the social rituals have ended. The mourner must now, for the most part, deal with his or her grief alone. Grief work involves coming to some type of reconciliation with the death, with one's relationship to the dead person, and with one's new future. There are as many ways of going about this work as there are people. Some people work through grief by seeing, holding, or smelling something that belonged to the deceased. For example, one widow kept her dead husband's shirt under her pillow. One mother would hug the kimono of her dead baby. A girl would go to the closet and smell her dead brother's shirts. These personal "rituals" helped the mourners find peace in their grieving.

In early America, some people worked through their grief by drawing watercolor mourning pictures, either on paper or silk. The artist painted family members somberly dressed standing near the tomb. Some women worked through their grief by making mourning quilts. Inscriptions resembling an epitaph were appliqued or embroidered on the quilt. Other people made mourning wreaths of human hair, which were then framed and put on display. Girls in school often made memorial pictures containing a sampler of different needlework stitches. Such creative expressions allowed the mourner a time for quiet reflection, as well as a sense of movement and progression through the grieving process.

Some people turn to a professional counselor for help in working through grief. Others seek help from one of the many grief support groups that may be found throughout the country. Still other people turn to prayer and a deepening of their religious faith.

While there is no one "right" way to work through grief, various psychologists do offer this advice to those who are grieving:

1. **Feel your grief. Don't run away from it.** No one else can feel your feelings for you or know exactly what you are feeling. But others have experienced similar feelings and have gotten through them. Not only can they listen to you, sympathize, and understand what you are feeling; their stories can encourage you to face your own grief and work through it with courage.

2. **Review the past in order to own it and then let it go.** Recall the brighter times in your life and embrace those things that have nurtured you through other hard times. Decide what in your relationship with the dead person you want to leave behind and what memories you want to carry with you. Then let go of your resentment and guilt. Realize that life will never be quite the same as before, and move on.

3. **Envision your future. Visualize what might be.** You do not have control over what happened to you, but you do have a choice about how you will respond to the death. You can withdraw from others, give up on life, and remain embittered and angry. Or you can reach out to others in the community and try to build a loving future. You can make this crisis a turning point, not an endpoint.

4. **Return to the present anew. Enter fully into the present moment.** Your pain can bring you wisdom, strength, compassion, healing, maturity, trust, and hope. Working through grief can make you more whole and can help you be more in touch with yourself, others, and God. Instead of asking "Why did this happen?" you can now resume life with the attitude found in the following poem of Dag Hammarskjold:

For all that has been—Thanks!
To all that shall be—Yes![4]

The ministry of consolation

The Israelites believed that their God was one who sympathized with them and gave them solace in times of sorrow. "You, O Lord, have helped and comforted me" (Psalm 86:17). The Israelites believed in a God who would someday save them from death and from mourning. "He will destroy death forever. The Lord God will wipe away the tears from all faces" (Isaiah 25:8).

Christians adopted these same beliefs as they developed their concept of God as Trinity. As St. Paul wrote, "Blessed be the God and Father of our Lord Jesus Christ, a gentle Father and the God of all consolation, who comforts us in all our sorrows" (2 Corinthians 1:3). "God will wipe away every tear from their eyes, and there shall be no more death or mourning, wailing or pain, for the old order has passed away" (Revelation 21:4).

Jesus, the Son of God, was also seen as compassionate and consoling. "Blessed are they who mourn," Jesus told his followers, "they shall be consoled" (Matthew 5:3; cf. Luke 6:21). Jesus comforted Mary and Martha at the death of their brother Lazarus (cf. John 11:1–44). Likewise, he consoled the synagogue official whose daughter had died (cf. Matthew 9:18–19, 23–26; Mark 5:21–24, 35–43; Luke 8:40–42, 49–56) and the widow of Nain whose son had died (cf. Luke 7:11–17). These events show not only Jesus' power over death, but his ability to change sorrow to joy.

The Holy Spirit is also a God of consolation. On the night before his death, Jesus tells his disciples that he must leave them. But he promises to send the Holy Spirit to support them in their time of mourning. "I will ask the Father and he will give you another Comforter, and he will never leave you. He is the Holy Spirit, the Spirit who leads into all truth" (John 14:16–17). "When the Father sends the Comforter instead of me—and by the Comforter I mean

---

4. Dag Hammarskjold, *Markings* (New York: Alfred A. Knopf, 1966), p. 89.

the Holy Spirit—he will teach you much, as well as remind you of everything I myself have told you" (John 14:26). "It is best for you that I go away, for if I don't, the Comforter won't come. If I do, he will—for I will send him to you" (John 16:7).

Not only are we like God when we show sympathy to others; as Christians, we have a responsibility to console those who mourn. This responsibility is listed as one of the Spiritual Works of Mercy. It is also called the Church's "ministry of consolation."

This ministry of consolation was present from the earliest days of the Church. As St. Paul told the Corinthians, God comforts us in our sorrows "so that we can offer others, in their sorrows, the consolation that we have received from God ourselves" (2 Corinthians 1:5). "Weep with those who weep" (Romans 12:15). For "if one member suffers in the body of Christ which is the Church, all the members suffer with that member" (1 Corinthians 12:26).[5]

This ministry extends to all Church members today. As the new *Order of Christian Funerals* asserts:

> When a member of Christ's Body dies, the faithful are called to a ministry of consolation to those who have suffered the loss of one whom they love. Christian consolation is rooted in that hope that comes from faith in the saving death and resurrection of the Lord Jesus Christ. Christian hope faces the reality of death and the anguish of grief but trusts confidently that the power of sin and death has been vanquished by the risen Lord. The Church calls each member of Christ's Body—priest, deacon, lay person—to participate in the ministry of consolation: to care for the dying, to pray for the dead, to comfort those who mourn.
>
> —General Introduction, #8

In addition to the actions listed above, the rite encourages Catholics to console mourners by writing letters of condolence and sending sympathy cards, bringing food to the house, praying for the dead at the general intercessions at Mass, and participating actively in the Church's death rituals—the vigil service, funeral, interment, and reception. By such actions we show support for others in their time of need, and we help them through the grieving process.

---

5. One of the titles of Mary is "Comforter of the Afflicted." Another translation of this same title is "Our Lady of Consolation."

What you can do

Most people feel very awkward around someone who is mourning. We want to do something to help, but we aren't sure what to do or what to say. And if the person starts crying, we really feel helpless. Perhaps we say words such as "Call me if you need me," but inside we hope the call never comes.

It is difficult to be around someone who is depressed or unpredictable or obsessed with a recent death. And yet as Christians, we are challenged to treat others as we would want them to treat us in a similar situation. What can you do to help someone who is grieving? Here is the answer: Put yourself in his or her shoes. Think about what would help you most if you were grieving. Then do the same for the other person.

Here are some specific ideas suggested by psychologists:

- Take the initiative. Get in touch with the grieving person, rather than wait for him or her to call you.
- Avoid cliches or cold impersonal statements, such as:
  —At least N._____ went fast.
  —N._____'s now out of his/her misery.
  —N._____'s with God now.
  —N._____ was old and had a good life.
  —Cheer up, it was for the best.
  —Keep busy, it'll help you forget.
- Soon after the death, write a personal letter of condolence, and include it in a sympathy card.
- Do something practical for the person. Offer to clean out the closets, take the deceased's clothes to a charitable organization, address envelopes to thank-you cards, baby-sit, cook a meal, etc.
- Continue to stay in touch, both by phone and by visits. Set up a specific time when you will spend time with the person, and then keep the date.
- When you are with the person, make sure you listen to what he or she is saying. Don't attempt to tell the person how he or she is feeling. And don't think that you have to fill up moments of silence with trivia about everyone you know. Remember, what is most important is your presence, not what you say.

- Affirm the grieving person as a good person, especially if he or she is feeling guilty.
- Be patient, especially if the person mourns longer than you would like. Try to include the person in an activity you are doing. If the person turns you down, don't take it personally and do remember to ask again later.

Because most people have difficulty writing, there is provided here a few extra tips about condolence letters. When you write a condolence letter, you should remember that it may be read by several members of the family. It may also be saved and passed down to future generations. But this does not mean that the letter needs to contain perfect spelling or grammar. Nor does it have to be formal. What is important is that you be yourself and express what you are genuinely feeling.

Amy Vanderbilt, in her book on etiquette, says that a good condolence letter has three key ingredients: (1) it expresses understanding and sympathy to the mourner; (2) it praises or says something positive about the deceased, in a personal way; and (3) it expresses a sincere desire to be of some help. To explain further, she quotes a condolence letter to a young Jewish widow from an eleven-year-old Catholic girl:

Dear Mrs. Wise,

It's just terrible that God desided to take Rabbi Wise so yung. It's really very meen of Him, because He must have knon we wanted Rabbi Wise to stay longer. I dont know if you believ in Purgatory and saints and all that stuff, but I do, and I just happen to know that with all our prayers Rabbi Wise went thru Purgtory awful fast, sort of like a car racer. So he's already in Heavn with God and His Saints. (my favrit Saint is Mother Seton). God will take care of Rabbi Wise and you, too, now that youre lone. I'll do your dishes or sit with the baby anytime. Tell Ralfie I have a new rattle for him anyway.

Love,[6]

The letter is far from perfect grammatically, and yet the young widow treasured it far more than the many purchased sympathy cards she received.

---

6. Letitia Baldrige, ed., *The Amy Vanderbilt Complete Book of Etiquette* (New York: Doubleday, 1978), p. 522. Used by permission.

For your journal

1. Think of a time when you grieved over a loss. Was your grief short lived or did it last for years? Was it overwhelmingly sad, or only mildly unpleasant? At this time, has your grief ended, or are you still experiencing it?

2. How do you act when you get angry?

3. What are some things that you feel guilty about? Do you think your guilt is reasonable (that you really are to blame) or unreasonable (you just feel that you are to blame)?

4. How has God comforted you in times of sorrow?

5. Who is someone in your life who is a good listener? How does this person let you know that he or she is truly listening?

6. On a scale of 1 to 10 (with 10 as the highest), how would you rank yourself as a good listener? How might you go about improving your listening skills?

7. Write yourself a condolence letter you wished you had received after the death of a loved one.

Discussion questions

1. What losses are a natural part of being an adult? of growing older?

2. Can you think of any examples where a person might begin grieving BEFORE someone dies?

3. Discuss a recent television show or movie in which one of the characters dies. How do the other characters react to the death? Do you think their responses are realistic?

4. Discuss each fear listed in this chapter that people might experience during the grieving process. Is it a reasonable or unreasonable fear? Do you have any suggestions about how to deal with this fear?

5. Can you think of any other fears that might be associated with grief?

6. What are some reasons a mourner might be angry with the person who died?

7. Some psychologists say that mourners are really grieving for themselves and what they have lost, rather than for the dead person. Do you agree or disagree?

8. Why do you think most of the social customs regarding mourning had to do with women? Do women grieve differently than men? Does society view mourning women differently than it views mourning men?

9. The widow's garb became the standard habit for religious women. Why do you think this was so?

10. How have other Christians tried to comfort you in times of sorrow? How did their words and actions make you feel?

11. Imagine that someone in your family has just died. How would you want your friends to respond? What would you want them to say and do?

12. Discuss each of the cliches given in this chapter. How would you feel if someone said this to you when you were grieving?

Part Five: Social Aspects

Many of the Jews had come to Martha and Mary to comfort them about their brother.

—John 11:19

9 Caring for the Sick and Dying

One family's story

Jeanne White's son Ryan was a normal kid, with just one exception: He was born with hemophilia. Periodically, he needed a blood transfusion. After the transfusion, life usually returned to normal again.

But this time was different. At age thirteen Ryan accidentally received a transfusion of tainted blood. As a result, he was infected with the AIDS virus. When students, parents, and school officials found out about Ryan's condition, hysteria broke loose. He was banned from attending school in Russianville. And for the next two years, Ryan was shunned by neighbors, relatives, schoolmates, and teachers. All the people mistakenly believed that they or their children could get AIDS just by being around Ryan.

As time went on, things got worse. No one would sit near the family in church. Then the family received threatening phone calls. Finally, a bullet was fired through the Whites' front window.

When the White family's story hit the news, a new group of friends came to the rescue: Michael Jackson, Phil Donahue, Marlo Thomas, Barbara Bush, Jesse Jackson, Elton John, and Donald Trump. Because of the influence of these friends, Ryan became a national spokesperson for AIDS education. Wherever he went, he told people the truth about AIDS and how it could and could not be spread.[1]

The Whites eventually won a court battle to permit Ryan to attend school. But when he returned to school, he found that he was the butt of "Ryan White jokes." Schoolmates flattened themselves against the walls as he passed them in the school corridor. Hardly anyone would talk to him. Because things were so bad, the Whites moved to Cicero, Indiana. Fortunately, Ryan was warmly welcomed there.

"I never really believed that Ryan would die of AIDS," Jeanne said a year after his death. "I thought that God would send us a miracle. I believe now that God did send us a miracle in Ryan. Miracles come in different forms—it's not always long life. Sometimes a miracle is what a person is able to do with life."[2]

---

1. Ryan White was born on December 16, 1971, in Kokomo, Indiana. He died of AIDS on April 8, 1990. His life was dramatized in the television movie "The Ryan White Story," and in the book *Ryan White: My Story* (New York: Dial Books, 1991). Both the movie and the book documented the prejudices Ryan encountered because of AIDS. The prejudice against Ryan did not end with his death. On several occasions, his grave has been vandalized.

2. From the Associated Press, May 12, 1991. Used by permission. All rights reserved.

Fear of the sick

Just as dying is part of life, so is sickness. In 1990, over 43 million people were treated for illnesses in the United States, and that number reflects only those who were served by Catholic hospitals. Although people frequently get sick, society tends to treat the sick as "untouchables." Our fear of the sick is just as strong as our fear of the dead, especially when the disease is infectious and fatal. And when the sick person is someone who is also dying—as in the case of someone who has AIDS—our fears multiply.[3]

Unfortunately, these fears often express themselves as prejudice and discrimination against the sick, the elderly, those who are mentally or physically disabled, or the terminally ill. We isolate these people in institutions because we don't want to deal with them or face what they represent.

In the next two chapters, you will explore the social dimensions of dealing with sickness and death. This chapter focuses on care of the sick. You will see how care of the sick has always been an important part of the Church's history and social teaching. You will also explore the meaning of the Sacrament of the Anointing of the Sick, and receive some tips about how to relate to those who are sick.

Stereotypes and fears

We often fear what we do not know. When someone becomes sick or disabled, our fear increases. The person no longer seems human; instead, he or she has become a giant label, "SICK" or "HANDICAPPED" or "TERMINALLY ILL." At best, we relate to the label and to our stereotypes of it, rather than relate to the individual person. At worst, we shy away from the people we have labeled, or we refuse to relate to them at all. Then, because we have isolated ourselves from these people, we tend to fear them even more. Stereotypes and prejudice become part of a vicious circle.

Stereotypes and prejudice reflect underlying fears. Some people fear the sick because they are afraid that they, too, will contract the disease. In cases of contagious diseases, such fears are justified. In most cases of sickness, however, the fears have no basis in reality.

---

3. In March 1991, the World Health Organization counted 334, 215 AIDS cases worldwide, although the true number was higher. In the United States, the Centers for Disease Control counted 171,876 AIDS cases. By 1991, over 108,000 Americans had died of AIDS. Nine million to 11 million people throughout the world were also thought to carry the AIDS virus.

Some people fear the machines, tubes, needles, pills, and other paraphernalia that go along with being sick. This is especially true if the person is in a hospital or convalescent home. The strange sights, sounds, and smells of the sick person's room can be frightening to those who are not used to them.

Other people fear the sick because sickness is a reminder of death. If you look at the major causes of death in the United States today, this fear seems appropriate. In 1988, for example, seven of the ten leading causes of death (excluding homicide) were some type of sickness—major cardiovascular diseases; cancer; pulmonary diseases, such as chronic bronchitis, emphysema, and asthma; pneumonia and flu; diabetes; liver disease; and AIDS.

Another reason we fear sickness is that we aren't as close to it as past generations. In former times, the sick were treated at home. Doctors made house calls. Now people are treated in doctors' offices or in hospitals. The elderly are sent to live in separate retirement communities or nursing homes. The mentally and physically disabled attend separate "special education" classes. Sickness has been removed from our ordinary experience of life; hence, we tend to fear what we do not know.

These fears are not new. The Hebrew Scriptures tell us that people hid their faces from the sick, spurned them, and held them in no esteem (cf. Isaiah 53:3). In the time of Jesus, most people considered persons with a mental disability, the mentally ill, and epileptics to be possessed by evil or unclean spirits. Lepers were avoided at all costs and had to live apart from others. The deaf, blind, and crippled were thought to be sinners. Because they were not accepted by society, they lived on the streets as beggars.

Jesus and the sick

Jesus countered the prevailing fears of his day with tangible action. He cared for the sick in ways that were compassionate and healing. Rather than relating to the sick on the basis of labels, Jesus treated them as people who had dignity.

Indeed, caring for the sick was an important part of Jesus' ministry; examples of it can be found in all four Gospels. Despite the prejudices of his day, Jesus reached out in love to heal all who came to him:

- lepers (cf. the leper—Matthew 8:2–4; Mark 1:40–45; Luke 5:12–16; ten lepers—Luke 17:11–18)
- Romans (cf. the centurion's servant—Matthew 8:5–13; Luke 7:1–10; the son of a royal officer—John 4:46–53)

- women (cf. Peter's mother-in-law—Matthew 8:14–15; Mark 1:29–31; Luke 4:38–39; woman with blood flow—Matthew 9:20–22; Mark 5:25–34; Luke 8:43–48; Syro-Phoenician woman—Matthew 15:21–28; Mark 7:24–30; stooped woman—Luke 13:10–17)

- the physically disabled (cf. cure of paralytic—Matthew 9:2–8; Mark 2:1–12; Luke 5:17–26; two blind men—Matthew 9:27–31; man with withered hand—Matthew 12:9–14; Mark 3:1–6; Luke 6:6–11; blind man at Jericho—Matthew 20:29–34; Mark 10:46–52; Luke 18:35–43; deaf mute—Mark 7:31–37; blind man at Bethsaida—Mark 8:22–26; cripple of thirty-eight years— John 5:1–9; man born blind— John 9:1–7)

- the sick (cf. man with dropsy—Luke 14:1–6; the sick—Matthew 4:23–24, 8:16, 10:8, 14:14; Luke 9:2, 10:9)

- those possessed by demons (cf. the Gadarene demoniac— Matthew 8:28–34; Mark 5:1–20; Luke 8:26–39; mute demoniac—Matthew 9:32–34; Luke 11:14–15; deaf-mute demoniac—Matthew 12:22; Luke 11:14–15; epileptic boy—Matthew 17:14–21; Mark 9:14–29; Luke 9:37–43a; demoniac in Capernaum—Mark 1:21–28; Luke 4:31–37)

Such actions were to be expected from Isaiah's suffering-servant Messiah. Thus Matthew includes the following dialogue in his Gospel:

> When John heard in prison of the works of the Messiah, he sent his disciples to him with this question, "Are you the one who is to come or should we look for another?" Jesus said to them in reply, "Go and tell John what you hear and see: the blind regain their sight, the lame walk, lepers are cleansed, the deaf hear, the dead are raised, and the poor have the good news proclaimed to them."
>
> —Matthew 11:2–5

In addition to his own actions of care toward the sick, Jesus gave his apostles the power to heal (cf. Matthew 10:1; Mark 3:14). This power continued in full force after Pentecost. Peter and John cured a crippled beggar (cf. Acts 3:1–10). The apostles cured the sick and those disturbed by unclean spirits (cf. Acts 5:12–16). Philip cured the paralyzed and crippled (cf. Acts 8:4–8). Ananias cured Paul of his blindness (cf.Acts 9:17–19). Peter healed a paralyzed man named Aeneas (cf. Acts 9:32–35), and Peter raised a woman who fell sick and died (cf. Acts 9:36–42). By their actions, the apostles called all members of the Church to pray for the sick and to show compassion toward them.

Church history and care of the sick

The early Christians became so good at caring for the sick that Constantine abolished all non-Christian hospitals in A.D. 331, thus making the care of the sick the sole matter of the Church. The first Christian hospitals were in monasteries. In A.D. 370, for example, St. Basil of Caesarea established a monastery in Cappadocia that included a hospital and a separate leprosarium. Early in the sixth century, St. Benedict founded the monastery of Monte Cassino, where care of the sick was placed above every other Christian duty. Later in the same century, St. John the Almsgiver built monastic hospitals for the poor in Alexandria. The manner in which monks cared for their own sick became a model for the laity. The monasteries had an infirmary, a pharmacy, and frequently grew their own medicinal plants.

In 1099, the Church built a hospital in Jerusalem for sick pilgrims. The hospital was capable of treating two thousand patients. Throughout the Middle Ages, the Benedictine order founded more than two thousand hospitals in Europe so that the sick could find help and the dying could die in peace and dignity.

In 1540, King Henry VIII dissolved all Catholic monasteries in England. The resultant loss of hospitals in England caused secular authorities to begin to provide for the sick, the injured, and the disabled. From that time on, two systems of hospitals developed side-by-side: private hospitals, sponsored primarily by the Church, and public, or government-run, hospitals.

Throughout the centuries, the Church continued to be a worldwide leader in care of the sick. Some noteworthy people involved in this work include the following:

- **St. John of God.** He started a hospital in Grenada in the early sixteenth century. This marked the beginning of the Brothers Hospitaller of St. John, an order devoted solely to the care of the sick. Today St. John of God is the patron of the sick, nurses, and hospitals.

- **St. Martin de Porres.** This Dominican lay brother first worked with the sick in the monastery's infirmary in Lima, Peru, in the early seventeenth century. Later, he served the sick and the poor throughout Lima.

- **St. Vincent de Paul.** He laid the foundations for a system of hospitals in Paris in the seventeenth century. He also started professional nursing.

- **Rose Hawthorne Lathrop.** She founded the Servants of Relief for Incurable Cancer in Hawthorne, NY, and opened the first cancer hospital there in 1900.
- **Mother Teresa of Calcutta.** She founded the Missionaries of Charity to work with the sick and the dying poor in Calcutta. Gradually her communities spread throughout the world, taking care of the sick and terminally ill. In 1979, Mother Teresa received the Nobel Peace Prize.

The first North American hospital was built in Mexico City in 1524 by Cortes. In 1639, the French established a hospital at Quebec City, Canada. Jeanne Mance, a French noblewoman, built a hospital in Montreal in 1644. This hospital was the beginning of the Order of the Sisters of St. Joseph, the oldest nursing group organized in North America. The first hospital in the United States was established on Manhattan Island in 1751. This hospital, however, was poorly equipped.

In the second half of the nineteenth century, the Church also became the leader in establishing mission hospitals throughout the world.

The hospice movement

Hospices were originally guest houses or "way stations" intended for pilgrims. Like hospitals, they were sponsored by religious communities. The most famous of these early hospices, the hospice of St. Bernard, continues to offer shelter for modern-day travelers passing over the Pennine Alps.

Today, hospices are retreats where the dying can live out their last days in a noninstitutional, homelike atmosphere. Patients are usually admitted only after they have received a prognosis of months or weeks to live. Friends and family can gather around the dying person, to help give as much support, comfort, and affection as possible. The hospice team includes doctors, nurses, social workers, consultants, and trained volunteers. Hospices may be in homes, hospitals, nursing homes, or separate facilities.

In 1905, the Sisters of Charity founded the St. James Hospice in London to care for the dying. The modern hospice movement, however, did not really begin until 1967, when Dr. Cicely Saunders founded St. Christopher's Hospice in London.

The Church today

Health care is an important part of the Church's social ministry today. Throughout the world, the Catholic Church runs 6,034 hospitals, 13,425 dispensaries, 649 leprosariums, and 10,811 homes for the aged or disabled. In the United States, there are 640 hospitals, 180 dispensaries, and 715 homes for special care that are operated as Catholic. Since 1915, the Catholic Health Association of the United States has existed as a national organization serving Catholic hospitals and long-term care facilities, their sponsoring organizations, and other health and related agencies and services.

Visiting the sick is considered one of the Corporal Works of Mercy, and is thus an important part of the life of every parish. When a person is confined by illness and is unable to go to church for reception of the sacraments, the parish priest, deacon, or Eucharistic minister visits the person. In addition to talking with the sick person, the minister also brings Holy Communion.

Parishes remember their sick each week in the general intercessions at Mass and periodically in celebrations of the Sacrament of the Anointing of the Sick—either in the parish or on an individual basis.

The Church's social teaching

The Catholic bishops of the United States periodically publish statements and pastoral letters to advise Catholics of the Church's social teaching. The following excerpts from some of these writings deal with four topics related to this chapter: the sick, the elderly, the disabled, and people with AIDS.

The Sick

3. We wish to call all Catholics to a fuller acceptance of their responsibility for their own health and for their share in the healing apostolate of the Church.

10. Because all human beings are created according to God's image, they possess a basic human dignity which calls for the utmost reverence. On the individual level this means a special responsibility to care for one's own health and that of others. On the societal level this calls for responsibility by society to provide adequate health care which is a basic human right.

12. The works of mercy call Christians to engage themselves in direct efforts to alleviate the misery of the afflicted.

15. . . . we must embrace every chance to help and to liberate, to

*heal the wounded world as Jesus taught us. Our hands must be the
strong but gentle hands of Christ, reaching out in mercy and justice,
touching individual persons, but also touching the social conditions
that hinder the wholeness which is God's desire for humanity.*

—Health and Health Care, *November 19, 1981*

The Elderly

3. *Society has come to take a negative view of the elderly. This can
be seen in the increasing tendency of families to rely on institutions
to care for their elderly members, and in repeated efforts by some
government officials to cut services and benefits for the elderly in
order to ease the burden of inflation on the rest of society.*

5. *In rejecting the elderly, we do more than perpetuate injustice:
When we reject any stage of human life, we are in effect rejecting a
part of ourselves and our connections with the human community.*

6. *The biblical commandment to "honor your father and mother"
(Deuteronomy 5:16) reminds us that, above all else, the family ought
to be a place of love, respect, and caring for the aging members of
society.*

8. *Our first task is to restore to the elderly the dignity and sense of
worth which they deserve.*

—Society and the Aged, *May 5, 1976*

Persons with Disabilities

11. *It is not enough merely to affirm the rights of persons with
disabilities. We must actively work to make them real in the fabric of
modern society. Recognizing that disabled individuals have a claim
to our respect because they share in the one redemption of Christ and
because they contribute to our society by their activity within it, the
Church must become an advocate for and with them. It must work to
increase the public's sensitivity toward the needs of disabled people
and support their rightful demand for justice. Moreover, individuals
and organizations at every level within the Church should minister
to disabled persons by serving their personal and social needs.*

—Pastoral on Persons with Disabilities, *November 15, 1978*

AIDS

*Part 2, #3. Persons with AIDS are not distant, unfamiliar people,
the objects of our misled pity and aversion. We must keep them
present to our consciousness as individuals and a community, and
embrace them with unconditional love. The Gospel demands reverence for life in all circumstances. Compassion—love—toward
persons infected with HIV is the only authentic Gospel response.*

Part 6, #1. Our response to persons with AIDS must be such that we discover Christ in them and they in turn are able to encounter Christ in us.[4] Although this response undoubtedly arises in the context of religious faith, even those without faith can and must look beyond suffering to see the human dignity and goodness of those who suffer.

— Called to Compassion and Responsibility: A Response to the HIV-AIDS Crisis, *November 30, 1989*

Anointing of the sick

For many centuries, Catholics perceived the sacrament of anointing as the "last rites" of the Church. Known as "extreme unction," it was thought to prepare a person for death. Thus, only a person who was in immediate danger of death took part in this sacrament. Extreme unction was usually celebrated in private, far away from the eyes and participatory prayers of the Christian community.[5]

The bishops of Vatican II called for a closer examination of this sacrament and for a revision that reflected its true meaning. The result was the 1972 revised rite, which called the sacrament by a new name: anointing of the sick. This name reflects the sacrament's dual purpose from biblical times: to offer the sick person the possibility of healing and to prepare the person for death.

According to the revised rite, the following people may receive the sacrament:

- Those whose health is seriously impaired by sickness or old age
- Those about to undergo surgery because of a serious illness
- Elderly people weakened by age, even if no serious illness is present
- Sick children who are sufficiently mature to be comforted by the sacrament

---

4. Pope John Paul II graphically demonstrated the call to compassion and care for the sick when he embraced four-year-old AIDS sufferer Brendan O'Rourke at Mission Dolores in San Francisco, on September 17, 1987.

5. In the past, when the priest arrived for the last rites, a bell was rung. The original purpose of this "passing bell" was to keep away any evil that might be lurking about the dying person. The bell was also rung at death, to announce the passing of the soul from this world to the next, and to invite the faithful to pray for its safe passage.

If possible, the sacrament is to be celebrated in the presence of the Christian assembly within Mass—either in church, in the home of the sick person, or in the hospital.

The liturgy of the sacrament includes the litany of the faithful for the sick, the laying on of hands, and the anointing with the Oil of the Sick. Under normal circumstances, the sick person is anointed both on the forehead and hands. In case of necessity, however, a single anointing can be given on the forehead (or another part of the body, depending upon the person's physical condition). The sacrament may be repeated if the sick person recovers and later becomes ill again.

The following is an outline of the sacrament.

Liturgy of anointing

Litany (The people respond: Lord have mercy.)

Let us pray to God for our brothers and sisters and for all those who devote themselves to caring for them.

- *Bless (the sick people) and fill them with new hope and strength: Lord, have mercy. (R)*
- *Relieve their pain: Lord, have mercy. (R)*
- *Free them from sin and do not let them give way to temptation: Lord, have mercy. (R)*
- *Sustain all the sick with your power: Lord, have mercy. (R)*
- *Assist all who care for the sick: Lord, have mercy. (R)*
- *Give life and health to our brothers and sisters on whom we lay our hands in your name: Lord, have mercy. (R)*

Laying on of hands (The priest silently lays his hands on the head of each sick person.)

Prayer over the oil (The priest either blesses the oil or, if it has already been blessed, says a prayer of thanksgiving.)

Anointing

Priest: (While he anoints the forehead)

Through this holy anointing may the Lord in his love and mercy help you with the grace of the Holy Spirit.

Person: Amen.

Priest: (While he anoints the hands)

May the Lord who frees you from sin save you and raise you up.

Person: Amen.

Prayer after anointing (The priest chooses one.)

(General)

Father in heaven,
through this holy anointing
grant our brothers and sisters comfort in their suffering.
When they are afraid, give them courage,
when afflicted, give them patience,
when dejected, afford them hope,
and when alone, assure them of the support of your holy people.
We ask this through Christ our Lord. Amen.

(In terminal illness)

Lord Jesus Christ,
you chose to share our human nature,
to redeem all people,
and to heal the sick.
Look with compassion upon your servants,
whom we have anointed in your name with this holy oil
for the healing of their body and spirit.
Support them with your power,
comfort them with your protection,
and give them the strength to fight against evil.
Since you have given them a share in your own passion,
help them to find hope in suffering,
for you are Lord for ever and ever. Amen.

(In advanced age)

God of mercy,
look kindly on your servants
who have grown weak under the burden of years.
In this holy anointing they ask for healing in body and soul.
Fill them with the strength of your Holy Spirit.
Keep them firm in faith and serene in hope,
so that they may give us all an example of patience
and joyfully witness to the power of your love.
We ask this through Christ our Lord. Amen.[6]

---

6. The International Commission on English in the Liturgy, *Pastoral Care of the Sick: Rites of Anointing and Viaticum* (Collegeville, MN: The Liturgical Press, 1983), pp. 107–112.

Visiting the sick and the elderly

Hospitals and convalescent homes always need volunteers to provide a variety of personal services. Here are just a few ideas of how you can minister to the sick and the elderly:

- Help with music and crafts.
- Read letters from friends or relatives to patients.
- Read to the patients a short story, the newspaper, or a passage from the Bible.
- Take a patient out for a drive.
- Talk with the patient about his or her family and about events that are going on in the world.
- Escort patients to an event at the home.
- Bring a birthday cake on the patient's birthday.
- Bring useful or silly presents.
- Bring in a pet for the patient to hold. (You must first make sure this is allowed.)

If you feel uncomfortable in the hospital or convalescent setting or if you can't think of anything to say to a sick or elderly person, here are some tips that might help:

- Learn the patient's condition in advance. This will prepare you for what to expect.
- Be sure the person is not too tired to have visitors. (Don't wake up someone in order to talk.)
- Show the sick person that you intend to spend some time. Take off your coat, put down your purse or newspaper.
- Sit down so that you are on the same eye level as the sick person. (This will help you talk to the person as an equal, rather than talking down to or treating the person like a child.)
- If you think you may feel awkward talking with the person, bring a bouquet of flowers or balloons, a card, a magazine, or a book to give to the patient. This will give you something to talk about right away.
- Encourage the patient to talk. Focus on him or her, not yourself. Ask questions that need more than a "Yes" or "No" answer.
- Talk loudly enough to be heard.
- Take the responsibility for keeping the conversation going.

- Communicate nonverbally as well as verbally. Maintain eye contact to show that you are genuinely interested. If appropriate, touch the person's hand or shoulder.
- Don't give advice unless it's asked for.
- Allow the patient to be honest about how he or she is feeling. If he or she is grumpy, don't say, "Cheer up."
- Ask if you can do anything for the patient—such as write a letter, make a phone call, water the plants, get some water.
- Leave when you see that the patient is getting tired.

If the sick person is terminally ill, here are some tips that might help you during your visit:

- Accept the person's death, as well as your own eventual death. If you can do this, you can help the person reduce his or her own anxiety about death.
- Be honest, not evasive. Answer any questions the person may have, especially regarding the chances for recovery or the expected amount of time left.
- Allow the person to accept the reality of the situation at his or her own pace. Do not withhold or force information upon the person.
- Be available (don't rush right off) and supportive. Use eye contact and physical touch.
- Remember to pay attention to family members you meet. They also need support before and after death occurs. Listen actively to what they say. If you feel comfortable doing so, express your own faith, but do not impose your religious beliefs on them.

If possible, try to find time to do volunteer work at a local hospital, nursing home, or hospice. People who do so say that the rewards are much greater than any sacrifices they make.

For your journal

1. How do you think Jeanne White felt when she learned her son had contracted the AIDS virus? when other people rejected him and shunned the family? How do you think you would feel in similar circumstances?

2. Do you know anyone who is elderly? sick? mentally disabled? physically disabled? dying? What is the person like? Does he or she fit the stereotype? How does your experience affect the way you perceive other people in the same group as this person?

3. If you were in one of these groups, how would you want people to treat you?

4. Do you have any fears about being around the sick or visiting a hospital, nursing home, or hospice? If so, try to identify the reasons behind your fears. What can you do to overcome these fears?

Discussion questions

1. Do you think employers, school officials, and other people have a right to know the names of persons who are HIV-positive? Or do you think the test results should be kept confidential?

2. Do you think students who are HIV-positive should be allowed to stay in school as long as possible?

3. Do you think AIDS patients are being punished by God for their sins?

4. What stereotypes do people tend to have regarding someone who is elderly? sick? mentally disabled? physically disabled? dying? What behaviors flow from these stereotypes? How could you and others begin to change the way you think about these groups of people?

5. If you have any elderly relatives, where do these people live? Do you have very much contact with them? Why or why not?

6. If another member of your family were dying, would you want that person to die at home or in a hospital? Why?

7. What do Jesus' actions show us about the attitudes and actions we should have toward the sick and disabled?

8. What do you think about present-day faith healers? Can prayer really cure a person?

9. Some people say that the gift of healing ended with the apostles. Do you think this is true or not? Are there ways that we, too, have the gift of healing?

10. What are possible ways that we—as individuals and as a society—can restore to the elderly their dignity and sense of worth?

11. Why are special ramps, parking places, and bathroom facilities for the disabled a matter of justice? How would a disabled person fare at your parish? at your workplace?

12. What are ways that people in your parish minister to the sick?

13. Have you ever attended a celebration of the sacrament of anointing that took place at church? What impressed you about the rite?

10 When Someone Dies

An open or shut case?

Funerals are social occasions in most cultures. What happens at funerals is not only a matter of socially prescribed etiquette, but may also be the source of contention. Consider, for example, the following letters to "Dear Abby."

DEAR ABBY: I am writing in response to the letter signed "Unfinished Business," from someone who had not seen his deceased friend for several years and was dismayed with the family's decision to have a closed-coffin funeral. I can relate to this situation whole-heartedly from the family's point of view.

When my father died of cancer 10 years ago, he had requested a closed-coffin funeral. What an uproar that created! Relatives and so-called friends who had not seen Dad in years were appalled. They said, "This is not customary! We wanted one last look at him." My response was, "Dad wanted you to remember him as robust and healthy, as he was before he became ill."

We found a picture of Dad taken when he was hale and hearty, and placed it on his closed coffin, surrounded by flowers.

HIS DAUGHTER IN CALIFORNIA

DEAR ABBY: I agree with "Unfinished Business" about closed-coffin wakes. Recently I drove 60 miles one way to pay my respects to a friend who had died of a heart attack, only to find a closed coffin. I was not very well acquainted with the widow, so I could have just as well paid my respects by sending her a sympathy card.

My point in writing is to suggest to families who feel that way that the words "Coffin will be closed" be added to the obituary in the newspaper. It may not be considered proper etiquette, but it will save a lot of hard feelings.

FINISHED BUSINESS IN BRYAN, OHIO

DEAR ABBY: I recall one funeral I attended a few years ago. It was for a loyal, longtime employee who had lingered with a terminal illness for a very long time. When his widow was asked why she wanted a closed-coffin funeral, she replied, "Nobody came to see him when he was alive, so why would anyone want to see him when he is dead?"

PINE BLUFF, ARK.[1]

---

1. From the "Dear Abby" column by Abigail Van Buren, copyright 1991. Reprinted with permission of Universal Press Syndicate. All rights reserved.

Knowing what to say and do

As social events, funerals bring diverse people together. They can sometimes be occasions of reconciliation between enemies. At other times, they are scenes of bitter fighting and hurtful dissension. Family members, who are already stressed because of the death, may be overly sensitive to what others say and do. Well-meaning friends—either because they are nervous or not sure what to say—may unintentionally say or do the wrong thing.

For all these reasons, each society establishes an accepted "ritual" that begins when someone dies. In the United States, this ritual includes meeting with the funeral director, notifying family members and friends, writing an obituary, planning and then attending the wake, funeral or memorial service, and final committal service, eating a meal together, and choosing a fitting tombstone or memorial. Knowing what to say and do at these times is not only a matter of social etiquette; it can help everyone involved get through this particularly difficult time.

Where to start

After someone dies, one of the first decisions that family members must make is the choice of funeral home. Once the phone call to the funeral director is made, the social rituals surrounding death begin. The funeral director will make sure that all legal requirements are met (these will be discussed at length in chapter 12), and will meet with the family to discuss the type of interment preferred—cremation, aboveground interment in a mausoleum, or ground burial.[2]

Regardless of the interment chosen, numerous details still need to be handled. For example, if the dead person is to be cremated, the family needs to decide whether to have the cremation after a wake and funeral (in which case the deceased is embalmed and placed in a casket) or to have the cremation first and a memorial service (without the casket) later. Another decision involves disposing of the ashes. Depending upon state law, the family may have several options: to purchase an urn and a niche in the columbarium of a crematorium, to bury the urn in a family plot or in an urn garden especially designed for the interment of ashes, to keep the cremains at home, or to spread the ashes over land or sea. If mausoleum interment or ground burial is chosen instead, the family needs to select a casket, vault, and a mausoleum space or interment plot.

---

2. In large urban areas, cemetery space may be very limited. This is leading to the building of high-rise mausoleums, some ten to twelve stories tall.

The funeral director, who has completed specializing training in mortuary science and grief counseling, guides the family through the decision-making process. He or she acts as an informed friend during this time of need, and can be of great help to people who are unacquainted with the "business" of death and the rituals surrounding it. He or she can help the family select with the priest the time and place for the wake (or vigil service), the funeral or memorial service, and the committal service. The actual planning of these services (Scripture readings, music, readers, etc.) is usually done by the family in consultation with a priest or parish minister.

Notifying others

Once the decisions about type of service, time, and place have been made, the family should notify other relatives, friends, employers, and business associates about the death. Many such people can be contacted by phone or telegram. In addition, the family can choose to write a death notice or an obituary for the local paper.

Death notices may be phoned to the classified department of one or more newspapers, but should always be checked carefully by the family for correct information. Age is not usually included in the death notice, unless the deceased is a child. The family's address is also not given, since thieves have been known to read about the death in the paper and then break in when the house is unattended during the funeral. Here is an example of a typical death notice:

> SMITH, Lloyd A.—May 22, 1991; beloved husband of Millie (Shepherd) Smith; devoted father of Daniel Smith and Patricia Trudell; proud grandfather of Patrick, Scott, Melissa, Nicole, and the late Brian; retired lieutenant in the San Francisco Fire Department.
>
> Visitation at Reilly Funeral Home, 29th and Dolores Sts, today after 2 P.M.; vigil service 8 P.M.; funeral Mass Friday, May 24, 9:30 A.M. at St. Catherine's Church, 1310 Bayswater Ave., Burlingame. Interment, Holy Cross Cemetery. Donations to Immaculate Conception Academy Memorial Scholarship Fund or spiritual bouquets preferred.

An obituary contains the same information as a death notice, with the addition of a biography of the deceased and a photograph (optional). The biography includes the name of the deceased, date and place of death (name of hospital or "at home"), the cause of death (this is optional; sometimes "after a long illness" is used), age, important education details, contributions made to society, military service record, awards and publications, and membership in social clubs and professional organizations.

Major newspapers maintain a file of readily accessible information about famous people. Television stations keep on hand a similar video file. When someone famous dies, the newspaper may run feature articles about the person. The television station may air a special program in memory of the person.

Expressions of sympathy

When friends and acquaintances learn of a death, social etiquette requires some type of expression of sympathy. The expression may be as simple as calling on the phone or sending a sympathy card that has a printed consoling verse, along with a handwritten letter of condolence. People often choose to send flowers to the funeral home or to the church, to be used during the vigil service, funeral, and committal service. The spray, wreath, or bouquet should have an attached plain white card with the name and address of the sender.

It should be noted that flowers are never appropriate at an Orthodox Jewish funeral; often they are not desired at Conservative or Reform funerals, either. In the past, the Catholic Church did not encourage the use of flowers at funeral services; now the *Order of Christian Funerals* allows for fresh flowers, used in moderation, in order to enhance the setting of the funeral rites.

Before sending flowers to any funeral, people should first check the death notice or obituary. If either says, "Please omit flowers," this request should be respected. The family may prefer to have only one floral bouquet that it purchases. Or the family may wish that the money be spent in another, more lasting, manner.

Often, the family will request that donations be made in the deceased's name to some charitable cause, such as the hospice where the person died, a heart fund, or a cancer foundation. Mourners make a check out to the charity, along with a note stating that this amount is contributed "in memory of" the deceased. The charity will then send the donor an acknowledgment, which may be used for tax purposes. The charity also notifies the family of the contribution.

Some Catholic families prefer Mass cards, or "spiritual bouquets," to flowers. In this case, friends and relatives arrange for a Mass to be said for the deceased. The priest accepts a Mass stipend and fills in a card stating that the Mass is to be said for the repose of the deceased. Sometimes the date and time of the Mass are included so that the family can attend. The donor then gives or mails the card to the family of the deceased, usually before the funeral. Masses may also be arranged on the anniversary of death.

Visitation at the funeral home

If you reread the death notice found in this chapter, you will see a time and place for visitation. This is an optional ritual, a time when friends can pay their last respects by viewing the deceased person in a casket in a room at the funeral home. Family members may also make themselves available at the funeral home during these "calling hours."

The coffin is usually open during the visitation. Traditionally, the embalmed corpse is dressed in his or her "Sunday best." Often, cosmetics have been applied to give the deceased the appearance of sleeping. The corpse may also be wearing eyeglasses and a wedding ring, as worn in life. Bishops and priests are dressed in their liturgical vestments. Religious men and women are usually dressed in their habits. A lay person may hold a Bible, crucifix, or rosary.

When a person arrives at the funeral home for the visitation, he or she should sign the guest register. The full name should be written legibly, in case the family later wishes to make an acknowledgment of the call. The visitor should express a few words of sympathy to the family. It is not appropriate to ask details about the illness or death, unless family members first bring it up. According to custom, the visitor is expected to pass by the open coffin and pay his or her respects to the deceased. This usually means standing for a moment with bowed head and saying an appropriate silent prayer. If passing by the coffin is too difficult or repugnant, however, the visitor does not have to do it. The entire length of the visit need not be longer than ten or fifteen minutes.

Before leaving, visitors should take a memorial card, if the family has had them printed. A memorial card may have a picture of the deceased or a picture of a biblical scene on one side. On the other side is the name of the deceased, the dates of birth and death, and a prayer or poem. The card is a way to help mourners work through their grief, and serves as a reminder to them to continue to pray for the dead person. Visitors frequently place the memorial cards they have been given in the family Bible at home.

The wake or vigil service

This ritual calls for a gathering of the family with friends and acquaintances in the presence of the deceased, either at the funeral home, the family's home, or in church. In some cases, the wake replaces the visitation. The coffin may be open or closed.

The wake ritual dates from the medieval custom of "rousing or waking the ghost," which was an attempt to bring the dead person back to life. These wakes were characterized by much drinking, dancing, calling out the dead person's name, and other types of raucous behavior. In early America, the purpose of the wake was threefold: to console relatives, to make sure the person was really dead and not just in a coma, and to prevent someone (oftentimes medical students who needed a cadaver to practice on) from stealing the body.

Wakes are found in numerous cultures. The Moluccans of Indonesia wake the body for the purpose of aiding the soul in its adjustment to the new way of life. Prayers, devotional acts, talking, and gossip are found at Basque wakes. Among the Merina people of Madagascar, the wake is a festive occasion with jokes, songs, dances, and games of dominoes. In Ireland, the wake may last for three days. The body is "laid out" in the person's best clothes as friends come to comfort the family. The wake is a major social occasion, with eating, drinking, dancing, singing, storytelling, and card-playing.

Traditionally at Catholic wakes, the priest led people in the rosary. The words of each Hail Mary, "pray for us now and at the hour of our death," were particularly meaningful to those who were mourning the loss of their loved one. While some Catholics continue to prefer a wake and rosary, the *Order of Christian Funerals* encourages Catholics to have a vigil service instead. This prayer service usually includes some Scripture readings, psalms, and singing. Variations may include poetry, the recitation of words that were written or spoken by the deceased, and "testimonies" from family members and friends.

The vigil service, with its theme of passing from death to new life, can provide a rich form of religious expression for all participants and can be an event of faith for them. It can also help family members to deepen their own religious faith in the resurrection.

The funeral service

The funeral service may be held either in a chapel at the funeral home or in a church. For Catholics, the funeral is almost always in a church as part of a Mass.

Anyone may attend the funeral, unless the death notice says that it is private.[3] While the wearing of black is no longer considered necessary at funerals, people should wear conservative, somber-colored clothes. Women may wear a hat. Men usually wear dark suits with conservative ties, white shirts, black shoes and socks.

---

3. A divorced spouse of the deceased may attend the funeral service if he or she so chooses. But he or she should not be seated with the present family unless the family requests it.

At Protestant funerals, the casket may be either open or closed. It is always closed for Jewish, Episcopalian, or Catholic funerals. In the United States, cremated remains cannot be brought to the Catholic funeral Mass; however, the Canadian bishops have given temporary permission for their pastors to do this.[4]

Ushers may be provided by the funeral home, the church, or by the family. Ushers should distribute programs or missalettes and escort people to their seats, walking on the left of those being seated. It is not proper to offer their arms, except to the old or infirm. Ushers should seat relatives and close friends toward the front of the church, keeping the front left pews free for the pallbearers.

In today's society, both men and women may serve as pallbearers. Pallbearers do not volunteer their services; they wait to be asked. Etiquette requires that a person accept the honor of being a pallbearer, unless there is some very valid reason (illness) for refusing. The family itself is often represented among the pallbearers. In most cases, the pallbearers do not actually carry the casket. They merely escort it into and out of the church. During the funeral, the pallbearers usually sit in the front pew to the left of the center aisle.

At Catholic funerals, unless it first gathers at the funeral home, the family gathers in the vestibule of the church before the funeral to meet the casket when it arrives from the funeral home. A large white cloth, or pall, is placed over the casket as a reminder of the deceased's baptism and membership in God's family. At the start of the funeral, the altar servers and priest lead the procession into the church. Pallbearers follow with the casket. Family members walk behind the casket.

During the funeral Mass, the priest gives a brief homily based on the Scripture readings. The *Order of Christian Funerals* says that there is never to be a eulogy at the time designated for the homily. However, the rite does allow for a member or friend of the family to speak in remembrance of the deceased following the prayer after communion and before the final commendation begins. The eulogy, which contains details or anecdotes from the person's life, should be short and should also refer to the mourners.

After the final commendation, the altar servers, priest, pallbearers and casket, and family members process out in the same order in which they came in. Outside the church the casket is put into the

---

4. If Catholics in the United States choose cremation and yet want the deceased at the funeral Mass, the body must be embalmed and in a casket. Cremation occurs after the Mass.

hearse. If the funeral has taken place in the evening, the casket is taken to the funeral home overnight and then to the cemetery for burial the next day. If the funeral has taken place during the day, burial usually follows immediately.

Members of the family may follow the hearse to the cemetery in their own cars or in limousines provided by the funeral home. Flowers may be taken to the cemetery in a separate car. Police on motorcycles or in cars usually lead the procession to the cemetery. Cars in the procession turn their lights on. Other drivers are not supposed to break into this cortege.[5]

At the cemetery, people park their cars and assemble at the grave site. Often, the ground near the grave will be covered with artificial turf. In inclement weather there may also be an outdoor tent to shelter the mourners. After a brief religious ceremony and blessing of the place of committal, the mourners are often invited to place a flower on the coffin. Mourners stay long enough to comfort family members. According to present-day custom, everyone leaves before the cemetery workers lower the casket into the ground. The *Order of Christian Funerals*, however, calls for a change in this custom.

The funeral rituals usually continue after the committal at the cemetery with the sharing of a meal in the home of a family member or in the parish hall.[6] Quite often, friends or volunteers from the parish funeral committee will band together to prepare this meal. Many post-funeral meals are accompanied by singing and storytelling.

Memorial services

Sometimes a memorial service (without the deceased's body) takes the place of a funeral service. Ordinarily, the Church encourages Catholics to have a funeral service, rather than a memorial service. But sometimes the family has no choice. For example, in January 1991, two navy planes collided at sea off the coast of San Diego. Twenty-seven crew members died; their bodies were never recovered. Later, a common memorial service was held at Moffett Field. Individual memorial services were also held by the church of each family.

---

5. Among traditional Italian families, priests, relatives, and friends of the dead person join in the procession after the funeral Mass. Children carry wreaths as the coffin is carried to its place in the cemetery.

6. It is traditional among Polish families to serve peas and noodles with poppy seeds and honey at a meal following a funeral.

A memorial service is sometimes held in addition to the funeral. This happens when a person dies in another part of the country or in a foreign country, and most of the family cannot attend the funeral. Memorial services may also be celebrated on the anniversary of death, for example, a month or year later. Memorial services usually take place in a church, but might also be held in a home or garden. The service itself consists of readings and prayers, a brief eulogy, and music. People speak briefly to the family, and then leave.

Memorials

By law, all graves must have a grave marker. Most families also prefer to purchase a tombstone. The size of the tombstone is often regulated by the cemetery. Epitaphs no longer are popular. Most tombstones today contain only the name of the person, birth date and date of death.

In addition to tombstones, Americans remember their dead in a great variety of tangible ways.[7] Libraries, college buildings, and hospital wings may be named after the wealthy philanthropist who financed them. The memorabilia of a famous person, such as Elvis Presley, may be collected together in a museum or parklike setting. Federal and state governments, too, will sometimes erect memorials to important leaders, heroes, and soldiers. Some examples include the Tomb of the Unknown Soldier in Arlington National Cemetery, the Vietnam Wall Memorial in Washington, DC, the Space Mirror Memorial at Kennedy Space Center, Cape Canaveral, and the Lincoln Memorial in Washington, DC.

Prayers for the dead

As you have learned, most Jews in the Hebrew Scriptures did not believe in life after death. Close to the time of Jesus, however, there is evidence that at least some Jews espoused a different belief—that the dead lived on and that the prayers of the living could affect their welfare. An example of this belief is found in 2 Maccabees 12:39–45. After a certain battle, Judas Maccabee, the Jewish leader, directed that the bodies of slain Jews be gathered from the battlefield for burial. When his soldiers did this, they found under the tunic of each fallen man a valuable amulet taken

---

7. During the second half of the nineteenth century, memorial photographs were popular. Family members assembled around the corpse to have their picture taken. One soldier in the Civil War who hurried home to have his photograph taken with his dead infant in his arms was James Garfield, later our 20th president.

from a temple at Jamnia. This was a serious religious violation (cf. Deuteronomy 7:25). Judas immediately prayed to God to forgive the sin of these men. He also took up money to send to Jerusalem so that a sacrifice could be offered for them.

The custom of praying for the dead was strong among Christians. From the inscriptions on second-century tombs, it is clear that the Christians prayed for the dead. The first mention of public prayers for the dead in worship was recorded by Tertullian in A.D. 211. These prayers were anniversary-day observances for the dead. In the third century, prayers for the dead were added to regular Eucharistic celebrations. When Constantine died in A.D. 337, his body was placed before the altar, and the people, together with the priests, prayed for his soul.

In 1274, the Council of Lyons declared—in connection with the doctrine on purgatory—that the dead could be assisted by intercessory prayers at Mass, almsgiving, prayers in general, and other devout practices according to the custom of the Church. In 1476, Pope Sixtus IV granted the first plenary indulgence applicable to the souls in purgatory. Unfortunately, some Catholics came to think that they could buy their way to heaven, regardless of how they lived. They paid stipends to priests to celebrate numerous Masses for the dead; wealthy Christians endowed monasteries so that Masses could be said regularly for the repose of their own souls and those of relatives. Needless to say, there was an overemphasis on indulgences and the money sometimes connected with them.

In 1840, the Sacred Congregation of Indulgences clarified the meaning of indulgences. It said that what is offered to God in the case of a plenary indulgence is fully sufficient to free the soul from purgatory, but what is actually effected will depend on the acceptance and the good pleasure of God. In other words, our good actions and prayers can influence God, but cannot control God.

In his 1967 apostolic letter, "The Doctrine and Practice of Indulgences," Pope Paul VI defended the custom of praying for the dead as one of the Spiritual Works of Mercy. "The faithful who apply indulgences as suffrages for the dead are practicing charity in a superior way." This work of mercy stems from two theological principles: membership of both the living and the dead in the communion of saints and the Body of Christ, and the role of human efforts in the building of God's kingdom.

The present Code of Canon Law states that in order to be capable of gaining indulgences, one must be baptized and in the state of grace. Proper disposition includes sorrow for sin, freedom from serious sin, performance of the required work, and the intention to gain the indulgence. A Catholic can gain a partial indulgence for the dead by praying customary prayers, by performing certain good works,[8] by prayerfully carrying out duties and bearing the difficulties of everyday life, by giving of one's time or money to serve others in need, and by abstaining from pleasures, according to a spirit of penance.

To gain a plenary indulgence, it is necessary for a person to be free of all attachment to sin, to perform certain good works, and to fulfill each of the following:

- celebration of the Sacrament of Reconciliation
- receiving Holy Communion at Mass
- prayer for the intention of the pope (This is fulfilled by praying one Our Father and one Hail Mary, and sometimes the Apostles' Creed, but other prayers may also be said.)

Some means of gaining a plenary indulgence for the dead include adoration of the Blessed Sacrament for at least one-half hour, devout reading of Scripture for at least one-half hour, making the Way of the Cross, and recitation of the rosary.

When you die

Before we end this chapter, imagine that you will die in three months. Use the following form to write an obituary you think would best describe you. Then, in your journal, write a poem or prayer that you would like included on your memorial card.

Far from being a morbid activity, this exercise can help you visualize the goals you want to accomplish in life, and how you want your life to affect others. Once we can envision such goals for ourselves (major achievements, affiliations, etc.), we can spend the rest of our lives trying to reach them.

---

8. Some means of gaining a partial indulgence for the dead include the following: praying the Magnificat or Hail Holy Queen; praying the Acts of Faith, Hope, and Love, as well as the Apostles' Creed; making the Sign of the Cross; visiting the Blessed Sacrament; and visiting a cemetery.

YOUR OBITUARY

Full name: _____

Date of birth: _____

Date of death: _____

Cause of death (optional): _____

Your biography—including major achievements, affiliations, and honors received:

Names of survivors and their relationship to you:

Date and hours of visitation: _____

Name of funeral home: _____

Time and place of vigil service: _____

Time and place of funeral ceremony: _____

Name of cemetery for burial: _____

OR cremation preferred: _____

Send flowers? _____

Send memorials to: _____

For your journal

1. Write about a funeral you have attended.

   • Did the ritual bring out the best in people or did it bring out the worst?

   • How comfortable did you feel at the wake, funeral service, committal, and/or meal? Why do you think you felt this way?

2. When you die, do you want a big funeral, a small (just family) funeral, or a memorial service?

3. When you die, do you want to be buried in the ground, placed in a mausoleum, or cremated?

4. When you die, do you want to have visitation hours? Why or why not?

5. When you die, do you want your casket to be opened or closed during the vigil service?

Discussion questions

1. How would you respond to each DEAR ABBY letter found in this chapter?

2. How have you felt when you have seen a dead person in a casket?

3. Describe your experience of being to a visitation at a funeral home. Did you view the deceased? Why or why not?

4. Think about your experience of attending a wake. What was it like? Where was it held?

5. Have you ever been to a vigil service? What was it like? What readings and songs were used? Where was it held?

6. Some people think that children should not attend a funeral. What do you think?

7. Do you think it is possible to buy your way into heaven? Does God discriminate between rich and poor?

8. Why are prayers for the dead an act of charity?

Part Six: Financial/Legal Aspects

*Then women who had come from Galilee with [Jesus] followed
behind, and when they had seen the tomb and the way in which his
body was laid in it, they returned and prepared spices and perfumed
oils. Then they rested on the sabbath according to the commandment.*

—*Luke 23:55–56*

11 The Cost of Dying

Bad taste or good business?

The world of business is based on the idea of supply and demand. Whenever there is a need for a product or a demand for a service, you will inevitably find someone who is willing to manufacture the product or provide the service. That someone will not only charge for the supplies and time, but will also attempt to make a profit.

Death and dying is perhaps one of the biggest businesses that exists worldwide. Just think of the doctors, hospitals, convalescent homes, estate lawyers, pharmaceutical companies, ambulance companies, florists, insurance companies, funeral homes, and cemeteries that deal in the business of death and dying. And then of course, there are newspapers, TV programs, and Hollywood movies that also "cash in" on death.

Many products and services surrounding death are good business. They are truly needed and show respect for human dignity. Other products and services are in bad taste. Here is one example of a business related to death. You decide: Is it bad taste or good business?

Grave Line Tours

Founded in 1988, Grave Line takes "mourners" on a tour of Hollywood in a 1969 silver Cadillac hearse. On the 2½ hour tour, mourners view such sites as:

- *Bungalow 3 of the Chateau Marmont, where actor John Belushi died from a lethal dose of heroin and cocaine in 1982.*

- *Highland Gardens Apartments, where singer Janis Joplin committed suicide in 1970.*

- *a carport on Holloway Drive were actor Sal Mineo was fatally stabbed in 1976.*

- *the high-rise apartment building on Shoreham Drive where Diane Linkletter leapt to her death from a sixth-floor window during a bad LSD trip in 1969.*

- *the house on Cielo Drive where Charles Manson and his "family" murdered pregnant actress Sharon Tate and several of her friends in 1969.*

While the tour no longer makes cemetery stops (people took too much time reading the gravestones), it does provide customers with a complimentary map to the Hollywood Memorial Park Cemetery.

The death business

In her book *The American Way of Death*, Jessica Mitford drew attention to the commercialization of death and the unethical procedures used by some funeral directors to hike up prices. The book created such a national uproar that the Federal Trade Commission passed a Funeral Rule in 1984. This rule attempts to regulate the business aspect of death in the following ways: by requiring funeral homes to quote prices over the phone so that consumers can more easily do comparison shopping; by requiring funeral directors to provide consumers with written itemized prices, including options; and by prohibiting funeral homes from making false statements about what the law requires.

In this chapter, you will learn about the financial aspects of death. You may think such knowledge is gruesome or not necessary. But think about it: everyone dies. The chances are almost 100 percent that, sooner or later, you will have to plan a funeral for a friend or relative. Waiting until death happens before considering the business side of death can put you at a great disadvantage. Stricken by grief and constrained by time, you may not realize all your options or ways to cut costs. You may end up making impulsive, expensive decisions you will later regret. This chapter will help you approach the business of death more reasonably.

Traditional funeral costs

A traditional funeral includes embalming, a casket, a funeral service, and burial in a cemetery. In 1991, the National Funeral Directors Association tabulated the cost of a traditional adult funeral as ranging from $3,725 to $6,870. This amount, however, was much smaller than the total amount of money spent. It did not include other expenses such as cemetery property, marker or monument, or floral expenses.

Most funeral homes offer "package plans" that cover everything for a traditional funeral except the casket. The price of the entire plan is roughly five times that of the price of the casket. One disadvantage to purchasing a package plan is that you may pay for services you don't want or choose not to have. One advantage is that package plans are often 15 percent less than the cost of buying each item separately. Today, all funeral homes must also provide customers with "itemized plans." In these plans, you pay only for the services you actually need and want.

The services you must pay for in a traditional funeral include the funeral director's services, the casket, embalming, transportation, cemetery expenses, the grave marker or tombstone, and miscellaneous expenses. We will look at each one separately.

The funeral director's services

Each funeral home charges a fee for its role in arranging and supervising the funeral. Because these fees vary widely, it is important to comparison shop between several funeral homes before selecting one. The funeral home fees include the following services:

- consultation with the funeral director
- use of funeral home facilities for storage of the body, visitation (optional), wake (optional), and funeral services (optional)
- death certificates (usually ten copies are needed for legal purposes) and other required permits
- six hired pallbearers (unless the family will provide them)
- thank-you cards and guest registry book
- cosmetics and hairstyling of corpse
- hearse and driver
- ushers for funeral
- bier upon which to rest the casket
- burial clothing or shroud (unless provided by the family)

Casket

The casket is the largest single expense of a funeral. Most funeral homes have selection rooms where caskets are displayed. The price will vary greatly, depending upon style and construction materials. Caskets come in three main styles, or types. On a full couch casket, the entire lid opens or comes off so that the entire body may be viewed. On a half couch casket, only the top half opens so that the body may be viewed from the waist up. A hinge cap casket is similar to the half couch, except for the placement of hinges.

The least expensive casket is a plain pine box. The next upgrades include caskets made of chestnut, cypress, or red cedar. These are usually covered with cloth. Caskets in the intermediate price range include the more expensive hardwoods: mahogany, walnut, oak, birch, maple, or cherry. They are treated with clear natural finish. The most expensive caskets are made of fiberglass or metal—specially treated iron, steel, copper, bronze, stainless steel, and zinc.[1] Such caskets may come with inner-spring mattresses and satin or velvet lining. If you don't see a casket in the funeral showroom in your price range or desired color, it is a good idea to ask.

---

1. Some casket manufacturers offer a thirty-year or even a fifty-year warranty on their metal coffins and say they will replace those that prove defective during that time.

Embalming

Embalming involves two processes: arterial embalming and cavity embalming. In arterial embalming, the body is drained of blood. Then the blood vessels are filled with formalin. In cavity embalming, fluids are removed from the thoracic and abdominal cavities and replaced with a preservative fluid.[2]

State laws vary regarding whether the corpse needs to be embalmed or not. (You will learn more about these laws in chapter 12.) If embalming is not performed, the funeral home may charge for refrigerating the body.

Transportation

These fees include the cost of transporting the body in a hearse or ambulance from the place of death to the funeral home, to the church for the funeral service, and to the cemetery. Extra fees will be charged for limousines to transport family members from the church to the cemetery, for transporting the body to another city or state for interment, and for police escorts.

Cemetery expenses

A cemetery may be either a traditional one or a memorial park. Traditional cemeteries allow grave markers or monuments to be put on a grave provided they meet size limitations. Memorial parks require uniform markers that are level with the grass. Some traditional cemeteries have a memorial park section; likewise, some memorial parks have traditional sections. As a general rule, cemeteries operated by nonprofit organizations such as cities, states, or churches are less expensive than privately owned cemeteries or memorial parks. Again, comparison shopping for a cemetery is a good idea if you want to keep funeral expenses down.

Basically, cemetery expenses include four things: the plot or mausoleum space, opening and closing a grave, the vault or grave liner, and perpetual care.

Plot or mausoleum space. A ground plot is less expensive than aboveground burial in individual, family, or community mausoleums. Many cemeteries allow people to buy a plot on a time-payment plan. Again, comparison shopping is a good idea. Some cemeteries charge no interest on their plans; others charge up to 20 percent per year. In some cases, it may be less expensive to get a bank loan than to accept the cemetery's financing.

---

2. Embalming is not mummification. Eventually an embalmed body will decompose.

Opening and closing a grave. Grave diggers and cemetery workers belong to a union, with strict rules regarding their hours and pay. For this reason, the cemetery will charge more to open and close a grave on weekends or holidays.

Vault or grave liner. Most cemeteries require that a casket be placed inside a concrete or metal container when it is placed in the ground. This container keeps the ground from caving in when the casket and body finally disintegrate. Usually, the container is simply called a vault. But sometimes a concrete enclosure is called a grave liner and a metal enclosure is called a vault. Concrete vaults are less costly than solid steel or copper ones that form an airtight seal. Vaults sold by cemeteries are less costly than those sold by funeral homes.

Perpetual care. Future maintenance of the cemetery may be an optional expense or part of the cost of the plot. If perpetual care is optional, you might ask to see graves that have it and those without it, for comparison. In some states, the money for perpetual care must be placed in a trust fund. The earnings from the fund are used to maintain the cemetery's grounds.

Grave markers or monuments

Some cemeteries require that you purchase their own markers or monuments. Others allow you to purchase them from independent monument companies. The cost will depend on size, material, design, and craftsmanship. Bronze markers are less expensive than granite markers. Markers are less expensive than monuments. Elaborate monuments can run into the thousands of dollars, depending upon the type of stone, the size, and the amount of engraving to be done. There may also be an extra installation fee.

Miscellaneous expenses

Numerous other expenses can contribute to the cost of the funeral. Among these are the following:

- attorney's fees regarding the will and estate taxes
- airline tickets, rental cars, and hotels, if the family has to travel to get to the funeral
- dry cleaning, if needed, for burial clothing
- newspaper death notices and obituaries
- honorarium for officiating minister or priest (It is usual for the minister to be given a fee for his services. Sometimes this fee is included in the funeral home's charge. More often, it is sent by a member of the family, along with a thank-you note.)

- music for the funeral service (Check with the clergyman about appropriate fees for the organist, vocalist, and any other musicians you may have.)
- flowers
- the post-funeral meal (In rural communities, neighbors may prepare food for the reception after the funeral. In cities, food will often be catered by a restaurant, at the family's expense.)
- postage for thank-you notes (Survivors should always send written notes of thanks for flowers, Mass cards, food, and donations to charity, and to the priest, pallbearers, ushers, and musicians. If hundreds of cards need to be written, the family may wish to pay the added expense of having cards printed or engraved.)

Financial resources

Now that you have an idea of the costs involved in a traditional funeral, another concern emerges: How to pay for it all. Fortunately, there are certain resources that you can tap, death benefits that will help to defray funeral expenses. Survivors must apply for almost all of these benefits; they are not sent automatically when someone dies.

Here are some resources for you to look into.

- **Social Security.** Death benefits are available under some conditions to the survivors of persons who were covered by Social Security. Consult your local Social Security office for more details about the benefits and how to apply for them.
- **Trade Unions and Fraternal Organizations.** Many trade unions and fraternal organizations provide death benefits to the families of their members. There are also benefits for the survivors of anyone who has ever been a railroad employee.
- **Life and Casualty Insurance.** If the deceased had life insurance, this money may be used by beneficiaries to pay for the funeral. Other possibilities include automobile-club insurance, accidental death insurance (available through some credit cards), and liability insurance.[3]
- **Employee's Benefits.** Depending on the nature of the death, survivors may be entitled to Workman's Compensation benefits. The families of state employees in some states are entitled to survivor benefits. Burial expenses for indigent families are commonly paid by the county.

---

3. When someone dies, it is important to notify insurance companies, including automobile insurance, for immediate cancellation and available refund. Survivors should also check promptly on all credit card payments. Some cards carry insurance clauses that will cancel debts in event of death.

- **Veterans Administration.** Veterans are eligible for death benefits if they served in the U.S. Armed Forces during the Spanish-American War, World War I, World War II, Korean War, Vietnam Conflict, Persian Gulf Crisis, and certain peacetime service, provided they have not been dishonorably discharged. For more information, contact the Veterans Administration.

The above resources are available in the United States. Canadian death benefits include the Canada Pension Plan (the equivalent of the Social Security System in the U.S.), which pays a lump sum death benefit to the estate of any person who has contributed to the plan for at least three calendar years. Veteran benefits in Canada are not guaranteed. The Last Post Fund is a private organization that arranges funerals and burial for veterans who die without the means to do so for themselves.

Some alternatives

One way to cut costs is not to have a traditional funeral and burial. Three of the most common alternatives are cremation, direct cremation or direct burial, and donation of one's body to science.

If cremation is chosen, the body is still laid out in a funeral home and there may still be a funeral. This involves fees for embalming, a casket, and transportation charges from the place of death to the funeral home and then to the crematory. There will also be an additional fee for the container the body must be placed in when cremated (usually a hardboard or cardboard box). The process of cremating a human body takes about ninety minutes. The water content of the body is evaporated, the carbon-containing parts of the body are disintegrated, and all that remains is the inorganic ash of the bone structure. The residue of the average-sized individual comprises about five to seven pounds of ash and bone fragments.

The advantage of cremation is that it usually eliminates the need for a cemetery plot, a vault or grave liner, opening and closing a grave, and a marker or monument. Total expenses for cremation will vary, depending upon the disposal of the cremains. Here are some options and their cost considerations:

- Ashes are stored at home (cost of urn only).
- Ashes are stored in a niche in a columbarium. (The price of a niche depends on its size, location, and quality. Perpetual care costs may or may not be included in the niche price.)

- Ashes are buried on private property, in a cemetery plot, or in an urn garden. (No urn is necessary; the cremains can be buried in the container provided by the crematory. But there will be a cost for opening and closing the plot, perpetual care, and a memorial plaque.)
- Ashes are scattered over land or sea, according to state law. (You will probably have to hire the services of a commercial pilot or boat.)[4]

In direct cremation or direct burial, the funeral director removes the body from the place of death (transportation cost), provides a container (for cremation) or plain coffin (for burial), and transports the body directly to the crematory or cemetery (transportation cost again), all within a matter of hours. Memorial services are usually arranged at a later date (fees for clergyman, music, flowers, food). Because this type of disposal is not very profitable, funeral homes may charge more for transportation. Other funeral homes that specialize in direct burial or cremation provide the same services at less cost.

People who wish to donate their body to science should make arrangements in advance with the chosen medical school, dental school, or research center. Thousands of cadavers are needed each year for the training of future doctors and dentists. Many schools require special embalming and will pay for the cost of transporting the body to the school. Transportation may take place either after visitation and funeral services, or immediately after death. After the school has finished with the body, it has a moral responsibility to dispose of it by burial or cremation.

Pre-planning

What do you do if you want a traditional funeral but you also want to keep expenses down? The most logical answer is to plan and pay for your funeral before you die. Today, 25 percent of funerals are paid with pre-need contracts. Such pre-planning has a number of advantages: (1) Since you have already taken care of the details, your family knows exactly what you want and how much it will cost. They won't have to make uninformed decisions or negotiate for a funeral during their time of grieving. (2) Planning ahead helps you and your family to accept death. (3) Paying for the funeral in advance freezes the cost at today's prices.

---

4. Reflecting traditional Church preference for burial, many Catholic dioceses insist that the cremains be interred or entombed and not merely dispersed or scattered somewhere or stored in the home.

Among the types of pre-need plans available are the following:

- **Funeral insurance.** Many families carry a small insurance policy (usually $10,000) on each member for the specific purpose of covering burial expenses. This is a term life policy, with premiums paid either all at once or in installments. The funeral director is the beneficiary of the policy.
- **Protection through a credit union.** Many credit unions have an arrangement whereby deposits made before age 55 are doubled (not to exceed $1,000 to $2,000) at the time of death. Check with your credit union to see what type of plan it offers.
- **Pre-need trusts.** The family funds a trust with a bank or savings institution. The trust's principal and interest pays for funeral expenses.
- **Mutual aid plans.** Some groups, including a number of Quakers and Mennonites, care for their dead without the assistance of a funeral director. Member families authorize the Church Burial Committee to act on their behalf to get the death certificate from the doctor and record it in the county court house, to get a transportation permit (if needed), and to get a burial permit or authorization to cremate. Following the disposition of the body, a Memorial Meeting is planned, to suit the needs of the family and community.

In addition to these church groups, there are now over 170 funeral or memorial societies in the United States, with over a million members. These societies are consumer groups organized to minimize funeral costs and to stress simplicity, dignity, and economy when dealing with death. Memorial and funeral societies are effective. They can save up to 50 percent in funeral costs, no matter what type of disposal is preferred, because they have the ability to bargain with funeral homes for reduced rates. Some societies even help nonmembers plan funerals on short notice.

Memorial societies were first formed in 1939. In 1963, the Continental Association of Funeral and Memorial Societies was formed in the United States. In 1971, a separate Memorial Society Association of Canada was formed. Membership in a memorial society is open to anyone for a small onetime family fee.

Because wills are usually not read until after the funeral service, it is important for anyone who has done pre-planning to let family members know about his or her intentions and wishes. Every person should have a computer file or paper file marked "In Case of Death." This file should contain the following information:

location of will; name and address of attorney; list of bank accounts, savings accounts; list of all securities and properties owned, and their whereabouts; insurance policies; location of safe-deposit box and key; name of preferred funeral home; information regarding burial plot; place where funeral should be held; choice of casket; list of pallbearers; location of all silver and jewelry; choice of burial or cremation; and note about organ or body donation. A family member should be told the location of the file so it will be available when needed.

Catholic cemeteries

It is natural to want to be buried near family members. Likewise, it makes sense to want to be buried near other members of the same community—people who share the same values and vision of life. That is why the major religions have their own cemeteries. Protestants of all denominations normally go to a local Protestant cemetery, and Jews usually are buried in their own burial ground. Catholics, too, have their own cemeteries.

When Constantine made Christianity the official religion in the fourth century, Christians were permitted to build cemeteries aboveground. Many of these cemeteries were attached to church buildings. They were seen as extensions of the church itself, and hence, as holy. When the cemeteries moved to other locations, they continued to act as an extension of the church.

Today, many parishes and dioceses own and operate Catholic cemeteries.[5] These cemeteries are nonprofit corporations that offer economical burial and columbarium services. Catholic cemeteries are a business; but they provide an important spiritual dimension as well. They are vital parts of the Church's mission. They differ from secular cemeteries in two ways: their sacredness and their witness.

Only churches and cemeteries are consecrated as sacred ground. In fact, a Catholic cemetery is considered to be holy just as a parish church in which the Blessed Sacrament is reserved in the tabernacle is holy. Like a church, a cemetery is a place where people can come to pray and meditate. It is holy because it contains the bodies of Christians who have been sanctified by their participation in the sacraments and by their life in the Christian community.[6]

---

5. The Catholic Cemetery Association was formed in 1949. It is an international organization, with members from Canada, Australia, and the United States. The nearly one thousand members come from about one half of the dioceses in these countries.

6. Canon Law #1205 defines sacred places as "those which are assigned to divine worship or to the burial of the faithful by dedication or blessing."

All Catholic cemeteries must have a cross that serves as a sign of their Christian identity and the Paschal Mystery—the passing from death to life. All Catholic cemeteries must also be blessed, either by the bishop or his appointed representative. The words of blessing summarize the Church's beliefs about death and resurrection:

Grant that this cemetery,
placed under the sign of the cross,
may, by the power of your blessing,
be a place of rest and hope.
May the bodies buried here sleep in your peace,
to rise immortal at the coming of your Son.
May this place be a comfort to the living,
a sign of their hope in unending life.
May prayers be offered here continually in supplication for those
*   who sleep in Christ*
and in constant praise of your mercy.
We ask this through Christ our Lord.
*   Amen.*[7]

The Catholic cemetery witnesses to three realities. First, it witnesses to the membership of both the living and the dead in the community of the faithful, the communion of saints, the Body of Christ. Catholic cemeteries exist as extensions of the living community of the faithful. They are a model of the Church's own community that is awaiting resurrection.

Second, the Catholic cemetery witnesses to social justice. Just as the Church serves the needs of people by sponsoring schools, hospitals, and social service agencies, so the Church sponsors cemeteries as a way to carry out one of the Corporal Works of Mercy: burying the dead. The Church provides a Christian burial for all its members, the very poor as well as those who can pay for it.

Third, the Catholic cemetery witnesses to our belief in the resurrection. The cemetery itself, with its art, architecture, and design, is a collective symbol of hope. Instead of testifying to the past, the Catholic cemetery looks forward to the future, when all the faithful will rise from the dead and enjoy life everlasting.

Following a tradition that predates the entombment of Christ by Joseph of Arimathea, Catholic cemeteries have traditionally buried

---

7. "Order for the Blessing of a Cemetery," *Book of Blessings* (Collegeville, MN: The Liturgical Press, 1989), p. 533.

people. While the Church continues to prefer burial over cremation, most Catholic cemeteries today do contain columbaria for
cremains. Catholics are encouraged, but not required, to be buried
in a Catholic cemetery. As Canon 1240 states, Catholics may be
buried in a non-Catholic cemetery, provided the grave is properly
blessed. Likewise, non-Catholic members of Catholic families may
now be buried in the Catholic cemetery.

Before you go . . .

You can help your survivors handle the business details of your
death by doing some research and making some decisions now. Take
some time to find out how much each of the following options costs.
Then, using the subsequent form, write down your funeral preferences.
Finally, discuss your preferences with your family.

Itemized Funeral Costs	Price Range
Funeral director's basic fees	
1) Funeral home #1	
2) Funeral home #2	
3) Funeral home #3	
Moving the remains to the funeral home	
Embalming	
Cosmetology and burial clothes	
Refrigeration (per day)	
Casket	
1) pine box or other soft woods	
2) hardwood types	
3) metal casket	
Visitation room	
Coordination of funeral service	
Chapel	
Hearse	
Limousine(s)	
Flowers	
Motorcycle escorts	
Clergy	
Music	
Cemetery plot	
Vault or grave liner	

Opening/Closing of grave
Perpetual care
Food
Alternatives
Cremation and columbarium niche
Direct cremation or burial
Memorial society plan

MY FUNERAL PREFERENCES

My funeral home preference is: _____

I want my body to be: buried _____ cremated _____ donated to

science _____ (state where)_____

I want my remains placed in: cemetery plot_____

mausoleum crypt _____ urn _____ elsewhere (describe) _____

_____

If I die in another state or country, I want (circle one)

 a) my body/remains shipped to: _____

 b) to be interred there

I would like an autopsy: yes _____ no _____ undecided_____.

If undecided, under what conditions would you want an

autopsy performed? _____

I would like my body embalmed: yes _____ no _____

I would like to have special cosmetics: no _____ yes _____

(Specify): _____

I would like my hair arranged in the following way:

_____

Clothing I would like: _____

Accessories I would like to be viewed with: (jewelry, glasses,

watch) _____

Accessories I would like to be buried with: _____

_____

The type of casket I would like:

pine box _____ other softwood (specify) _____

hardwood (specify) _____

metal (specify) _____

full couch _____ half couch _____ hinge cap _____

sealed? yes _____ no _____

Expressions of sympathy I would prefer: flowers _____

memorial fund or charity (specify) _____

My cemetery preference is: _____

The type of vault I would like:

concrete _____ metal _____ sealed _____ unsealed _____

For your journal

1. How much could your family afford or want to pay for the funeral costs of one of its members?

2. What are the names of funeral homes in your area? How do they differ in terms of providing services? Do Catholic parishes work with one home more than others? If so, why?

3. In planning a funeral, would you choose a package plan or an itemized plan? Why?

4. Is it important to you that a casket is sealed (airtight) to prevent water leakage? Why or why not?

5. To what extent do you believe in buying life insurance? burial insurance? What life insurance or burial insurance policies does your family have?

6. What death benefits would be available to your family if you or your spouse died?

7. How many of your ancestors are buried in a Catholic cemetery? Would you want to be buried in a Catholic cemetery? Why or why not?

Discussion questions

1. Is Grave Line Tours good business or bad taste?
2. Can you think of any death-related business that may be in bad taste?
3. What are some of the ways that death is commercialized in today's society?
4. How much does a traditional funeral cost in your community today?
5. Have you ever been to a crematorium? Have you ever seen a container of cremains? What was your experience like?
6. If someone in your family was cremated, what would you do with the ashes? Why?
7. Would you ever consider donating your body to science? Why or why not?
8. What might be some disadvantages to pre-need planning?

12 The Law and Death

And the answer is . . .

Is a building without a door and windows and access by the living still a mausoleum? The answer to that question was the center of a year-long legal battle between St. Agnes Catholic cemetery officials and the executors of Kate Smith's estate.[1] Meanwhile, the famous singer's body remained unburied (stored in a temporary receiving vault) more than a year after her death.

The reason for the dispute was a clause in Smith's will, stating that she wanted to be interred in St. Agnes Cemetery "in a hermetically sealed bronze casket in a mausoleum sufficient to contain my remains alone."

The executors interpreted the clause to mean a traditional mausoleum. So they submitted plans for an eleven-foot high, rose-granite structure that visitors could walk into. The leaders of the cemetery, which has traditionally forbidden aboveground crypts and large headstones, objected. Instead, they were willing to make an exception for Smith by allowing an aboveground sarcophagus-style tomb.

The executors fought back, accusing the parish of wanting to keep the money Smith had bequeathed to it, rather than spend it on the mausoleum she wanted. Parish officials and friends of Smith countered, saying that Smith would have respected the cemetery rules. The main intent of her will was not a traditional mausoleum, but the desire not to be buried underground. (She had an obsessive fear of being underground.)

Public pressure mounted on both sides to settle the dispute. By the time another mausoleum could be designed, the ground at Lake Placid would be frozen and the cemetery would have to wait until the following spring to inter Smith's body.

Finally, the executors agreed to accept the cemetery's proposal. In November, 1987, Kate Smith's body was put in its last resting place in an aboveground tomb. The inscription on her tomb contained President Franklin D. Roosevelt's heartfelt words, "This is Kate Smith. This is America."

---

1. Kate Smith, also known as Kathryn Elizabeth Smith, was born on May 1, 1909, in Greenville, Virginia. She died June 17, 1986, in Raleigh, North Carolina. She was a renowned singer, known nationally as the "First Lady of radio." She had her own radio shows in the 1930s and 1940s, as well as her own television shows in the 1950s. She is best known for her renditions of the songs "When the Moon Comes Over the Mountain" and "God Bless America." In 1982, she was awarded the U.S. Medal of Freedom.

The last say

Since ancient times, a person's dying words have been regarded as sacred. In the Hebrew Scriptures, a father divided his property among his heirs on his deathbed. As the stories of Isaac's and Jacob's death tell us, being present at a father's death and receiving his last blessing were very important. What a father said determined the future for everyone in the family. No one dared to act contrary to these wishes (cf. Genesis 27:1–45; 47:27–49:33).

In modern times, death is often removed from the family setting. The family doesn't always gather around the deathbed. Consequently, major fights sometimes erupt over what a person's last wishes really were. For this reason, a person's will has evolved into a legal document. It is just one of the many aspects of death that are treated under the law.

This chapter will introduce you to some of the laws relating to death. For the most part, such laws come under the health and safety codes of each state. You will learn what these laws have to say about death certificates, autopsies, cremation, and burial. You will also learn about universal organ donation and the Church's laws regarding death and ecclesiastical burial.

The death certificate

A death certificate is a legal document stating the person's identity, the time of death, and the cause of death. In all states, a death certificate is required before a body can be buried or cremated. This is to prevent the destruction of evidence, if it turns out that a crime was committed. If the deceased was under a doctor's care, that doctor or another licensed physician issues the death certificate. If the deceased was not under a doctor's care or if there is a question of death by violence, a coroner or medical examiner is called in to examine the body and to issue the death certificate.

Identification. Under usual circumstances, family members or friends identify the deceased person. This may happen at the scene of death or in a morgue. In cases where an unknown person dies, the coroner must make every effort to identify him or her. This requires detective work—a search through fingerprint files, dental records, missing persons' photographs, blood and genetic matching. If the body is never identified, it is buried with a marker saying "John Doe" or "Jane Doe." If the body is identified but no one claims it, the coroner buries it "in the manner provided for interment of the indigent dead." According to the law, the unclaimed dead may be embalmed and used for scientific and educational purposes.

Time of Death. Despite advances in medical science, determining the time of death is not always easy. As you learned in chapter 1, a person is considered dead when (1) total brain function, (2) spontaneous function of the respiratory system, and (3) spontaneous function of the circulatory system cease permanently. But what about the person whose brain waves are flat, yet who continues breathing on his or her own? Or what about the person whose brain is alive, but whose other bodily functions must be sustained by machines? Are these people dead, or are they alive?

Knowing the exact time of death is important in forensic science, which deals with deaths where murder or violence has occurred. It is also important if any vital organs are to be donated to a transplant program. The organs must be taken as soon after death as possible in order to ensure healthy tissue for a successful transplant.

In December, 1990, Pope John Paul II called on scientists to keep trying to "determine as precisely as possible the exact moment and the indisputable sign of death." He also cautioned them to be prudent in deciding when to remove organs for transplant. "Neither individuals nor society are permitted to endanger life, whatever benefits might possibly accrue as a result," he said. According to Christian moral principles, doctors cannot sacrifice one person, "even though it may be for the benefit of another human being who might be felt to be entitled to preference."[2]

Cause of Death. All states have laws that require an autopsy of the deceased in cases of sudden or unexplained death.[3] When a coroner is required to investigate the cause of death, he or she is entitled to custody of the corpse until the conclusion of the autopsy or medical investigation. It is a misdemeanor to perform an autopsy without written authorization. This authorization must be obtained from the deceased (before death), the survivors, the public administrator of the deceased's estate, or the coroner.

NOTE: Over eight thousand Americans die each year in foreign countries. Because of the expense involved in bringing back the body, about half of these Americans are buried or cremated in the countries in which death occurred. In the other cases, the United States Consulate in the country of death has custody over the corpse and arranges for it

---

2. Quoted in Felican A. Foy, ed., *1991 Catholic Almanac* (Huntington, IN: Our Sunday Visitor, 1990), p. 70.
3. Autopsies, which are not mentioned in Canon Law, are not morally objectionable to the Church, except in the case of the pope. Even though John Paul I died suddenly in 1978 after serving only 33 days as pope, Vatican officials—following ancient Church custom—refused to allow an autopsy.

to be flown home. The consul must provide the next of kin with a "report of death," which has the same legal status as a death certificate. Anyone who is traveling abroad should always keep his/her passport on his/her person, to serve as a means of identification in case of death. The traveler should also carry with the passport instructions to be followed in event of death.

Common law in the United States and England says that a person may be declared legally dead if he or she has disappeared and cannot be located for seven years. In the case of disappearance resulting from military action or a travel accident, the presumption of death may be made sooner.

Disposition of the body

Believe it or not, you have no legal say in how your body will be disposed after death, unless you donate your body or parts of it for anatomic research or organ donation. Even if you state in writing that you want to be buried in the ground or buried in a mausoleum or cremated, your family has no legal obligation to carry out your wishes. Once you die, your body is treated under the law as property or quasi-property that belongs to your surviving spouse, your surviving children, your surviving parents, your next of kin, or the executor of your will. These people can decide how your remains will be interred.

Regardless of what your family or executor decides, your estate is financially liable. This means that you must pay for the funeral, burial, or cremation. If there is not enough money in your bank account to cover these costs, responsibility for payment falls to all family members.

Disposal by Cremation. Some states require a special permit or authorization for cremation. The crematorium requires the signature of the next of kin or the executor before the actual cremation. This authorization usually includes instructions for disposition of the ashes or for shipping them to some other community. Some crematoriums are insured against lawsuits that might arise from performing a cremation without proper authorization. In some states, when it is impossible for a crematorium to secure all of the necessary signatures, an affidavit attesting to the desire of the deceased to be cremated acts as proper authorization.

In several states, cremation may not take place for forty-eight hours following death, unless a health officer orders immediate cremation in the case of contagious disease. Only two states— Massachusetts and Michigan—have laws that require the corpse to be placed in a casket for cremation. In all other states, the corpse may be cremated in a cardboard container.

In most states, a person can inurn, inter, or scatter cremains so long as they do not create an offense to anyone or violate another's property rights. The exceptions to this are California, Washington, and Nevada, all of which prohibit the scattering of ashes. The National Park Service also forbids the strewing of ashes in the national parks because of the possible creation of a public nuisance. In 1965, California permitted scattering of ashes beyond the three-mile limit at sea and from an airplane flying more than five thousand feet above non-populous areas. In some states, it is necessary to secure a permit before shipping cremains to another state.

Disposition by Burial. Most states, for health reasons, limit burials to sites designated as cemeteries. In California, for example, it is against the law to bury someone within the city limits except in a cemetery. One exception to the cemetery rule is found in New York. There, a person may be buried in any family burying ground, provided it is no longer than three acres and no closer than one hundred feet to a residence whose owner has not given permission for the burial. Many states require a grave liner or concrete vault if one is to be buried in the ground.

Other laws exist regarding the cemetery itself and disinterment. In most states, for example, it is a misdemeanor to vandalize a cemetery. California law states that it is a felony to remove unlawfully, to mutilate, or to disinter human remains. No remains can be legally removed from any cemetery except upon written order of the health department or superior court.

Embalming

Laws of each state and even some cities specify the conditions under which a corpse may or may not be embalmed. For example, in most states it is against the law to embalm a corpse if the cause of death is unknown or if the death is related to a car accident or crime, except by permission of the coroner or justice of the peace. On the other hand, embalming is not always a legal requirement. In Arkansas, Hawaii, Louisiana, Maryland, Nevada, New Hampshire, New York, South Dakota, Vermont, West Virginia, and Wyoming, embalming is not mandatory under any circumstances. In those states, the decision to embalm a corpse is solely at the discretion of the executor or next of kin.[4]

---

4. Embalming is neither prescribed nor prohibited by Canon Law. Church custom, however, prohibits the embalming of a pope. When a pope dies, his body is washed, clothed, and then made available for public viewing. This custom was problematic in the case of Pope Paul VI. The heat caused his skin to turn green.

What follows is a summary of the embalming laws of the other states, as well as those of Washington, DC, and Puerto Rico. As you can see from this summary, which is condensed from a 1984 report by the National Funeral Directors Association, embalming is required in these states only for certain reasons: (1) the death is due to a communicable or infectious disease, (2) the final disposition is not made within a prescribed period of time, or (3) the body is to be transported between states in a common carrier (airplane, train, etc.). In the state laws, the term "specially prepared" refers to washing the body in a disinfectant solution, closing the orifices with absorbent cotton, and wrapping the body in a clean sheet.

Embalming Laws

Alabama If the body is moved across the state line by common carrier, it must be either embalmed or cremated. The body must also be embalmed or cremated if final disposition does not take place within thirty hours after death.

Alaska In case of death by unusual or communicable disease or suspected communicable disease, the body must be embalmed.

Arizona If a body is to be stored or transported longer than twenty-four hours, it must be embalmed or refrigerated. If a body is to be transported outside the state, it must be embalmed unless transportation is to be provided by a family member or by a licensed undertaker within twenty-four hours after death. If death is from a communicable disease, the body must be embalmed.

California A body must be embalmed when it is to be transferred by common carrier. If death is a result of a contagious disease, the county health officer may order the body to be embalmed.

Colorado When a body is to be held for more than twenty-four hours, it must be embalmed or refrigerated. If the body is to be shipped by common carrier, it must be either embalmed or in a hermetically sealed container.

Connecticut When a body is to be transported over state lines by common carrier, it must be embalmed.

Delaware When a body is to be kept for more than twenty-four hours, it must either be embalmed or placed in a hermetically sealed metal or metal-lined coffin.

District of Columbia A body must be embalmed if death results from a communicable disease.

Florida If a body is held in any place or in transit over twenty-four hours after death or pending final disposition, it must be refrigerated, embalmed, or specially prepared. Embalming is required when death results from a highly contagious disease or the body is transported outside the state.

Georgia Embalming is required in the case of a contagious disease or when the body will be transported and the final destination cannot be reached within twenty-four hours.

Idaho A body must be embalmed when it is to be transported by common carrier.

Illinois A body must be embalmed if death results from a communicable disease or is to be transported or shipped by common carrier.

Indiana A body must be embalmed if death is from a communicable disease (such as leprosy, plague, or smallpox) or if it is ordered to be embalmed by the county health officer.

Iowa A body must be embalmed if death occurs from a communicable disease or if the body is transported.

Kansas All bodies that are not buried within twenty-four hours of death must be embalmed. All bodies shipped by private hearse further than an adjacent county must be embalmed.

Maine If a body is to be transported by common carrier, it must be embalmed.

Massachusetts If death occurs from a highly contagious disease, the body must be embalmed. If death occurs from a different disease dangerous to public health, the body must be embalmed or, if it is to be buried within twenty-four hours, must be specially prepared and refrigerated. In other cases of death, a body cannot be transported unless embalmed or specially prepared and sealed in an airtight coffin.

Michigan If death occurs from a communicable disease and a body is to be transported, it must be embalmed. Otherwise, a body must be embalmed if the destination cannot be reached within forty-eight hours.

Minnesota Embalming is required if death occurs from a communicable disease, the body is transported out of state via airplane, or if burial or cremation will not be accomplished within seventy-two hours.

Mississippi If burial or cremation is not to take place within forty-eight hours after death, a body must be embalmed or refrigerated. Bodies that are transported must be embalmed in cases of communicable diseases if the destination cannot be reached within twenty-four hours.

Missouri If death results from a communicable disease and a body is to be transported by common carrier, it must be either embalmed, in an airtight sealed container, or specially prepared. If death results from a communicable disease and there is to be a public funeral, the body must be embalmed or permanently encased in a sealed casket. If death results from another cause, the body must be embalmed or encased in an airtight container that is hermetically sealed.

Montana If death results from a communicable disease and a body is to be transported, the body must be embalmed. If death results from another cause and the body is to be transported by common carrier and will be en route more than eight hours or will reach its destination more than thirty-six hours after death, the body must be embalmed, refrigerated, or specially prepared. If death results from a cause other than a communicable disease and a body is to be transported by private conveyor and will not reach its destination within forty-eight hours after death, the body must be embalmed, refrigerated, or specially prepared.

Nebraska If a body is to be transported intrastate by common carrier, it must be either embalmed or placed in a sealed container. If it is to be transported by private carrier under the supervision of a licensed funeral director, the body must reach its destination within twenty-four hours following death if not embalmed and must be refrigerated; if refrigerated, the body must reach its destination within twenty-four hours following removal from storage. Exception: If a body is placed in a metal or metal-lined sealed container immediately after death, it may be considered the same as an embalmed body. If death occurs from a communicable disease, a body shall be promptly embalmed or encased in a metal or metal-lined hermetically sealed container.

New Jersey If a body is not to be buried or cremated within forty-eight hours after death, it must be embalmed or refrigerated. If death occurs from a communicable disease and a body is not to be buried or disposed of within twenty-four hours after death, it must be embalmed. If death occurs from other causes and a body is to be transported by common carrier, the body must be embalmed if the destination cannot be reached within twenty-four hours after death.

New Mexico If death is a result of a contagious disease, a body must be embalmed. If the body is shipped out of state, it must be embalmed.

North Carolina All bodies, regardless of cause of death, shall be embalmed if condition permits; otherwise a strong, tightly-sealed outer case is needed.

North Dakota If a body is not to be buried within seventy-two hours after death, it must be embalmed. If death occurs from a communicable disease, a body must be embalmed unless there is no viewing and it is immediately buried. If a body is to be transported by common carrier or if it is to be transported for more than seventy-five miles or in interstate commerce, it must be embalmed.

Ohio If death occurs from a communicable disease and if the body is transported longer than twenty-four hours after death, it must be embalmed.

Oklahoma If death results from a contagious disease or if a body cannot be disposed of within a reasonable time, the body must be embalmed.

Oregon If a body is to be held longer than twenty-four hours, it must be embalmed or refrigerated. If death is a result of a communicable disease and the body is to be transported, the body must be embalmed if transportation to its destination cannot be completed within twenty-four hours after death. Regardless of cause of death, if there is to be a funeral more than twenty-four hours after death, the body must be either embalmed or refrigerated.

Pennsylvania If death is from a contagious disease or if a body is to be held twenty-four hours after death, it shall be embalmed, placed in a sealed container, or refrigerated.

Puerto Rico If a body is not to be buried within twenty-four hours after death, it must be embalmed. If the body is to be transported and disposition cannot be completed within twenty-four hours after death, the body must be embalmed.

Rhode Island If a body is to be shipped by common carrier, it must be embalmed. If death is a result of a communicable disease and if a public funeral is to be held somewhere other than the place of death, the body must be embalmed and permanently enclosed; if not embalmed, it must be buried or enclosed in a tightly sealed outer case within twenty-four hours.

South Carolina If a body is to be shipped by common carrier, it must be embalmed.

Texas If a body is to be held in any place or is to be in transit for more than twenty-four hours after death and pending final disposition, the body must be refrigerated or embalmed.

Utah If a body is to be shipped by common carrier, it must be embalmed. If a body is to be held in any place or is to be in transit for more than twenty-four hours after death and pending final disposition, it must be either refrigerated or embalmed. If there is to be a public funeral and death results from a communicable disease, a body should be embalmed.

Virginia If a body is to be shipped by common carrier, it must be embalmed.

Washington If death results from a communicable disease, a body must be embalmed or cremated. If death is a result of an infectious disease and a body is to be transferred outside the jurisdiction of the local health department or if a body is to be transported by common carrier, the body must be embalmed. If a body is to be transported pending final disposition more than twenty-four hours after death, the body must be embalmed.

Wisconsin If a body is to be shipped by common carrier, the body must be embalmed. Regardless of type of carrier, if a body is to be transported and if death was the result of a communicable disease, the body must be embalmed.

(Used by permission of the National Funeral Directors Association, 11121 W. Oklahoma Ave., Milwaukee, WI 53227)

The Uniform Anatomical Gift Act

The Uniform Anatomical Gift Act is a law adopted by Washington, DC, and all states, except Delaware, Massachusetts, Mississippi, Nebraska, Ohio, Rhode Island, and West Virginia. This act says that any individual of sound mind and eighteen years of age or older may give all or any part of his or her body after death to one of the following: (1) a hospital, surgeon, or physician for medical or dental education, research, advancement of medical/dental science, therapy, or transplantation; (2) any accredited medical school or dental school, college, or university for education, research, advancement of science, therapy, or transplantation; (3) any bank or storage facility for education, research, advancement of science, therapy, or transplantation; or (4) any specified individual for therapy or transplantation needed. The anatomical gift is usually made in a person's will or by a donor card or recorded message, and may be taken immediately after death. The recipient may accept or reject the gift.

Most states now have anatomical donor forms on the back of driver's licenses. These should be used in addition to Uniform Donor wallet cards that may be obtained from various organ banks. A person may donate one, several, or all of the following vital organs.

Eyes. In the United States alone, the sight of thirty thousand people could be restored if enough corneas were available. Corneal transplant operations are now effective in restoring sight in 90 percent of all patients. (At the present time, it is not possible to transplant the entire eye.) Eyes must be removed within two to four hours after death. Airlines will fly them to their destinations without charge.

Ears. More than 18 million people in the United States suffer partial or total deafness. Persons with hearing problems or other ear disorders are urged to bequeath their inner ears to temporal bone banks for research.

Kidneys. Severe diabetics and people suffering from renal failure desperately need kidneys. While kidney transplant operations are becoming more successful, not enough kidneys are available for all those who need them.

Tissues. Body tissues, such as bone, ear, eye, heart, heart valve, and arteries are needed by regional tissue banks for transplantation.

Pituitary Glands. An estimated ten thousand children in the United States suffer from serious pituitary deficiency that retards growth. Donated pituitary glands can help to produce the hormones these children need.

Skin. A donation of skin can be extremely valuable to persons suffering from serious burns.

The Church considers the donation of organs to be an act of Christian charity.

Writing a will

Most people spend their entire lives accumulating possessions, real estate, and bank accounts. But in the end, the popular saying, "You can't take it with you," holds true for everyone. A legal will is a way of dispersing one's possessions according to one's wishes.

The person who makes out the will is called the legator, or settlor. The person or charitable organization that receives the benefits is called the beneficiary. When a person dies, his or her lawyer should be contacted for a reading of the will. The administrator or executor sees that the will is carried out. Before the beneficiaries can receive their inheritance, the probate court makes sure that the deceased's funeral expenses and all outstanding bills are paid.

Everyone should write a will. The will can be changed and updated at any time, either with an entirely new document or with codicils. Waiting until you are old or ill to write a will not a good idea. By procrastinating, you may end up dying intestate, or without a will.

What happens if you die without a will? Then the state will write your will for you. Your possessions and money will be distributed in accordance with the laws of your state. The probate court will appoint an administrator to see that the state's laws are carried out. If the person is a married adult, most state laws stipulate that one third to one half of the person's estate goes to his or her spouse and two thirds to the children. If the person is a single adult or child, the law stipulates that the entire estate goes to the deceased's parents.

The probate process is both time-consuming and costly. It takes an average of six months to a year to process an estate. Probate fees can range anywhere between 8 ½ percent to 20 percent of the entire estate.[5] This means your beneficiaries will receive significantly less than you may have intended. If this is not the way you want your possessions and money to be distributed, then you need to make out a will.

Writing a will is more than a legal procedure. It is also a psychological challenge to the writer to accept, rather than to deny, the reality of death. Furthermore, it is an expression of love for one's spouse, relatives, charitable organizations, and friends.

Church law

When the Code of Canon Law was revised in 1983, it reduced to ten the forty previous canons (from the 1917 Code) dealing with death and burial.[6] As you will see, these laws allow local bishops a great deal of latitude.

Canon 1176

Pt.1: The Christian faithful departed are to be given ecclesiastical funeral rites according to the norm of law.

Pt. 2: Through ecclesiastical funeral rites the Church asks spiritual assistance for the departed, honors their bodies, and at the same time brings the solace of hope to the living; such rites are to be celebrated according to the norm of liturgical laws.

---

5. When President Franklin D. Roosevelt died, the probate lawyers and administrator were paid 11 percent of his estate.

6. The former law (CIC 1203) forbade cremation. Now cremation is to be denied only when it is based on a sectarian spirit, hatred for the Catholic religion or Church, or a denial of the resurrection of the body. Funeral rites are not to be performed at the place of cremation.

Pt. 3: The Church earnestly recommends that the pious custom of burying the bodies of the dead be observed; it does not, however, forbid cremation unless it has been chosen for reasons which are contrary to Christian teaching.

Canon 1177

Pt. 1: As a rule the funeral rites for any of the faithful departed must be celebrated in his or her own parish church.

Pt. 2: However, any member of the Christian faithful or those commissioned to arrange for his or her funeral may choose another church for the funeral rites with the consent of its rector and after informing the departed person's pastor.

Pt. 3: If death has occurred outside the person's own parish, and the corpse has not been transferred to that parish and another church has not been legitimately chosen for the funeral, the funeral rites are to be celebrated in the church of the parish where the death occurred unless another church has been designated by particular law.

Canon 1178

The funeral rites of a diocesan bishop are to be celebrated in his own cathedral church unless he has chosen another church.

Canon 1179

As a rule the funeral rites of religious or members of societies of apostolic life are to be celebrated in their own church or oratory by their superior if it is a clerical institute or society, otherwise by the chaplain.

Canon 1180

Pt. 1: If a parish has its own cemetery, the faithful departed are to be interred in it unless another cemetery has been legitimately chosen either by the departed person or by those who are responsible to arrange for his or her interment.

Pt. 2: However, everyone, unless prohibited by law, is permitted to choose a cemetery for burial.

Canon 1181

The prescriptions of can. 1264 are to be observed in regard to the offerings given on the occasion of funerals;[7] precautions are nevertheless to be taken in funeral rites against any favoritism toward persons and against depriving the poor of the funeral rites which are their due.

---

7. Canon 1264 states that the bishop should fix the amount or set a limit on the amount to be given on the occasions of funerals. No one is to be denied Christian burial because of lack of money.

Canon 1182

After the interment an entry is to be made in the (parish) death register in accord with the norm of particular law.

Canon 1183

Pt. 1: As regards funeral rites catechumens are to be considered members of the Christian faithful.

Pt. 2: The local ordinary can permit children to be given ecclesiastical funeral rites if their parents intended to baptize them but they died before their baptism.

Pt. 3: In the prudent judgment of the local ordinary, ecclesiastical funeral rites can be granted to baptized members of some non-Catholic church or ecclesial community unless it is evidently contrary to their will and provided their own minister is unavailable.

Canon 1184

Pt. 1: Unless they have given some signs of repentance before their death, the following are to be deprived of ecclesiastical funeral rites: (1) notorious apostates, heretics, and schismatics; (2) persons who had chosen cremation of their own bodies for reasons opposed to the Christian faith; (3) other manifest sinners for whom ecclesiastical funeral rites cannot be granted without public scandal to the faithful.[8]

Pt. 2: If some doubt should arise, the local ordinary is to be consulted, and his judgment is to be followed.

Canon 1185

Any funeral Mass whatsoever is also to be denied a person excluded from ecclesiastical funeral rites.[9]

In addition to these canons, the Church says that major amputated members (arm, leg, etc.) which maintain some recognizable human quality are to be disposed of in consecrated ground by burial or by cremation. With proper consent, the amputated member may be used by medical schools for purposes of study and dissection.

---

8. At one time in Church history, criminals, suicides, strangers, and the illegitimate could not receive ecclesiastical burial.

9. The Canon Law Society of America, trans., *The Code of Canon Law: Latin–English Edition* (Washington, DC: Canon Law Society of America, 1983), pp. 837–40.

Your will

The laws of many states require a person to be twenty-one years of age in order to execute a legal will. This age requirement may differ in the same state with regard to real property and personal property. Real property is land and buildings (house, commercial building). Personal property includes clothes, automobiles, furniture, mortgages, promissory notes, stocks and bonds. Generally, the minimum age is lower for personal property than it is for real property. The minimum age may also differ, depending on one's gender.

Many people consult a lawyer to write their will. It is also possible, however, to write one without a lawyer. Both books and computer programs are available to assist people who wish to do this. It is important that the person making a will be of sound mind, good memory, and under no coercion from others. There are other considerations as well.

Ordinarily, a will is drafted with a typewriter, computer, or pen. Some states even allow a will to be in the form of an audiotape or videotape. A will written in pencil is not legally binding. The final copy needs to be perfect, with no erasing or crossing out. No special form is needed as long as the intentions of the person are clear. The will, however, does need to be dated and signed in the presence of two witnesses, and notarized. The following states, as well as the Philippines and Puerto Rico require a person to have three witnesses to a will: Connecticut, Georgia, Louisiana, Maine, Massachusetts, New Hampshire, South Carolina, and Vermont.

Unless all of your possessions are to go to one person or charity, your will should list all properties (real or personal) by name (purple sweater, automobile, etc.) or by categories (jewelry, books, CD collection). The will should also clearly specify the name of the person or charity that is to inherit each item. It is not enough to omit the name of a family member if the intention is to disinherit that person. The family member must be mentioned in the will, along with the express statement that he or she will inherit nothing.[10]

On the next page, you will find a sample outline for a will.

---

10. In Louisiana, a parent is prohibited from disinheriting a child.

Last Will and Testament

I, _____ , a resident of

(your legal name)

_____ ,

(city)   (county)   (state)

declare that this is my last will. I hereby revoke all wills and codicils that I have previously made.

I make the following cash gifts:

Amount   Beneficiary

I make the following gifts of personal property:

Property   Beneficiary

I give the rest of my estate to _____ .

I nominate _____ as executor. If he/she shall for any reason fail to qualify or cease to act as executor, I nominate _____ as executor.

I subscribe my name this _____ day of _____ , 19 ____ , at

_____ ,

(city)   (county)   (state)

and do hereby declare that I am of sound mind and that I voluntarily sign this instrument as my last will.

_____

(your signature)

Witnesses (signed names and addresses):

_____

_____

_____

For your journal

1. What real property (land, house, commercial buildings) do you own? What do you want to happen to this property after you die?

2. What personal property (clothes, automobiles, furniture, mortgages, promissory notes, stocks and bonds) do you have? What do you want to happen to this property after you die?

Discussion questions

1. How would you have interpreted the words of Kate Smith's will?

2. Who do you think has the right to decide when a person is dead?

3. Why are identification, time of death, and cause of death important to life insurance companies?

4. California law forbids the scattering of ashes at sea at any point less than three miles from shore. Why do you think this law exists?

5. California law also mandates that cremains be removed from their container before scattering. Why do you think this law exists?

6. Do you think the scattering of ashes is environmentally safe or do you think it is a form of pollution?

7. Do you think people should donate organs when they die?

8. In the 19th century, it was the custom of rich European families to leave the entire inheritance to the oldest son. Discuss the advantages and disadvantages of this custom. Do you think it was fair?

Part Seven: Moral Aspects

I have set before you life and death, the blessing and the curse.
Choose life, then, that you and your descendants may live. . . .

—Deuteronomy 30:19

13 Some Life and Death Issues

Important Choices

Imagine each of the following situations. Then identify what life-and-death issue is involved.

Situation 1: A husband and wife are expecting their first child. Tests on the fetus have shown that it has Down's syndrome and will be mentally handicapped.

Situation 2: The McCarthys' son, who is a senior in high school, has just been told by his girlfriend that she is pregnant.

Situation 3: An obstetrician's patient has just given birth to twins. The babies, however, are Siamese twins, joined at the waist and horribly deformed. It will not be possible to separate them.

Situation 4: Mr. Smith is 80 and has cancer. The pain has gotten so bad that he pleads with his wife to help him commit suicide.

Situation 5: The Jones' teenage daughter was in a terrible car accident. She has been in a coma for three months and cannot breathe without a respirator. The doctors have given Mr. and Mrs. Jones little hope that she will recover.

Situation 6: An elderly patient has kidney disease and must spend several hours each day attached to a dialysis machine. The procedure is both frightening and painful. The patient begs his doctor to take him off the machines and to let him die in peace at home.

Working through life-and-death issues requires more than a knowledge of medicine. It also requires an application of moral principles. Each of the six situations you just considered belongs in an area of morality known as bioethics. In this highly sensitive area, doctors, nurses, patients, families, and the Church must all work together to reach a decision that is not only legal, but also respects life and human dignity.

Respect for life is a basic Christian principle. It is also a tenet of the Hippocratic oath, an oath doctors used to take in which they promised to uphold and sustain life. Before the advent of modern medicine, respecting life was more of a black-and-white proposition. The doctor did his or her best to keep the patient alive. If the patient died, resuscitation was usually impossible.

Modern scientific technology—with its invention of sophisticated diagnostic tools, organ transplants, respirators, heart and brain monitors, genetic engineering, and so forth—has opened a new set of moral dilemmas and questions. Who will live? Who will die? And who has the right to decide? These are just a few of the tough questions posed by present-day medical situations.

In this chapter, you will examine four specific topics in the area of bioethics: abortion, infanticide, euthanasia, and the right to die. You will also learn what the Church has to say about each topic.

Abortion

"Abortion" refers to the expulsion of the fetus from the womb, with resulting death. In some cases, an abortion is spontaneous; it is then referred to as a "miscarriage." In other cases, the abortion is deliberately induced. The reasons for inducing abortion vary greatly—financial distress, "bad timing," birth defects found in the fetus, rape, incest, endangerment of the mother's health, too many children already. According to the *Roe v. Wade* decision of the Supreme Court (1973), a woman is not required to have ANY reason in order to end a pregnancy in the first trimester. Under the law, she may seek a legal abortion simply because she doesn't want the child.

In 1985, American women between the ages of fifteen and forty-four aborted 422 fetuses for every 1,000 live births. This amounted to approximately 1,588,600 abortions. By far, the women who had abortions were unmarried and white. Most had no prior children or abortions. Sixty percent of the women were under twenty-five; almost half of this group were teenagers.

Since the Church teaches that life begins at conception, it considers induced abortion—for any reason—morally wrong. Thus Code 1398 of Canon Law states: "A person who procures a successful [completed] abortion incurs an automatic excommunication." Excommunication due to an abortion can be remitted by the local bishop. Confessors have been delegated by many bishops to absolve from this penalty—at least in the case of a first abortion. Nevertheless, abortion continues to be considered a very serious sin by the Church.

What the Church condemns is a "completed abortion"—a case where the abortion has taken place and the fetus has been killed as a result of a procedure whose primary purpose is to end the life of the fetus. The Church, however, does take into consideration a moral principle called the "double effect." A certain action may have two effects, one that is intended and one that is not intended. For example, suppose a pregnant woman is found to have cancer.

In order to save her life, she must have chemotherapy or radiation treatments. In such a case, the Church would allow the medical treatment, even though the secondary (unintended) result might be the killing of the fetus. However, every possible effort would have to be made to save and protect both lives.[1]

Abortion has become one of the most controversial and emotional moral issues of our time. Basically, it has divided people into two camps: those who oppose abortion (pro-life), and those who favor it (pro-abortion). The fundamental stance of each group may be summarized as follows:

Pro-Life

1. Human beings are required to respect the nature of their bodies, including the reproductive process.
2. Life begins at the moment of conception.
3. All life, especially that of the most vulnerable and the unborn, is sacred.
4. The unborn have a right to be born.
5. It is wrong to kill an innocent human being, and wrong to legalize an action that is immoral.
6. If abortion were not legal, fewer women would seek it.
7. There are not enough babies for all the people who want to adopt them.

Pro-Abortion

1. Human beings are free to do whatever they think is right with their bodies.
2. It is unclear when life actually begins.
3. Quality of life determines whether life is sacred or not.
4. A woman has a right to determine what happens to her own body.
5. It is wrong to put one's moral position (anti-abortion) into law.
6. Women will always want abortions. It is safer to obtain an abortion legally than illegally.
7. Unwanted children are often abused, neglected, or grow up to be criminals.

---

1. According to Church law, an aborted human fetus, which is a human being with body and soul, has a right to Christian burial. If the parents consent, the Church considers it all right to donate the fetus to medical schools for the education of future doctors.

The controversy between the two groups has become so intense that some political campaigns are run on this one issue alone. Politicians may or may not be elected to public office, depending on their abortion stance. Likewise, justices of the Supreme Court may or may not be voted for by members of the Senate, depending on their abortion views.

Since the 1973 Supreme Court decision, numerous pro-life groups have sought to get the decision reversed. Their efforts seem to be having some success. In its 1989 *Webster v.Reproductive Services* ruling, a more conservative Supreme Court upheld the legality of some new state restrictions on abortion. Where the legal battle surrounding abortion will end is anyone's guess. But one thing is clear: The Catholic Church will always be on the side of life rather than the side of death.

Infanticide

Infanticide is the deliberate killing of babies and infants. This immoral practice has been around for centuries. In biblical times, the worshipers of the god Baal sacrificed infants as part of their religious rituals (cf. Genesis 22:1–18). The Egyptians, around the time of Moses' birth, killed male Hebrew babies as a way to control the Hebrew population (cf. Exodus 1:15—2:10). In the time of Solomon, some Jewish women killed their own children as a means of population control and as a means of ridding the community of its weak and deformed children (cf. 1 Kings 3:16–28). The Christian Scriptures, too, recount the practice of infanticide. Matthew's Gospel says that Herod ordered the killing of male Hebrew babies in an attempt to kill Jesus (cf. Matthew 2:1–18).[2]

Other cultures practiced infanticide as well. The Spartans, for example, regularly inspected all newborn babies and eliminated those who were weak by hurling them off Mount Taygetus. The Romans drowned their deformed infants. The Eskimos and Polynesians killed female babies out of fear that they would not find husbands to support them. Still other cultures killed children who were born as the result of incest, fornication, or adultery.

In contrast, the Hebrews and Christians forbade infanticide. This is one of the reasons the following story about Jesus was included in the Gospel of Mark.

---

2. The Feast of Holy Innocents (December 28) honors the many babies that Matthew's Gospel says Herod slew in an attempt to eliminate Jesus, whom he perceived as a dangerous rival to his throne.

And people were bringing children to him that he might touch
them, but the disciples rebuked them. When Jesus saw this he became
indignant and said to them, "Let the children come to me; do not
prevent them, for the kingdom of God belongs to such as these.
Amen, I say to you, whoever does not accept the kingdom of God like
a child will not enter it." Then he embraced them and blessed them,
placing his hands on them.

—Mark 10:13–16

Children were important to Jesus and were respected by him. Thus the leaders of the early Church argued in favor of the baptism of children and for their full membership in the Christian community.

Throughout its history, the Church fought against infanticide by establishing orphanages and adoption agencies. The first known instance of a Christian foundling hospital was Datheus House, established in Milan in A.D. 787. In the Middle Ages, a religious order known as the Hospitalers of the Holy Ghost devoted itself to the care of abandoned babies. The order fitted its hospices with "turning cradles" at the gate to allow mothers to leave their babies there anonymously.

Today in the United States, infanticide is found primarily in instances of extreme child abuse (neglect or bodily harm) and in a passive-type of murder known as pediatric euthanasia, in which some badly deformed babies or premature babies have been refused nutrition and left to die. Most of these cases have involved the following types of children: (1) babies born with Down's syndrome, a severe mental retardation often complicated by fatal heart defects and other physical problems; (2) babies born with spina bifida, in which the spinal cord is deformed and protrudes outside the body; (3) babies born with AIDS; and (4) Siamese twins, in which two babies are joined together and share common vital organs or limbs.

Both child abuse and pediatric euthanasia are illegal and are deplored by Catholic moralists. Teaching that even deformed children have a right to life, the Church continues to sponsor pediatric hospitals, facilities for children with disabilities (including the deaf and hearing impaired, the emotionally or socially maladjusted, the developmentally disabled, the orthopedically disabled, and the visually disabled), child welfare programs, day care centers, adoption agencies, and shelters for abused children.

Also in contrast to those who advocate killing children who have severe mental or physical disabilities, is the development of a relatively new field of medicine known as neonatal care. Not many

years ago, a newborn weighing less than three pounds was un-
likely to survive. Now, because of advances in technology, babies
as small as 1 pound, 10 ounces, can be saved. Also emerging is
another branch of medicine that deals with the medical treatment
of the unborn.

Euthanasia

The word *euthanasia* means "good death." Another term often
used is *mercy killing*. The term commonly refers to the direct taking
of human life in order to relieve suffering. Cases of euthanasia
usually involve someone who is elderly or who is suffering terribly.

Some people, such as members of the Hemlock Society and the
Euthanasia Society, argue that simply being alive is not a good in itself,
especially when someone can no longer live with meaning and dignity
or live without pain. According to the philosophy of these societies,
each person should have the right to choose the time of his or her
death, especially if a truly human life as they define it is no longer
possible. So they encourage those with terminal illness to plan their
own deaths. They also urge doctors and family members to exercise
"compassion" by helping terminally ill people die.

Currently, euthanasia is against the law in the United States. If
the doctor or family member intentionally causes the person to die,
it is considered to be murder. If the person ends his or her own life,
it is basically a form of suicide. But what about the situation where
a doctor or family member assists a person in committing suicide?
In this case, the controversy regarding the morality or immorality
of euthanasia takes on another dimension.

Aiding and abetting a suicide is a felony in twenty-six states. Nevertheless, nothing legally prevents a person from moving from a state
that prohibits assisted suicide to a state that allows it. This happened in
1990, when Dr. Jack Kevorkian of Michigan built a machine to assist in
the suicide of a 54-year-old Oregon woman named Janet Adkins, who
had Alzheimer's disease. Because the action was illegal in Oregon, the
woman went to Michigan, where she committed suicide using
Kevorkian's machine. The Michigan court seized Kevorkian's machine
and barred him from using it. First-degree murder charges against him,
however, were dropped. Dr. Kevorkian proceeded to build a second
machine, which was used to help two other women commit suicide.
Once again, the doctor was charged with murder; once again, the
charges were dropped.

Kevorkian's actions provoked loud cries of alarm and disap-
proval from both the Catholic Church and the American Medical

Association. Both groups were adamant: No reason can ever justify the causing of one's own or another's death. No one has the right to decide when a person, terminally ill or not, should die.[3]

The right to die

Modern scientific technology has complicated the issue of euthanasia considerably. Now it is possible to keep a brain-dead person alive on machines for years on end. Ethicists as well as the families of such a person are rightfully asking if such extraordinary measures to sustain life are going too far. Should hospitals use all the technological tools at their disposal to prolong lives that can't be saved? Is such treatment prolonging life, or is it merely prolonging the person's suffering and dying? In other words, when does a hopelessly ill person have the right to die? When is it morally permissible to end treatment and let the person die?

The stopping of extraordinary means to keep a patient alive involves some difficult decisions. The toughest decisions in this regard occur in situations where the patient is permanently unconscious. Such a patient is sometimes described as being in an irreversible coma or in a persistent vegetative state. He or she cannot speak, walk, swallow, or perform other normal functions, and has no likelihood of recovery. Such a patient also is unable to express his or her wishes about continuing or ending treatment.

The first such case that attracted nationwide legal and ethical debate was that of a young Catholic named Karen Ann Quinlan (1954–1985). On April 14, 1975, Karen lapsed into an irreversible coma after taking a combination of tranquilizers and alcohol. The lower court in New Jersey refused to give her parents permission to remove her respirator. This decision was later reversed by the Supreme Court. With the support of their local pastor, Karen's parents had the respirator removed. To everyone's surprise, Karen continued breathing on her own. For nine more years, she was kept alive on antibiotics and high-nutrient feedings through a tube. Her father visited her daily; her mother visited two or three times a week. When Karen finally died of pneumonia, she weighed only sixty pounds.[4]

---

3. A 1991 Illinois study showed that elderly suicide victims seldom took their own lives because they were desperately ill, broke, or isolated. Only 13 percent of a group of fifty-four elderly suicide victims had fatal diseases, and only 24 percent had chronic diseases. Instead, the vast majority had mental health problems. Sixty-five percent were depressed, and 19 percent were alcoholics.
4. You can find more information about Karen Ann Quinlan in the book *Karen Ann* or the TV movie *In the Matter of Karen Ann Quinlan*.

In Karen's case, a distinction was made between the respirator (extraordinary means) and assisted nutrition and hydration (an ordinary form of health care). In the years following Karen's death, families involved in similar situations have taken a closer look at the definition of "extraordinary." When a patient is unconscious, seriously ill and/or dying, food and water must be provided with the assistance of some form of medical technology, such as intravenous lines, a nasogastric tube (a tube inserted through the nose to the stomach), or a gastrostomic tube (a tube inserted directly into the stomach). Is such assisted nutrition and hydration considered "normal," or is it an "extra-ordinary" means of keeping someone alive? In other words, is it ever moral to withhold or withdraw food and water from a patient?

This ethical issue was raised in the case of Nancy Cruzan (1957–1990), a young woman from Missouri. On January 11, 1983, she was injured in a car crash that left her with irreversible brain damage. For eight years, she lay in a coma in a hospital. The hospital refused to let the family stop life-sustaining treatment without court approval. In June, 1990, the United States Supreme Court upheld the Missouri court's insistence that the state had the right to require Nancy's family to produce "clear and compelling evidence" that she would not want to continue treatment. After the family did this, a Missouri judge allowed doctors to remove Nancy's feeding tube. She died December 26, twelve days later.

Was the removal of the feeding tube moral or immoral? The answer is not clear. The Missouri bishops issued a statement about Nancy's death, in which they said the following:

> *The moral theology of the Catholic Church on this question is based on some careful distinctions. On the one hand, we believe that no person has the right to directly take his or her own life or to take the life of another innocent person. On the other hand, in the light of modern medical technology, it is not always necessary to use every possible measure to prolong life indefinitely. Pope Pius XII has taught in the name of the church that "extraordinary means" need not be taken to prolong life when such means offer no real benefit and when such extraordinary means are onerous to the patient or even to others (for example, the family).[5]*

---

5. The Missouri Bishops, "Statement on Ending Nancy Cruzan's Nutrition and Hydration," *Origins* Vol. 20: No. 31, January 10, 1991, p. 495.

The bishops' statement could be interpreted to mean that they considered assisted nutrition and hydration as extraordinary means in Nancy's case. They stated that the decision about cases such as hers should be made in light of moral principles and "should be taken with great deliberation."

Bishop James McHugh of Camden, New Jersey, on the other hand, offers very specific guidelines in dealing with the termination of food and water to different types of patients. His guidelines are as follows:

1. Unconscious, Imminently Dying Patient (i.e., progressive and rapid deterioration): The dying process has begun and cannot be reversed. Nutrition and hydration are now useless and, all things considered, no longer a reasonable burden.

2. Conscious, Imminently Dying Patient: Nutrition and hydration are useless, possibly burdensome and need not be artificially provided but may be if desired by the patient.

3. Conscious, Irreversibly Ill, Not Imminently Dying Patient (the person is conscious, beyond cure or reversal of the disease, but able to function to some degree): Nutrition and hydration sustain life, so they are not useless; and usually they are not unreasonably burdensome. Nutrition and hydration should be provided unless or until there is clear evidence that provision constitutes an unreasonable burden for the patient.

4. Unconscious, Non-Dying Patient: Nutrition and hydration should be supplied. Feeding is not useless because it sustains a human life. . . . Withdrawal of nutrition/hydration brings about death by starvation/dehydration . . . and is not morally justifiable.[6]

As you can see, the moral dilemmas surrounding the right to die are complicated. Undoubtedly, the Church will continue to issue statements on the subject as further reflection occurs and future situations arise. Regardless of that reflection on the specifics of these situations, however, the Church's stance will always reflect a recognition of the sanctity of life and the belief that the life of a person who is physically or mentally diabled is no less important than that of a person without such a disability.

---

6. Bishop James McHugh, "Principles in regard to Withholding or Withdrawing Artificially Assisted Nutrition/Hydration," *Origins* Vol. 19: No. 19, October 12, 1989.

Church doctrine and bioethics

One of the functions of the magisterium is to guide Catholics in matters of Christian morality. The magisterium does this by issuing periodic statements about principles and about specific topics. On the next two pages, you will find excerpts from official Church documents that deal with the issues of abortion, infanticide, euthanasia, and the use of extraordinary means.

Abortion

The direct interruption of the generative process already begun, and, above all, directly willed and procured abortion, even if for therapeutic reasons, are to be absolutely excluded as licit means of regulating birth.[7]

From the time that the ovum is fertilized, a new life is begun which is neither that of the father nor of the mother; it is rather the life of a new human being with his or her own growth. . . . Right from fertilization is begun the adventure of a human life, and each of its great capacities requires time . . . to find its place and to be in a position to act.[8]

Followers of Christ are obliged not only to be personally opposed to abortion, but to seek to remove circumstances which influence some to turn to abortion as a solution to their problems, and also to work for the restoration of a climate of opinion and a legal order which respect the value of unborn human life.[9]

Respect and reverence for human life arise from the dignity of the human person made in God's image and likeness. Life is a precious gift from the creator. Through its laws and institutions, society must respect the life of every human being from conception to natural death. Direct attacks on human life—such as abortion, infanticide, euthanasia, and certain forms of fetal experimentation (cf. Declaration on Procured Abortion, Sacred Congregation for the Doctrine of the Faith, 1974*)—are gravely immoral.*[10]

Infanticide

For God, the Lord of life, has conferred on humans the surpassing ministry of safeguarding life—a ministry which must be fulfilled in a

---

7. "On the Regulation of Birth," #14 (also known as *Humanae Vitae*) encyclical letter of Pope Paul VI, in 1968.

8. "Declaration on Procured Abortion," #s12–13, issued by the Sacred Congregation for the Doctrine of the Faith, in 1974.

9. *Sharing the Light of Faith: National Catechetical Directory for Catholics of the United States,* #105b, issued by the U.S. Catholic Conference, in 1979.

10. *Ibid.,* #167.

worthy manner. Therefore from the moment of its conception life must be guarded with the greatest care, while abortion and infanticide are unspeakable crimes.[11]

Every human being is of priceless value: made in God's image, redeemed by Christ, and called to an eternal destiny.[12]

The child has the right to be conceived, carried in the womb, brought into the world and brought up within marriage: It is through the secure and recognized relationship to their own parents that children can discover their own identity and achieve their own proper human development.[13]

Euthanasia

Nothing and no one can in any way permit the killing of an innocent human being, whether a fetus or an embryo, an infant or an adult, an old person, or one suffering from an incurable disease, or a person who is dying. Furthermore, no one is permitted to ask for this act of killing, either for himself or herself or for another person entrusted to his or her care, nor can he or she consent to it, either explicitly or implicitly.[14]

Extraordinary Means

While euthanasia or direct killing is gravely wrong, it does not follow that there is an obligation to prolong the life of a dying person by extraordinary means. At times the effort to do so is of no help to the dying and may even be contrary to the compassion due them. People have a right to refuse treatment which offers no reasonable hope of recovery and imposes excessive burdens on them and perhaps also their families. At times it may even be morally imperative to discontinue particular medical treatments in order to give the dying the personal care and attention they really need as life ebbs.[15]

11. "Pastoral Constitution on the Church in the Modern World," #51, issued by the Bishops of Vatican II, in 1965.

12. *Sharing the Light of Faith,* #105b.

13. "Instruction on Respect for Life in Its Origin and on the Dignity of Procreation," #II:A1, issued by the Sacred Congregation for the Doctrine of the Faith, in 1987.

14. "Declaration on Euthanasia," #19, issued by the Sacred Congregation for the Doctrine of the Faith, in 1980.

15. "To Live in Christ Jesus: A Pastoral Reflection on the Moral Life," #58, issued by the National Conference of Catholic Bishops, in 1976.

A living will

Both the Karen Quinlan and the Nancy Cruzan cases made people aware of some of the moral and legal dilemmas that modern medicine and medical technology create. As a result of these cases, people began making what are now called living wills. In living wills, people make known their wishes about what medical or healthcare treatment they would or would not want if they came to be seriously ill.

A living will usually expresses the person's wish not to receive extraordinary means if he or she becomes mentally or physically disabled and there is no reasonable expectation of recovery. A living will may also state that the person is to be given medication to lessen pain, even if it hastens the moment of death. The purpose of the document is to ask that one's dying not be unreasonably prolonged.

As the courts hand down rulings in cases involving right-to-die issues, living wills are evolving.[16] This process is necessary so that living wills can stand up in court should they be put to the test in a particular case. This refinement process has created not only better living wills, but a second document known as a durable power of attorney for healthcare. Both documents come under what are called advance directives for healthcare.

Advance directives for healthcare

Both a living will and a durable power of attorney for healthcare ensure that a patient's wishes about medical treatment will still be carried out even if he or she can no longer communicate what those wishes are. A living will usually applies to the case of a person who has a terminal condition that will result in death within a short time. Depending on the state in which a person lives, a living will may also cover the case of a person in a persistent vegetative state. On the other hand, a durable power of attorney for healthcare addresses any situation where medical or healthcare treatment is needed and the person cannot speak for himself or herself.

While a living will expresses a person's wishes, it does not name anyone to see that those wishes are carried out. In addition, a living will may be too general to speak to every situation that may arise in a given case. Thus, problems can arise. For example, whose wishes does a doctor honor if a patient's family is not in agreement about what is to be done? Furthermore, there is the question of whether the doctor may

---

16. In 1991, thirty-four states and the District of Columbia recognized living wills as legal documents.

legally honor the wishes of any family member. A durable power of attorney for healthcare, however, takes care of the shortcomings in a living will. It legally authorizes someone by name (the agent) to make medical or healthcare treatment decisions for another. Thus, the decisions of the agent have the same legal force as if it were the patient speaking on his or her own behalf.

On December 1, 1991, a federal law known as the *Patient Self-Determination Act* went into effect in the United States. Under this law, any adult who is admitted to a hospital, nursing home, or healthcare program is to be asked if he or she has any advance directives for healthcare. The response is to be noted on his or her records. The *Patient Self-Determination Act* also mandates that a patient be given written information concerning his or her rights under state law to make decisions about treatment options. A patient must also be told about a program's or healthcare facility's policy in matters of advance directives.

If and when the time comes that you execute an advance directive for healthcare, be sure to do the following:

1. Discuss it with your physician and your family members.
2. Place a copy in your medical records.
3. Give copies to family members, close friends, and neighbors.
4. Keep a reduced-size copy in a purse or wallet.
5. In the case of a durable power of attorney, give a copy to the agent and the alternate agent, if you have named one.

Taking these actions now can save your family a lot of anguish should you become unconscious or seriously ill. They can also ensure that your wishes are carried out.

For your journal

1. Do you want a living will? Why or why not?
2. Who would you name now as the agent of your durable power of attorney? alternate agent? Why would you choose these people?

Discussion questions

1. Why do some people think that state or federal money should be used to fund abortions?
2. What can Catholic parishes and high schools do to support women who are pregnant?

3. How do your elected officials (senators, congresspersons, governor, mayor) stand on abortion?

4. What is your diocese doing to support women who are pregnant?

5. Do you consider direct or assisted euthanasia to be humane or to be dehumanizing (like shooting a lame horse or putting a rabid dog to sleep)?

6. Do you think there should be a federal law regarding euthanasia that applies to all the states?

7. Why do some people think that a person has a right to choose when he or she will die? Why does the Church say that this decision rightfully belongs to God?

8. What is the difference between euthanasia and stopping the use of extraordinary means to keep alive a patient who is hopelessly ill?

9. A fair number of people *do* recover from a coma. How should this affect one's attitude toward withdrawing food and water from people who are comatose?

10. What are the reasons the Church gives for saying that abortion is wrong?

11. What are some ways in your community that Catholics can "seek to remove circumstances which influence some to turn to abortion as a solution to their problems, and also to work for the restoration of a climate of opinion and a legal order which respect the value of unborn human life"?

12. Why is the Church opposed to infanticide?

13. What is the underlying moral principle of the Church's stance on euthanasia?

14 Violence: A Way to Live, A Way to Die

No place is safe

Violence is fast becoming an American way of life and death. It seems that no place is safe from, or immune to, violence. Consider the following story, found in the *San Francisco Chronicle* on May 31, 1991.

> A bloody gunfight erupted during a "quiet hour" at an Oakland mortuary Wednesday night when a teenage widow pulled a pistol and opened fire on some of her late husband's friends after they ripped up a photo of the couple that had been placed atop the casket, police said yesterday.
>
> When the furious widow, Delicia Hodges Hines, 18, started shooting, several of the mourners drew their own pistols and returned fire, investigators said.
>
> After the melee, Hines, a 5-year-old girl and another bystander were rushed to a hospital with injuries. The widow and two gunslinging mourners were arrested.
>
> The gunplay occurred at about 8 P.M. at the C. P. Bannon Mortuary, located in the heart of an East Oakland area notorious for drug-dealing, where mourners had gathered to remember Derlin Hines.
>
> Hines, who police say was a drug dealer, was shot to death last week during an argument with his wife's brother, 19-year-old Dale Hodges, who remains in jail on suspicion of murder. . . .
>
> Police officers said Delicia Hines went into a rage after some of her husband's associates grabbed a photo of the couple and ripped her image out of the picture.
>
> Lieutenant Mike Sims of the Oakland Police Department said Mrs. Hines went outside, got a gun, then ran back into the chapel and tried to shoot the people who tore up the picture.
>
> "All hell broke loose," Sims said. . . . "People saw her with a handgun, and everyone started to run. It was a general panic."[1]

---

1. Peter Fimrite, "Gunbattle Shatters 'Quiet Hour' at Mortuary," *San Francisco Chronicle*, May 31, 1991, p. A 17.

Unfortunately, the gunfight just described is not that unusual in certain parts of the United States. As a 1991 national survey revealed, 14 percent of all Americans carry a pistol with them or in their car.[2] More and more teenagers are bringing guns, knives, and other weapons with them to school. Violent crimes, especially homicides committed by strangers, relatives, and gang members, are on the upswing.

Is violence inherent in human nature, or is it something we teach our children? Just view the cartoons found on Saturday morning TV and decide for yourself. Everywhere you turn, violence seems to be an integral part of our social network. Such violence is a far cry from the gospel message of peace and "turning the other cheek" (cf. Matthew 5:39).

In this chapter, you will explore four different expressions of violence—warfare (conventional and nuclear), the Holocaust, capital punishment, and domestic violence. You will read sections of specific Church documents that call us, in contrast, to be peacemakers. Finally, you will explore the existence of violence in your own life and discover ways that you can live as a peacemaker.

War

Since the beginning of time, human beings have fought and killed one another. The first weapons of war were stone axes, spears, maces, wooden clubs, and flint daggers. In later ages, weapons were made of iron and bronze. People banded together in cities and built high walls around themselves as protection against enemies. By the time of the ancient Greeks and Romans, war technology included helmets, shields, body armor, chariots, and horses. In the fourth century B.C., the Persians used elephants in war. In 218 B.C., Hannibal's army also used elephants to cross the Alps into Italy.

Throughout the Hebrew Scriptures, the Israelites waged many battles in the name of Yahweh. Before the building of the Temple, the Israelites took the ark of the covenant with them into battle, as a sign of God's presence. Salvation did not mean everlasting life in heaven, but victory over one's enemies. God himself was the shield that delivered the Israelites from their enemies. Victory was a sign of faithfulness to the covenant; defeat (such as when the Babylonians

---

2. The 1991 national survey was published in a book entitled *The Day America Told the Truth: What People Really Believe about Everything That Matters.* In the survey, 7 percent of the people said they would kill a stranger for ten million dollars.

captured most of the Israelite survivors and held them in Babylon) was a sign of punishment for sinning against the covenant.

The technology of conventional warfare changed significantly with the invention of gunpowder by the Chinese in the ninth century. Eventually the battlefield became the scene of cannons, pistols, muzzle-loaders, and other forms of artillery. But even these weapons seem primitive when compared to those used in the 1991 Persian Gulf Conflict: Scud missiles, Patriot antimissiles, F-14 Tomcat bombers, A-10 Thunderbolts and Warthogs, computerized "smart" bombs, Tomahawk cruise missiles, and spy satellites.

Indeed, present-day warfare involves a sophisticated death machine that knows no comparison. In addition to automatic weapons, grenade launchers, amphibious vehicles, and submarines, there has been the development of chemical, biological, and nuclear warfare. Because of modern communications satellites and the "first-strike" capacity of several nations, regional wars can quickly escalate to worldwide dimensions. The nuclear arsenals of a few countries now have the capacity to destroy all life on earth many times over.

The killing force of nuclear weapons is derived from either fission (the breaking apart of atomic particles) or fusion (the combining of hydrogen atoms to form helium). Fusion weapons are also called thermonuclear weapons. One type of fusion weapon, the neutron bomb, can kill people while doing only limited damage to buildings. In addition to the destruction caused by the initial blast, nuclear explosions produce blinding light, searing heat, and lethal radiation ("fallout") that may persist in the air, ground, and water for hundreds or thousands of years.

The devastating capacity of nuclear weapons was seen on August 6, 1945, when the United States Army Air Forces dropped an atomic bomb on Hiroshima, Japan. Most of the city was destroyed, and seventy to eighty thousand people were killed. Thousands more died in subsequent years due to radiation poisoning. Today Hiroshima is a spiritual center of the peace movement for the banning of atomic weapons. Peace Memorial Park contains a museum and monument dedicated to those who died in the atomic explosion.

The United States dropped a second atomic bomb on Nagasaki, Japan, on August 9, 1945. It killed thirty-nine thousand people outright and injured about twenty-five thousand more. About 40 percent of the city's buildings were completely destroyed. Today Nagasaki, like Hiroshima, is a spiritual center for movements to ban nuclear weapons.

The first atomic bombs were large. Today's nuclear devices can fit inside missiles and artillery shells. The development of computerized missile-guidance systems has made multiple nuclear warheads possible on intercontinental ballistic missiles, with each warhead being able to strike a different target. If such weapons are ever used in large numbers, scientists suspect that the earth would enter into a long-term nuclear winter. It is theorized that conditions of semidarkness, killing frosts, and subfreezing temperatures, combined with high radiation, would destroy most animal and plant life. Humans would die in large numbers, due to starvation, exposure, and disease.

Fear of worldwide death caused by a nuclear war has prompted international arms control, disarmament, and arms limitation agreements. In 1963, the Soviet Union, United Kingdom, and United States signed a Nuclear Test-Ban Treaty that banned tests of nuclear weapons in the atmosphere, outer space, and underwater. This treaty was subsequently signed by 120 countries. In 1968, the Nuclear Non-Proliferation Treaty, which was signed by 140 countries, sought to reduce chemical, biological, and nuclear weapons. The 1972 Strategic Arms Limitation Talk I (SALT) between the United States and the Soviet Union limited both the size of nuclear arsenals and the development of more advanced strategic weapons. In the 1987 Intermediate Range Nuclear Forces Treaty, the United States and the Soviet Union agreed to eliminate medium-range, land-based missiles.

Christian ethics and warfare

Two moral positions regarding war exist within the Church. The first position, known as pacifism, interprets the gospel as forbidding all use of violence. The second position, known as the just-war theory, acknowledges some legitimate use of force. To understand these two positions, it is important to consider them separately.

Pacifism

A pacifist is someone who refuses to bear arms or to use force as a means of settling disputes. This refusal is usually based on religious beliefs. Many pacifists, for example, cite biblical passages to support their position. The Messiah shall be the Prince of Peace (cf. Isaiah 9:4). In the kingdom of God, all nations will live in peace.

They shall beat their swords into plowshares
and their spears into pruning hooks;
One nation shall not raise the sword against another,
nor shall they train for war again.

—Isaiah 2:4

As followers of Jesus, we are to turn the other cheek, love our enemies, and pray for those who persecute us (cf. Matthew 5:38–48). "For all who take the sword will perish by the sword" (Matthew 26:52). We are called to live as peacemakers. (cf. Matthew 5:9).

During the Civil War, members of the Society of Friends absolutely refused to bear arms because they believed that God forbids warfare and military service. As a result, laws were passed that exempted Quakers, Mennonites, and others who were conscientious objectors from military service. Since the Civil War, there have been some pacifists who objected to each war that was occurred. Some gave alternative nonviolent service; some went to jail. These pacifists raised national consciousness during the Vietnam War. Many of them burned their draft cards and moved to Canada. Many stopped protesting the war when the draft was stopped.

In 1948, an international group of Catholics known as *Pax Christi* was founded to work for disarmament, to educate people for peace, and to provide alternatives to violence. There are over nine thousand members of *Pax Christi* in the United States today.

Just-war theory

Other Catholics in today's world espouse what is known as the just-war theory. This theory says that war may be waged by Christians if it is a just war. In order to be considered just, the war must meet the following six criteria:

- It must be waged for a just cause. (To liberate an occupied country is a just cause. To invade a country for its oil is not a just cause.)
- It must be declared by the proper authority. (In the United States, the president is the commander-in-chief of the armed forces; Congress alone can declare war.)
- It must be waged for a right intention. (For example, freedom rather than personal gain.)
- It must be a last resort. (All peaceful means to resolve the conflict must have been tried.)
- It must have a likely outcome of success. (It is not moral to risk the lives of soldiers if you can't possibly win.)
- Proportional means must be used. (No more force than is necessary may be used. According to Catholic teaching, the use of nuclear weapons is immoral and may not be permitted.)

Using this theory, some Christians become selective conscientious objectors (COs). They are not opposed to war in general, but they oppose a specific war because it is not just. One example of a selective CO was Franz Jaegerstaetter, a Catholic peasant in Austria. On August 9, 1943, he was beheaded in Berlin because he refused to serve in what he was convinced was an unjust war being waged by an immoral regime.

Once a "just" war has been entered, the countries involved are expected to follow a set of moral principles known as the Geneva Conventions. These international treaties between 1864 and 1949 call for the protection of civilians during war and for humanitarian treatment of prisoners of war (POWs). Specifically, the Conventions say that all Red Cross establishments and personnel are to be immune from attack and capture. All wounded combatants are to receive impartial reception and treatment. No physical or mental torture or other means of coercion can be used on POWs. Civilian targets cannot be deliberately bombed or attacked.

The Holocaust

One of the reasons the Geneva Conventions are considered so important today is that they are precautions against a repeat of the overwhelming atrocities that were committed during World War II. Underlying World War II was another type of war, too horrible to imagine. This second war, known as the Holocaust, consisted of twelve years of Nazi persecution of Jews and other minorities. The purpose of this war was the "Final Solution," or genocide of all Jews in Europe.

The Holocaust began in 1933, shortly after Adolf Hitler became chancellor of Germany. It started with a national boycott of Jewish businesses and with government-sponsored vandalism of Jewish property. Next, Jews were fired from government, legal, and university positions. Under the Nurmberg laws of 1935, German Jews lost their citizenship and were forbidden to intermarry with other Germans. In 1938, almost every synagogue in Germany was destroyed. Jews could no longer attend public schools, own businesses or land, or go to museums. By 1941, all Jews were required to wear the yellow Star of David badge.

When the German armies invaded Poland, Russia, and the Baltic states, SS death squads rounded up the Jews, shot them, and buried them in mass graves. In 1942, fifteen leading Nazi bureaucrats inaugurated the "Final Solution." This meant transporting Jews in crowded railroad cars to distant concentration camps, where they would be either exterminated at once or worked to death. Gas chambers disguised as showers were the most frequent method of extermination. The naked corpses were then incinerated in adjacent crematoriums.

Four million Jews died in this way in the death camps of Ausch-witz, Mejdanek, Treblinka, Chelmno, Dachau, Buchenwald, Sobi-bor, and Belzec. About two million additional Jews were killed by the Nazis in other ways. By the end of World War II, the Nazis had succeeded in killing approximately 72 percent of the Jewish popu-lation in Europe.

The world reacted with shock and repugnance when it discov-ered what had happened. Since that time, the Catholic Church and other Christian Churches have banded with Jewish groups to make sure the Holocaust never happens again. Each year, *Yom HaShoah*, Holocaust Memorial Day, is observed April 19 or 20. Increasingly, people are observing this day with Christian-Jewish memorial services.

Capital punishment

Another type of violence that ends in homicide is capital punish-ment. Capital punishment is based on a sense of justice that says, "an eye for an eye, a life for a life." The criminal must "pay" for his or her crime. Formerly in history, a person could be put to death for committing a wide range of crimes. As John 8:1–11 tells us, women in the time of Jesus could be stoned to death according to Jewish law for committing adultery. (Roman law did not permit the Jews actually to carry this out.) According to Roman law, non-Romans and slaves could be crucified for committing such crimes as murder, robbery, piracy, treason, and rebellion.

In colonial America, a person suspected (not necessarily convicted) of arson could be burned at the stake. Couples caught in adultery could be hanged. Men or women suspected of witchcraft could also be burned or hanged. In eighteenth century England, several hundred different offenses could warrant the death penalty. Enlightenment writers of the eighteenth century brought about many reforms in the way criminals were punished. Limits were placed also on the number and type of crime that might merit the death penalty.

In its 1972 *Furman v. Georgia* decision, the United States Supreme Court ruled that capital punishment as it was then practiced in Georgia and other states violated the Eighth Amendment because it was cruel and unusual punishment. In 1976, however, the Supreme Court upheld the constitutionality of revised state laws calling for capital punishment. Some states now have the death penalty; others do not.

Are there crimes so horrible that the death penalty is warranted? And if so, should television cameras be allowed to broadcast the death?

These are heated questions being asked by more and more people. The debate over capital punishment deals with four important values: respect for the sanctity of human life, the protection of human life, the preservation of order in society, and the achievement of justice through law. The people who cite these values to argue against capital punishment are called abolitionists. Among such people are the United States bishops. People who use these same values to support capital punishment are called retributionists. A summary of both positions follows.

Arguments for Capital Punishment

1. Capital punishment acts as a deterrent to crime. If a person is sentenced to life in prison, he or she has nothing to lose by committing additional crimes. No further punishment can be given. But if the person knows that he or she could get the death penalty, the person may not commit the crime.

2. Most capital crime offenders are beyond reform or rehabilitation. If they should escape, be pardoned, or be paroled, the community would be at risk.

3. Justice calls for punishment or retribution in order to restore the order that has been violated by the criminal. Murder requires a like punishment.

4. The jail system is already too crowded. The cost of maintaining a murderer runs into the thousands of dollars each year.

Arguments against Capital Punishment

1. Capital punishment does prevent a criminal from committing any more crimes. But it does not necessarily deter a criminal from committing a capital crime, nor does it deter other criminals.

2. It is never too late for God's grace to touch and transform hearts. It is possible for even the worst criminal to reform and to be rehabilitated. Capital punishment deprives a criminal of further time in which to reform.

3. Justice may not be served by capital punishment. An innocent person may be executed. (During the twentieth century, eight innocent men in the United States were executed.) An execution, once it has occurred, cannot be revoked. Furthermore, the death penalty is socially discriminating. It is applied much more often to the poor, who cannot afford lawyers and appeals.

4. Every human life (even that of a criminal) has unique worth and dignity. Respect for life is more important than money. The fifth commandment tells us that it is wrong to kill another human being. People should not become killers in order to punish a murderer. Executions are cruel and unusual punishment.

Domestic violence

Domestic violence refers to the violence that takes place in a wide range of family and other intimate relations (siblings, parent-child, other relatives, married and unmarried partnerships, terminated partnerships, and the abuse of elderly parents by their adult children). The violence itself may involve physical contact between persons, use of a weapon, a threat with a weapon, explicit verbal threat of bodily harm, and other actions causing mental or psychological harm. All too often such violence ends in death. Among the fatal crimes associated with domestic violence are fratricide, matricide, parricide, patricide, sororicide, and uxoricide.

In 1974, the first shelter for battered women was opened near London. During the next ten years, five hundred shelters for battered women were established in the United States. In 1990, the Journal of American Medicine reported that intimate violence was the leading cause of injuries to women. More women were battered that year than the total number of women involved in car crashes, rapes, and muggings. A 1984 Atlanta report on fatal domestic violence showed that 52 percent of the victims were women and 74 percent of the perpetrators were male.

Other studies in the United States have shown that marital violence occurs in one out of four marriages. One million children are physically abused by parents or caretakers every year. And one million elderly people are abused every year by their adult children. From these statistics, it is clear that domestic violence is commonplace, and that the perpetrators and victims of such violence are ordinary people.

The Judeo-Christian ethic of peace contrasts strongly with such violence. "I will establish peace in the land, that you may lie down to rest without anxiety" (Leviticus 26:6). The importance of loving and trusting family relationships is also clear. "Your wife shall be like a fruitful vine in the recesses of your home; your children like olive plants around your table" (Psalm 128:3). "Christ's peace must reign in your hearts, since as members of the one body you have been called to that peace" (Colossians 3:15).

In 1980, the World Synod of Bishops emphasized the love and caring that are to characterize Christian families. Such family love finds its roots in the Sacrament of Marriage and is strengthened by the Eucharist, by shared prayer, and by the support of the Christian community. For these reasons, the bishops deepened their commitment to family ministry.

The Church's stance

Here are some excerpts from official Church documents relating to the types of violence discussed in this chapter.

War

Preventing nuclear war is a moral imperative.[3]

Under no circumstances may nuclear weapons or other instruments of mass slaughter be used for the purpose of destroying population centers or other predominantly civilian targets.[4]

Peace cannot be limited to a mere absence of war, the result of an ever precarious balance of forces. No, peace is something built up day after day, in the pursuit of an order intended by God, which implies a more perfect form of justice among men and women.[5]

The Holocaust

Furthermore, whatever is opposed to life itself, such as . . . genocide, . . . whatever violates the integrity of the human person, . . . whatever insults human dignity, . . . all these things and others of their like are infamies indeed. They poison human society, but they do more harm to those who practice them than those who suffer from the injury. Moreover, they are a supreme dishonor to the Creator.[6]

The Church repudiates all persecutions against any (hu)man. Moreover, mindful of her common patrimony with the Jews, and motivated by the Gospel's spiritual love and by no political considerations, she deplores the hatred, persecutions, and displays of anti-Semitism directed against the Jews at any time and from any source.[7]

(The Holocaust) will forever remain a shame for humanity. . . . Once again I issue an appeal to all people, inviting them to overcome their prejudices and to combat every form of racism by agreeing to recognize the fundamental dignity and the goodness that dwell within every human being and to be ever more conscious that they belong to a single human family, willed and gathered together by God.[8]

---

3. "The Challenge of Peace: God's Promise and Our Response," #234, issued by the National Conference of Catholic Bishops, in 1983.

4. *Ibid.*, #147.

5. "The Development of Peoples," #76, an encyclical letter of Pope Paul VI, in 1976.

6. "Constitution on the Church in the Modern World," #27, issued by the Bishops of Vatican II, in 1965.

7. "Declaration on the Relationship of the Church to Non-Christian Religions," #4, issued by the Bishops of Vatican II, in 1965.

8. "The Fiftieth Anniversary of World War II," #5, an apostolic letter of Pope John Paul II, in 1989.

Capital Punishment

We believe that in the conditions of contemporary American society, the legitimate purposes of punishment do not justify the imposition of the death penalty. Furthermore, we believe that there are serious considerations which should prompt Christians and all Americans to support the abolition of capital punishment.[9]

Abolition sends a message that we can break the cycle of violence, that we need not take life for life, that we can envisage more humane and more hopeful and effective responses to the growth of violent crime.[10]

Abolition of capital punishment is also a manifestation of our belief in the unique worth and dignity of each person from the moment of conception, a creature made in the image and likeness of God.[11]

Domestic Violence

We must have a coherent national firearms policy responsible to the overall public interest and respectful of the rights and privileges of all Americans. The unlimited freedom to possess and use handguns must give way to the rights of all people to safety and protection against those who misuse these weapons.[12]

The love between husband and wife and, in a derivatory and broader way, the love between members of the same family—between parents and children, brothers and sisters and relatives and members of the household—is given life and sustenance by an unceasing inner dynamism leading the family to ever deeper and more intense communion, which is the foundation and soul of the community of marriage and the family.[13]

Another task for the family is to form persons in love and also to practice love in all its relationships. . . .[14]

---

9. "Statement on Capital Punishment," #9, issued by the U.S. Bishops, in 1980.
10. *Ibid.*, #10.
11. *Ibid.*, #11.
12. "Handgun Violence: A Threat to Life," #8, issued by the U.S. Catholic Conference and the Committee on Social Development and World Peace, in 1975.
13. "The Apostolic Exhortation on the Family," #18, issued by Pope John Paul II, in 1981.
14. "A Message to Christian Families in the Modern World," #12, issued by the World Synod of Bishops, in 1980.

Being a peacemaker

Christian peacemaking has three dimensions: The recognition of violence, the avoidance of violence, and the day-by-day working at peace. To help you grow as a peacemaker, complete the following two exercises.

Use the questions on this page to reflect on the presence of and the potential for violence in your own life. Choose a quiet spot away from others while you do your reflecting.

Violence questionnaire

1. What percentage of the TV programs you like to watch are violent?
2. On a scale of 1 to 10, how often do you get angry?
3. Do you act in nonviolent or violent ways when you get angry?
4. Have you ever felt so angry that you wanted to kill someone?
5. On a scale of 1 to 10, how peaceful was/is the relationship between your parents?
6. Did one or both of your parents ever abuse you physically?
7. Has anyone ever threatened to cause you physical harm?
8. Have you ever threatened to harm a spouse or a child?
9. Have you ever hit a spouse or a child?
10. Have you ever threatened to harm someone else?
11. Has anyone ever hit you?
12. Have you ever tried to get revenge after a relationship has broken up?
13. Do you or any member of your family belong to "the mob" or to a gang?
14. Do you or other family members have access to guns or other weapons?

Now, in your journal, identify specific ways that you can build community and eliminate hostility in the following relationships: parents; siblings; children; other relatives; spouse; friends; neighbors; coworkers.

For your journal

1. As a child, did you ever play war games, or did you ever play with toy guns, tanks, and so forth.? How do you think such toys (or lack of them) affected your attitudes toward war and violence?
2. Would you be willing to give up your life for your country? Why or why not?
3. Would you ever march in a peace protest or take part in a peaceful demonstration? Why or why not?
4. What are your views on capital punishment? What has shaped those views?

Discussion questions

1. Why do you think so many people in our society own and carry guns?
2. Do you think people are naturally violent or do we learn violence?
3. Do you find the violence in TV shows and movies to be entertaining? Why or why not?
4. Why do some teenagers and young adults join gangs? What are the reasons gang members seek to kill one another?
5. Benjamin Franklin once said: "There never was a good war nor a bad peace." Do you agree or disagree? In other words, do you think war is ever justified?
6. Do you think pacifists truly object to war, or are they just cowards?
7. Review what you learned about Jewish burial customs and beliefs. Then discuss how the Nazi death camps violated not only the Jews' physical rights, but their spiritual beliefs as well.
8. In 1991, KQED television station in San Francisco applied to the United States District Court for permission to televise the execution of criminals in the gas chamber. Debate whether such permission should be granted. Also debate what effect you think televised executions would have on people's opinions about the death penalty.
9. Does your state have a death penalty? If so, for what crimes is it given? How are the criminals executed? Do you think your state's law should be changed?

10. What do you think are some of the factors that might contribute to domestic violence?

11. Discuss how each of the following can help families grow in love: the Sacrament of Marriage, the Eucharist, shared prayer, the Christian community.

12. Debate whether all people should have access to firearms.

13. Brainstorm about just punishments for crimes and effective ways to rehabilitate criminals.

14. Why do you think many victims of family violence never tell anyone?

Part Eight: Religious Aspects

I am the resurrection and the life; those who believe in me, though they should die, will come to life; and those who are alive and believe in me will never die.

—*John 11:25–26*

15 Life Everlasting

Close encounters

Here are some stories of people who have had close encounters with death or a premonition of some type of afterlife. After reading each story, tell whether you have had any similar experiences.

• Daniel started reading a book on English knights, because he had always been fascinated by that period in history. Before long, he realized that what he was reading seemed very familiar. It wasn't that he had read about the same thing before; it was more like he had actually been there as a knight himself. The more Daniel read, the more he felt that he had stumbled onto a former identity, someone he might have been in a past life.

• Carol, who had just gotten off work, got into her car to begin the long commute home. Along the way, she began daydreaming. All of a sudden, she found her car in the path of an oncoming semi. In the panic that engulfed her, Carol felt that she entered a different time zone. Every minute was an hour; every action was in slow motion. As the truck rushed closer, Carol saw her whole life flash before her. Then, at the last minute, the semi swerved and missed the car. Carol was safe, but she never forgot her experience.

• José accidentally hit his head on a rock after diving into the lake. The next thing he knew, he was out of his body, watching his friends try to rescue him. José continued to watch as the paramedics came. Then he saw his dead father, beckoning him toward a brightly lit tunnel. José was filled with warm and loving feelings, and was just about to enter the tunnel when he was jerked back into his body. José opened his eyes and found himself staring up at the face of a paramedic. He felt glad to be alive, but angry too. The world of his father seemed so appealing that he hadn't wanted to come back.

Almost everyone has had some type of deja vu experience, the sensation of being in a place or situation before. Some people, such as the Hindus and Buddhists, believe that such experiences are proof that life continues on after death and are evidence of reincarnation. Some people say such experiences can be explained as being caused by the time gap between the moment we first "see" an event and the moment it is fully processed by the mind or brain. (We have seen it "before"!) Other people are not quite sure what to think of these experiences.

In the early 1970s, Dr. Raymond Moody interviewed over one hundred people who had near-death experiences, who were "clinically dead" but then revived. His findings, which were recorded in the book *Life After Life*, included factors such as out-of-the body experiences, encounters with deceased loved ones, a light at the end of a tunnel, and overwhelming feelings of love and warmth. Most people said they didn't want to come back. All said they were no longer afraid of death.

Although Dr. Moody's findings do not prove the existence of life after death, they can be interpreted as pointing to it. Indeed, belief in some type of afterlife is widespread among almost all cultures throughout the world.

In this chapter, you will be studying a branch of theology known as eschatology. Eschatology deals with the "last things," which the Catholic Church defines as death, judgment, heaven, and hell. You will learn not only what the Church believes about each of these topics, you will also see how the Church celebrates its belief in an afterlife in the solemnities of the Ascension and the Assumption. Furthermore, you will reflect on how your own beliefs about the afterlife influence your motivation to live by gospel values.

Resurrection of the dead

Resurrection of the dead is one of the fundamental teachings of the Catholic Church (cf. Hebrews 6:2). This teaching is expressed in the Apostles' Creed with the words, "I believe in . . . the resurrection of the body and life everlasting," and in the Nicene Creed with the words, "We look for the resurrection of the dead, and the life of the world to come."

From the time of the Babylonian exile onward, the Jews used the phrase "resurrection of the dead" as a metaphor for the future restoration of Israel as a people. Isaiah's prophecy that "your dead shall live, their corpses shall rise" reflected a belief in Israel's corporate survival, rather than individual life after death (cf. Isaiah 26:19). So too, Ezekiel's vision of God bringing dry bones to life reflected Israel's hope for new life after the exile (cf. Ezekiel 37:1–14).

As you learned earlier in this book, Jewish belief in individual resurrection of the dead did not show itself until around the time of Jesus. According to the Gospels, the Pharisees believed in the resurrection, but the Sadducees did not. The Pharisees, however, were not united in their belief. Some believed that everyone would be raised after death. Others limited resurrection to Israelites; still others limited it to the just.

All three Synoptic Gospels record Jesus' views on the resurrection (cf. Matthew 22:23–33; Mark 12:18–27; Luke 20:27–40). Here is the account from Matthew:

> *On that day Sadducees . . . put this question to him, saying, ". . . Now there were seven brothers among us. The first married and died and, having no descendants, let his wife to his brother. The same happened with the second and the third, through all seven. Finally the woman died. Now at the resurrection, of the seven, whose wife will she be? For they all had been married to her." Jesus said to them in reply, ". . . At the resurrection they neither marry nor are given in marriage but are like the angels in heaven. . . . (God) is not the God of the dead but of the living."*

The passage makes two important points: (1) the whole person (body and soul) rises from the dead and is somehow recognizable as that same unique person, and (2) the resurrected person is somehow changed. He or she is a new being, a new creation, "like the angels in heaven."

These two beliefs about the resurrection are also found in the biblical accounts of the post-resurrection appearances of Jesus. The risen Jesus is recognizable by his disciples, and yet he is changed. He still eats and drinks, but can appear or disappear instantly.

Like Jesus, all believers will be raised up (cf. John 6:55). As St. Paul tells the Corinthians, how this will happen is not entirely clear. In answer to the questions, "How are the dead raised? With what kind of body will they come back?" Paul writes:

> *Behold, I tell you a mystery. We shall not all fall asleep, but we will all be changed, in an instant, in the blink of an eye, at the last trumpet. For the trumpet will sound, the dead will be raised incorruptible, and we shall be changed. For this which is corruptible must clothe itself with incorruptibility, and this which is mortal must clothe itself with immortality.*
>
> *—1 Corinthians 15:51–53*

When we are raised up, we will not merely survive death, but we will be changed radically.

In the early days of the Church when the Apostles' Creed was being formulated, the gnostics taught that only the soul lived on after death. The body, which was physical matter, was evil and therefore irredeemable. To counteract this belief, the wording of the Apostles' Creed clearly affirms belief in the resurrection of "the body" as well as the soul. The entire person lives on after death. All of God's creation—material and spiritual—is good. Likewise, all

people—both believers and unbelievers, the good and the bad—
pass through death to an afterlife.

Particular judgment

According to Catholic thought, passing through death to an
afterlife requires an intermediate step—that of particular judgment.
In this step, the person who has died is judged by God and then is
rewarded or punished accordingly.

Our present-day concept of particular judgment originated in
the Hebrew Scriptures.[1] In numerous instances, the judgment of
God is presented as merciful, righteous, and faithful to the covenant with Israel. God will not treat the innocent and the guilty
alike (cf. Genesis 18:25) because God is a God of justice and up-
rightness (cf. Jeremiah 9:23).

Unfortunately, the Israelites' conception of the justice of God
became tangled up with feelings of wrath and vindication against
their enemies. As the psalmist writes,

They shall be destroyed who seek my life,
they shall go into the depths of the earth;
They shall be delivered over to the sword,
and shall be the prey of jackals.
—*Psalm 63:10–11*

If God could destroy Israel's enemies, then it followed logically
that God's anger could also turn against Israel. Instead of loving
God, many of the Israelites lived in fear and dread that God would
judge them unfavorably.

It is interesting to note how the Gospels present Jesus' views of
God's judgment. On the one hand, Jesus upholds the image of God
as a just Judge who will separate the wheat from the chaff (cf.
Matthew 13:24–30), the goats from the sheep (cf. Matthew 25:31–
46), the just from the unjust (cf. Matthew 18:23–35), those who use
their talents wisely from those who waste their talents (cf. Matthew
25:14–30). And as Jesus tells us in the parable of Lazarus and the
rich man, God's judgment of us at death is permanent (cf. Luke
16:19–31). It cannot be changed.

---

1. Particular judgment after death is found outside the Christian tradition as
well. The Egyptian Book of the Dead shows an illustration in which a man is
weighed against a feather. The feather is a symbol of truth and freedom from the
burden of sin. As you have already learned, Muslims believe that immediately
after death, a person is judged by two angels named Munkar and Nakir.

On the other hand, Jesus adds two very important dimensions to the concept of personal judgment. First, Jesus tells us that God does not really judge us; instead, we judge ourselves. The punishment or reward we choose after death reflects a lifetime of other choices:

- how well we loved others (cf. Matthew 25:31–46)
- our sincerity in following God's Word (cf. Matthew 23:1–36)
- how we applied ourselves in building God's kingdom (cf. Luke 19:11–27)
- the strength of our belief in Jesus (cf. John 11:25).
- our willingness to forgive others (cf. Matthew 6:14–15)

The way God will judge us at death holds no surprises. In essence, what happens to us then is chosen by us long before we die.

Second, Jesus stresses the mercy of God rather than human justice. This concept of God's mercy is seen clearly in the parable of the laborers in the vineyard (cf. Matthew 20:1–16) and in the parable of the prodigal son (cf. Luke 15:11–32). Jesus himself expresses the mercy of God in his forgiveness of Peter (cf. John 21:15–19), his crucifiers (cf. Luke 23:34), the good thief (cf. Luke 23:39–43), and the woman caught in adultery (cf. John 8:1–11).

These two teachings of Jesus are seen in the Catholic belief about particular judgment after death. If we have lived according to the gospel and to the promptings of the Holy Spirit, then we will go to heaven, an afterlife of eternal bliss and happiness with God. If we have fallen short of our Christian commitment, but are still basically oriented toward the gospel message, then we will go to purgatory, a place of further purification before we enter heaven. If we have lived in sin and have chosen to reject the gospel, then we will go to hell, an afterlife of eternal suffering and separation from God.

Heaven

When the word *heaven* was first used by biblical writers, it referred to the skies above the earth. It was a definite place in the universe created by God (cf. Genesis 1:1). More important, it was the place where God lived (cf. Deuteronomy 26:15; Psalm 2:4). Because the number seven was important in Jewish numerology, some early Jewish writers referred to "the seven heavens." Being in "seventh heaven" was the highest possible degree of bliss. Later writers spoke of only three heavens; the last of these was God's dwelling. St. Paul alluded to the popular belief in three heavens (never formally adopted by the Church) when he wrote, "I know someone in Christ who, fourteen years ago (whether in the body or out of the body I do not know, God knows), was caught up to the third heaven" (2 Corinthians 12:2).

According to the biblical view of the universe, God rules all things from heaven, where he is surrounded by his heavenly court. The heavenly hosts are nine choirs of angels, each with different ranks and duties. From highest to lowest, these choirs are known as Seraphim (the closest angels to God), Cherubim (wise guardians and protectors), Thrones (who kneel in adoration before God's throne), Dominations (who move the stars and planets), Virtues (responsible for working miracles), Powers (who fight against evil), Principalities (who watch over whole countries), Archangels (messengers from God in significant matters), and Angels.[2] These heavenly hosts are referred to in each Mass in the preface to the Eucharistic Prayer.

Heaven is described as the place from which Christ came and to which he returned (cf. Matthew 3:16; Acts 2:2). It is also the ultimate home of the blessed who die in the Lord. Christians, after all, are citizens of heaven (cf. Philippians 3:20). We look forward to this home (cf. 2 Corinthians 5:1–5), this inheritance (cf. 1 Peter 1:4), this reward (cf. Matthew 5:12), and treasure (cf. Matthew 6:20; Colossians 1:5).

While heaven is not necessarily a geographic place, it is a state of complete and permanent happiness in which we will enjoy the beatific vision. In heaven we will know God firsthand as Father, Son, and Holy Spirit. Because of this union with God, we will know unending joy. A second reason for our joy will be our continuing knowledge and love of others with whom we had relationships during life. We join them, as well as the company of all the elect (Mary, the angels, and the saints), in a communion of one Spirit.

Hell

Traditionally, hell has been described as the kingdom of evil, which is ruled by the devil. Even a cursory look at today's world suggests the existence of such a kingdom. Daily in some part of the globe people are the victims of moral evils, such as famine due to war, death squads, and crime. We are also aware that within us there sometimes wages a personal battle between good (virtue) and evil (vice).

---

2. The Church celebrates the feast of the Archangels Michael, Gabriel, and Raphael on September 29.

Although belief in hell is not specifically included in either the Apostles' Creed or the Nicene Creed, the creedal statement that Christ will return to judge the living and the dead implies the existence of hell.[3] What is hell? It is the state of eternal separation from God. The Bible calls it "Gehenna." The name comes from an actual place southwest of Jerusalem that was formerly the site of a gentile cult that offered human sacrifice.

Jewish writings refer to Gehenna as a place of punishment and suffering after death. In the Christian Scriptures, it is a place of fire (cf. Matthew 5:22; 18:9; James 3:6) that is unquenchable (cf. Mark 9:43); a pit (cf. Matthew 5:29f; Mark 9:45,47; Luke 12:5) in which the wicked are annihilated (cf. Matthew 10:28); a place of eternal torment (cf. Matthew 18:8; 3:10,12; 7:19; Luke 3:9, 17) where the worms of decay never die (cf. Mark 9:48). Hell is a place of darkness (cf. Matthew 22:13; 25:30) where there will be continual weeping and gnashing of teeth (cf. Matthew 13:50; 24:51).[4]

Such descriptions of hell, figurative though they may be, seem hard to reconcile with Jesus' teaching about a God of love and mercy. That is why some Christians question whether hell really exists. But the Church teaches that hell is a real possibility because of human free will. Hell, basically, is eternal separation from God and participation in God's kingdom. During life, we can choose not to believe the gospel nor to accept God's love nor to follow Jesus' example. Likewise in death we can choose to reject God and communion with God's People. Hell, then, is not God's choice, but our own.

The Last Judgment

Catholic teaching has always held to a belief in two separate judgments—the particular judgment that takes place at the moment of death, and the Last Judgment that will take place at the end of the world. Belief in this second judgment is found both in the Apostles' Creed, which states, "He ascended into heaven and sits at the right hand of God, the Father Almighty. From thence he

---

3. An older translation of the Apostles' Creed says of Jesus that "he descended into hell." These words mean that Jesus truly died and remained dead for a short time. The new translation says of Jesus that "he descended to the dead"; thus, it renders more accurately the meaning of the Apostles' Creed in its original language, where Jesus is said to have gone to *Sheol* when he died. *Sheol* is the underworld, the realm of the dead; hell, the place of fire and eternal separation from God.

4. Throughout history, the devil has had many names: Satan, Beelzebub, the Anti-Christ, Lucifer, Belial, Old Gendy, Old Harry, Old Nick, Old Scratch, Serpent, Old Gooseberry, Apollyon, and Prince of Darkness.

shall come to judge the living and the dead," and in the Nicene Creed, which states, "He ascended into heaven and is seated at the right hand of the Father. He will come again in glory to judge the living and the dead, and his kingdom will have no end."

The Last Judgment is a general judgment at end of the world. It embraces all humans living and dead, good and bad, baptized and unbaptized. (It is unclear whether "living" refers to those who are spiritually alive or to those who are physically alive.) Sometimes this event is called the "judgment of God," because the Trinity passes judgment and achieves the completion of God's plan for creation. At other times, this event is called the "judgment of Christ," the parousia, or the Second Coming (cf. Matthew 16:27; 25:31; 24:30; 26:64). This judgment is Jesus' last and greatest act as Savior. In it, he completes the work assigned to him in the moment of his Incarnation. Finally, the Last Judgment is sometimes referred to as the apocalypse. At this event, God's entire plan of salvation will be revealed to us; God's kingdom will become a reality.

At the Last Judgment, two major tasks will be accomplished. The dead shall rise again to be reunited with their bodies, and God's kingdom will be established in its entirety and fullness. Although both of these events are considered mysteries, beyond human understanding, we can get a sense of what they will be like by looking at Scripture.

Resurrection of the Body. Those who are physically alive when the Last Judgment takes place will somehow be changed in accordance with their relationship to God. For them, particular judgment and final judgment are the same. But for all those who have died, the final judgment will mark a never-ending reunion of body and soul. As St. Paul tells the Philippians, "(Christ) will change our lowly body to conform with his glorified body by the power that enables him also to bring all things into subjection to himself" (Philippians 3:21).

Our bodies, Paul tells us, will be like the glorified body of Jesus. They will have splendor and will appear beautiful to behold (supernatural radiance or lucidity). They will have agility (the ability to move through space with the speed of thought), subtlety (the ability to pass through matter, just as Christ passed through the closed doors of the upper room), and impassibility (they will not suffer or age).

The Kingdom of God. At the Last Judgment, Christ will usher in his everlasting kingdom (cf. Matthew 16:28; Luke 1:33; 9:27). As a future reality that Christians are supposed to make their highest priority during life (cf. Matthew 6:33; Luke 12:31), the reign of God will become a full, present reality at the end of the world. Jesus describes this kingdom in many of his parables. Essentially, it is a kingdom of love, joy, peace, and justice.

The early Christians in the community of Thessalonica believed that the Last Judgment would happen in their lifetimes. They based their belief on prophecies that said the disciples would not finish their preaching before the Second Coming (cf. Matthew 10:23) and the present generation would not die before the Last Judgment (cf. Matthew 24:34; Mark 13:30; Luke 21:32; 1 Thessalonians 4:13ff; 1 Peter 4:7; Revelation 3:11; 22:20).

Biblical scholars have argued that such passages predict the fall of Jerusalem rather than the Last Judgment. They point instead to other Scripture passages in which Jesus warns that the Last Judgment will come without warning, like a thief in the night. As the parables of the wise and foolish virgins (cf. Matthew 25:1–13) and the talents (cf. Matthew 25:14–30) tell us, we should be prepared at all times to face judgment.

Celebrating belief in eternal life

The Church celebrates its belief in eternal life in many different ways. Among them are the solemnities of the Ascension of the Lord and the Assumption of Mary. Both of these feasts are holy days of obligation in the Church year. Here is a closer look at each of them.

The Ascension

This feast, which is observed forty days after Easter, commemorates the ascension of Christ into heaven with a glorified human nature (cf. Mark 16:19; Luke 24:51; Acts 1:1–11). Since the fifth century, the Church has celebrated the solemnity of the Ascension as a pledge that we too will be glorified at the Last Judgment.[5] This hope in our own resurrection is expressed in the opening prayer for the Mass of the day:

> *God our Father,*
> *make us joyful in the ascension of your Son Jesus Christ.*
> *May we follow him into the new creation,*
> *for his ascension is our glory and our hope.*
> *We ask this through our Lord Jesus Christ . . .*
> *Amen.*

---

5. The Church also celebrated the Ascension before the fifth century, but it was observed in connection with Easter and Pentecost.

The Scripture readings for the day are filled with allusions to the Last Judgment. Psalm 47 tells us that God will mount his throne amid shouts of joy and reign over all nations (cf. Psalm 47:6, 9). Jesus will sit at God's right hand, above every "principality, power, virtue, and domination" (cf. Ephesians 1:21). In the first reading, from the Acts of the Apostles, the disciples ask Jesus when they could expect God's kingdom to come. Jesus tells them that the time is not for them to know. Meanwhile, they are to be his "witnesses in Jerusalem, throughout Judaea and Samaria, and to the ends of the earth" (Acts 1:8) and know that he is with them "until the end of the world" (Matthew 28:20).

The Easter candle is lit at the Ascension liturgy, as it is at every liturgy during the Easter season, both as a reminder of Christ's resurrection and of the hope we have for our own resurrection from the dead. The Rite of Christian Initiation of Adults suggests that a celebration be held on this day for the neophytes (the newly baptized) and their godparents. In union with these new members, the Church prays that all may receive the gift of the beatific vision (cf. Ephesians 1:17–19).

The Assumption

The Assumption, which is observed on August 15, celebrates the taking into heaven of Mary—body and soul—at the end of her life on earth.[6] The feast was first celebrated in the sixth century in the East; Christians in the West began celebrating it in the seventh century. It was popularly known as the *Natale* (the falling asleep) or the Dormition of Mary. The Assumption was not actually proclaimed a dogma of the Church, however, until 1950.

The Assumption honors Mary for her role in salvation history. "She gave birth to a son, a male child, destined to rule all nations with an iron rod" (Revelation 12:5). The solemnity also honors Mary as the first disciple of Jesus, as someone who "trusted that the Lord's words to her would be fulfilled" (Luke 1:45). She is the first of Christ's followers to experience reunion of body and soul after death (cf. 1 Corinthians 15:22–23). The Assumption also gives witness to the hope of all Christians in the glory that awaits us at the Last Judgment. Thus the opening prayer of the Mass states:

> *All-powerful and ever-living God,*
> *you raised the sinless Virgin Mary,*
> *mother of your Son,*

---

6. Our Lady of the Assumption is the patron saint of France, India, Malta, Paraguay, and South Africa.

body and soul to the glory of heaven.
May we see heaven as our final goal
and come to share her glory.
We ask this through our Lord Jesus Christ, your Son,
who lives and reigns with you and the Holy Spirit,
one God, for ever and ever.
Amen.

Since ancient times, it has been a custom in the Church to bless the produce of fields, gardens, and orchards on the feast of the Assumption. Just as the harvest is a time of reaping the seeds sown by human hands, so the Last Judgment is seen as a time when God reaps the fullness of Christ's kingdom. "Then your people, enriched by the gifts of your goodness, will praise you unceasingly now and for ages unending" (*Order of Blessings*, p. 360).[7]

A life of virtue

In almost every time in history, some preachers have used the afterlife to motivate people to live good Christian lives. These preachers quote biblical verses describing the excruciating torments of hell in what are referred to as "fire and brimstone" sermons. Such sermons are intended to put the "fear of God" into people so that they persevere in virtue rather than vice.

The logic is the same as the arguments used by retributionists, who favor capital punishment. Just as the death penalty is thought to deter crime, so the fear of eternal punishment is thought to deter sin. There is a big problem, however, with using hell in this way. Such motivation, even if it works, keeps people at an infantile stage of spiritual development. They never really "grow up" as Christians.

To understand this better, think about your own life and your motives for doing good. When you were a small child, you most likely kept a family rule or obeyed your parents because you knew you would get a spanking or be sent to your room if you didn't. You were motivated by something outside yourself: the pain of punishment. You didn't do the good action because you valued it as good. You did it simply because you wanted to avoid punishment.

Think again about your childhood. If your parents were always consistent in punishing you when you did something bad, then you probably stopped doing the bad thing. But if your parents

---

7. Another custom on the solemnity of the Assumption has been the blessing of harbors and fishing boats. This custom is still observed today by the Portuguese Catholics in New England.

were like most parents, they probably slipped up now or then, or didn't always catch you "in the act." You learned that sometimes you could get away with acting bad. So what did you do? If the punishment was the only thing motivating you, you probably kept right on doing bad. And you saw your parents mostly as disciplinarians, as the dispensers of punishment. You probably feared them; you may even have hated them at times.

As you grew older, you probably were motivated to do good in order to get a reward. You may have done your chores in order to get an allowance. Or you may have worked hard in school because you wanted your parents to praise you when they saw your report card.

This second motivation is definitely more mature than acting out of fear of punishment. That is why some religious educators and homilists have stopped talking about hell and, instead, have capitalized on the wonders of heaven. They try to use future union with God and eternal life as the motivating force for living a virtuous life now.

The problem with this approach is that it still leaves people at an infantile stage of spiritual development. The motivation for following the gospel remains on the outside, in the future. Heaven becomes something we "earn," and God is a distant Boss. We still haven't grown up spiritually.

The change from childhood to adulthood is not just physical; it is a moral change as well. What this means is that our adult selves are no longer motivated to do good solely because we fear punishment or desire a reward. We have somehow internalized what it means to be virtuous, and we choose to do good, regardless of whether others know about it or not.

This internalization of Christian virtues is what following Jesus is all about. Mature Christians choose to keep the Ten Commandments and to live the Beatitudes because such actions are good in themselves. Furthermore, they are part of an ongoing and dynamic relationship with God. Such actions express personal identity: friendship with Jesus and membership in the people of God.

So what does this all mean in practical terms? St. Paul spells it out to the Galatians in this way: When we live in the Spirit, we act with "love, joy, peace, patience, kindness, generosity, faithfulness, gentleness, and self control" (Galatians 5:22). These virtues make up the kingdom of God—not just the kingdom of God that will come in completeness at the end of time, but the kingdom of God that is already taking shape within us (cf. Luke 17:20). For this reason, St. Paul urges us to put aside the motivation of childhood morality and to mature spiritually (cf. 1 Corinthians 13:1–11).

For your journal

1. What are your feelings about being judged after death? Do you find judgment to be scary or is it comforting?

2. If you were to die one minute from now, how do you think you would be judged?

3. When have you been the happiest? Describe what prompted the happiness and what being happy felt like. How long did your feelings of happiness last?

4. In your own words, try to describe what you think it would be like to be completely and permanently happy.

5. Have you ever felt the struggle between good and evil within you? Describe a specific example of this struggle and which side "won."

6. What are some examples from your childhood of decisions you made that were based on fear of punishment?

7. How consistent were your parents in carrying out their threats of punishment?

8. On a scale of 1 to 10, how much of the gospel message do you think you have internalized? How much of your moral behavior is still motivated by external influences (fear of punishment or desire for approval)?

9. Suppose there were no heaven or hell. Would that make a difference in the way you choose to live? Why or why not?

Discussion questions

1. Have you ever had a deja vu experience? Describe the feeling.

2. Have you ever had an "out of the body" experience? Do you know someone who has had such an experience?

3. Do you know anyone who was "clinically dead" and then revived? What did the person tell you about his or her experience?

4. Do you think a person who lost a parent at a young age and then lived a full life will be younger, older, or the same age as the parent in the afterlife?

5. Do you think the resurrected body of those with mental disabilities or those who are paraplegic will be made whole in heaven?

6. What are the similarities and differences between the following concepts: resurrection of the soul, resurrection of the body, resurrection of the just, and resurrection of all people?

7. Whom do people judge more harshly: themselves or others? Do you think it's harder or easier to forgive yourself than to forgive someone else?

8. What are some examples of evil in the world today?

9. Do you think there is more evil now, or less evil, than there was five years ago?

10. Do you think there is more evil now, or less evil, than there was five centuries ago?

11. How can Mary be a role model for today's Catholics?

12. What songs do you think would be appropriate for Mass on the feast of the Assumption?

13. How were you punished as a child when you did something bad? Was the punishment effective in stopping your behavior? How did the punishment affect your attitude toward your parents?

14. How were you rewarded as a child when you did something good?

15. "Virtue is its own reward." What do you think this saying means? Give examples if possible.

16. You have learned in this book that we die as we have lived. Debate whether we can find happiness in the afterlife if we have not been happy in this life.

16 From Death to Life: Catholic Rituals

Celebrating new life

Throughout this book, you have looked at death from many different perspectives—philosophical, historical, cultural, psychological, social, financial/legal, moral, and religious. You have seen how belief in life after death has permeated almost all cultures. And yet you have also seen how no proof can be offered for the existence of such an afterlife. Belief in the resurrection remains simply that: a matter of faith.

And yet it is this belief—both in the resurrection of Jesus and in our own resurrection at the end of time—that remains the cornerstone of Christianity. "Christ has died, Christ is risen, Christ will come again," is proclaimed by millions of Catholics throughout the world at each Eucharist. Our belief is so strong that it must be celebrated.

In this chapter, you will explore some of the Catholic rituals that celebrate the passing from death to life. You will look first at the liturgies of the Easter Triduum and then at the *Order of Christian Funerals*. Finally, you will look at the Church's Rite of Baptism and spend time planning your own funeral liturgy.

The Easter Triduum

The Church's main celebration of the Paschal Mystery is three days, not one. The Easter Triduum, which begins at evening Mass on Holy Thursday and ends with evening prayer on Easter Sunday, celebrates the Passover of Christ from death to new life. It is simplistic to say that Holy Thursday celebrates the Last Supper of Jesus and the institution of the Eucharist or that Good Friday commemorates Jesus' dying on a cross or that Easter Sunday celebrates his rising from the tomb. Each liturgy of the Easter Triduum celebrates the entire Passover event: Christ's dying and rising, as well as the promise of our own dying and rising. It is within this context of the whole that the Church focuses on particular moments during the Easter Triduum.

Holy Thursday

The first moment of the Easter Triduum is the Mass of the Lord's Supper, which is celebrated in the evening on Holy Thursday.[1] We remember Jesus' self-sacrifice so that we could have new life, and we give thanks in the Eucharistic meal of love. Both of these sentiments are found in the opening prayer:

God our Father,
we are gathered here to share in the supper
which your only Son left to his Church to reveal his love.
He gave it to us when he was about to die
and commanded us to celebrate it as the new and eternal sacrifice.
We pray that in this eucharist
we may find the fullness of love and life. . . .
Amen.[2]

The Scripture readings remind us that the Eucharist is rooted in the Exodus experience of the Israelites, who were set free from slavery in Egypt and given a new life in the Promised Land. The readings recount how the angel of death passed over the houses of the Israelites as they were preparing to leave Egypt and how the angel struck instead the houses of the Egyptians.

After the homily, people representing a cross section of the community have their feet washed. In this symbolic action we remember that we are to give our lives in selfless service of others, just as Jesus did.

As the prayer after communion expresses, the sacred bread and wine we share is a foretaste of the heavenly banquet.

Almighty God,
we receive new life
from the supper your Son gave us in this world.
May we find full contentment
in the meal we hope to share
in your eternal kingdom. . . .
Amen.

---

1. During the singing of the Gloria on Holy Thursday, the church bells are rung. They remain silent until the Gloria at the Easter Vigil. This ancient custom marks the solemnity of the passion and death of Jesus, as well as the joy of the resurrection.

2. This prayer and all the other prayers from the celebrations of the Church used in this chapter, unless otherwise noted, are taken from the English translation of *The Roman Missal.*

Following this prayer, the Holy Eucharist is transferred to another location, to an altar of repose. The ciborium of consecrated hosts is carried through the church in procession while the people sing the *"Pange Lingua."* Adoration of the Blessed Sacrament continues at the altar of repose until midnight. Meanwhile, the main altar is stripped. All crosses in the church are removed or covered.

Good Friday

Good Friday (the celebration especially of the Lord's passion and death) is the only day of the year in which the sacraments are not celebrated.[3] The liturgy of Good Friday is not a Mass, but rather a communion service that consists of three parts: the liturgy of the word, the veneration of the cross, and Holy Communion.

The Scripture readings present Jesus as Isaiah's suffering servant, as one who "learned obedience from what he suffered" and thus became "the source of eternal salvation for all who obey him" (Hebrews 4:9). The passion account presents Jesus as the king of a heavenly kingdom that is greater than any earthly one. The liturgy of the word concludes with prayers of intercession for the Church, the pope, the clergy and laity, those preparing for baptism, the unity of all Christians, the Jewish people, non-Christians, atheists, all in public office, and those in need.

During the veneration of the cross, people are asked to show reverence to a cross that is unveiled. After all have had a chance to venerate the cross—either individually or collectively by kissing it, genuflecting, bowing, or the like—the communion service begins with the Lord's Prayer. The bread that is used for Communion was consecrated on Holy Thursday. The prayer after communion recalls not only Christ's death, but also his resurrection and our own restoration to life.

At the conclusion of the service, all depart in silence. The altar is stripped; only the cross remains, with four candles.

Holy Saturday

To commemorate the time Jesus spent in the tomb, the Church spends this day in prayer and meditation. No Mass is celebrated. Communion is given only as Viaticum. The altar is left bare throughout the day.[4]

---

3. The Church asks Christians to fast and abstain from meat on Good Friday to honor the suffering and death of Jesus and to enter more deeply into the experience of his dying and rising.

4. On Holy Saturday, Mexican Americans have a custom of blessing the animals—dogs, pigeons, parakeets, turtles, cats, roosters. It may be an adaptation of the Roman custom of blessing animals to encourage fertility, a rite that took place in early April when homage was paid to Venus, the goddess of love.

Easter

The liturgy of Easter Sunday begins after dark on Saturday with the celebration of the Easter Vigil. This service has four parts: the service of light, the liturgy of the word, the liturgy of baptism, and the liturgy of the Eucharist. The symbols and actions of the Easter Vigil attest to the Church's belief in the resurrection and serve as a climax to the Triduum and as the focal point of the entire Church year.

The Service of Light. The liturgy begins in darkness, reminiscent of the darkness of the tomb. Outside the church, the priest and ministers light the new fire, saying:

Dear friends in Christ,
on this most holy night,
when our Lord Jesus Christ passed from death to life,
the Church invites her children throughout the world
to come together in vigil and prayer.
This is the passover of the Lord:
if we honor the memory of his death and resurrection
by hearing his word and celebrating his mysteries,
then we may be confident
that we shall share his victory over death
and live with him for ever in God.

The Easter candle is then lit from this fire and taken in procession into the church. All the people light their smaller candles from the Easter candle (if local fire regulations allow it). The Proclamation that is sung calls on the choirs of angels and all creation to praise the risen Christ.

Liturgy of the Word. Nine readings may be read—seven from the Hebrew Scriptures and two from the Christian Scriptures. These readings recall how God saved people throughout history and then finally sent a redeemer. Each reading is accompanied by a responsorial psalm and prayer. For pastoral reasons, the number of Hebrew Scripture readings may be reduced; however the reading from Exodus must always be used. After the last reading from the Hebrew Scriptures, the Gloria is sung while the church bells are rung. The liturgy of the word then proceeds as usual, with the epistle reading, alleluia, Gospel, and homily.

Liturgy of Baptism. Throughout Lent, the catechumens who have been "elected" to Church membership prepare for baptism. This baptism takes place at the Easter Vigil. The rite begins with the singing of the Litany of the Saints, which asks all the saints of heaven to pray for the Church and for these new members. The priest then blesses the water by lowering the Easter candle into it and saying:

> *May all who are buried with Christ*
> *in the death of baptism*
> *rise also with him to newness of life.*

He then baptizes all the candidates. Adult neophytes are confirmed immediately if a priest with the faculty to confirm or a bishop is present. The Rite of Baptism concludes by a renewal of baptismal promises by the entire community. All baptized Catholics once again promise to reject Satan and his works, and to believe all that the Church teaches, including the resurrection of the body and life everlasting. This renewal takes the place of the Creed.

Liturgy of the Eucharist. After the Rite of Baptism, the liturgy continues in the same way as all Masses. The prayer over the gifts alludes to the coming of God's kingdom at the end of time:

> *Lord,*
> *accept the prayers and offerings of your people.*
> *With our help may this Easter mystery of our redemption*
> *bring to perfection the saving work you have begun in us.*

According to custom, food may be blessed either before or after the Easter Vigil service or on Easter Sunday morning for consumption at the family's Easter meal. This custom arose from the traditional Lenten fast. Easter was the first day when meat, eggs, and other foods could be eaten again. The prayer of blessing, which may be given by a priest, deacon, or lay person, is as follows:

> *God of glory,*
> *the eyes of all turn to you*
> *as we celebrate Christ's victory over sin and death.*
> *Bless us and this food of our first Easter meal.*
> *May we who gather at the Lord's table*
> *continue to celebrate the joy of his resurrection*
> *and be admitted finally to his heavenly banquet. . . .*
> *Amen.*[5]

---

5. International Committee on English in the Liturgy, *Book of Blessings*, p. 641.

The custom of blessing food is especially prevalent among Polish Americans and the Croatian-Slovenian community. Favorite Easter foods among these cultures include ham, homemade sausage, *potica* (a crescent-shaped pastry filled with nuts and spices), *nadev* (a pig's stomach stuffed with meat; it's something like salami), hard-boiled eggs, yeast bread, and cake shaped as a lamb.

Order of Christian Funerals

Since All Souls' Day, 1989, the *Order of Christian Funerals* has been mandatory in the United States. This order contains the liturgies approved by the Church for celebrating the death of Catholics. As directed by Vatican II, these revised funeral rites clearly express the paschal character of a Christian's death. All three rites—the vigil service, the funeral liturgy, and the rite of committal—confidently proclaim "that God has created each person for eternal life and that Jesus, the Son of God, by his death and resurrection, has broken the chains of sin and death that bound humanity."[6]

The vigil service

The vigil service is celebrated by the family and Christian community sometime after death and before the funeral liturgy. A priest, deacon, or lay person (in the absence of a priest or deacon) presides. The *Order* includes two types of services: the vigil for the deceased (to be used when the vigil is celebrated at the home of the deceased, in a funeral home, or in some other suitable place) and the vigil for the deceased with reception at the church (to be used when the vigil is celebrated in church). Both types of vigil services consist of introductory rites, the liturgy of the word, intercessory prayers, and a concluding rite.

Introductory Rites. The purpose of these rites is to gather the community and prepare all to listen to God's word. In the vigil for the deceased, the introductory rites include a greeting by the presider, an opening song that expresses belief in eternal life, an invitation to prayer, and an opening prayer. In the vigil with reception at the church, the presider greets the family at the entrance of the church, sprinkles the casket with holy water, and spreads the pall over the casket. An opening song is sung as the family and casket process into church. Then an invitation to prayer and an opening prayer follow.

---

6. International Committee on English in the Liturgy, *Order of Christian Funerals*, #1.

Liturgy of the Word. This part of the service consists of a Scripture reading, a responsorial psalm (preferably sung), a Gospel reading, and homily. As the *Order* makes clear, the purpose of the liturgy of the word is "to proclaim the paschal mystery, teach remembrance of the dead, convey the hope of being gathered together in God's kingdom, and encourage the witness of Christian life."[7]

Prayers of Intercession. The community prays to God to have mercy on the deceased person. It does this first in a litany, to which people respond, "Lord, have mercy." After everyone prays the Lord's Prayer, the presider says a concluding prayer. At this time, a member or friend of the family may speak in remembrance of the deceased.

Concluding Rite. The vigil ends with a blessing and may be followed by a closing song.

The Church encourages mourners to have a vigil service, rather than a simple wake. Members of the local parish are encouraged to attend the vigil to show concern and support for the mourners, and thus take part in the Church's ministry of consolation. In addition, parishioners are encouraged to participate fully in the prayers and songs of the vigil service.[8]

The funeral liturgy

For hundreds of years, the priest wore black vestments at funeral liturgies. The color black emphasized mourning for death, but did little to symbolize the joy of resurrection. In 1970, the United States Bishops' Committee on the Liturgy allowed white vestments to be worn for funeral liturgies, besides purple or black.

The *Order of Christian Funerals* provides two forms of liturgies: the funeral Mass (which is preferred) and the funeral liturgy outside Mass. The main parts of the funeral Mass are the reception of the body, the liturgy of the word, the liturgy of the Eucharist, and the final commendation and farewell.[9] The funeral liturgy outside Mass has the same structure, except for the liturgy of the Eucharist.

---

7. *Order of Christian Funerals,* #60.

8. In addition to the vigil service, the Church provides three brief rites that may be used on occasions of prayer with the family before the funeral. These rites are to be used after death, when the family gathers in the presence of the body, and when the body is transferred to the church or place of committal.

9. For centuries, the funeral Mass was called a Requiem Mass because of the first Latin word of the Introit, which translated as "Eternal rest grant unto them, O Lord." Despite the new emphasis on the resurrection, the "Mass of the Resurrection" is an incorrect title for a funeral Mass and is reserved only for the Easter liturgy itself.

Reception at the Church. The funeral Mass begins at the entrance of the church, where the priest and family members welcome the casket.

The reason for gathering at church is given as follows:

Since the church is the place where the community of faith assembles for worship, the rite of reception of the body at the church has great significance. The church is the place where the Christian life is begotten in baptism, nourished in the eucharist, and where the community gathers to commend one of its deceased members to the Father. The church is at once a symbol of the community and of the heavenly liturgy that the celebration of the liturgy anticipates.[10]

The priest begins by greeting the family members. Then he sprinkles the casket with holy water in remembrance of the deceased person's baptism. Family members then help to place the funeral pall over the coffin. This white cloth is a reminder of the garment given at baptism. After the pall is in place, the priest and altar servers lead the entrance procession. The casket, with pall-bearers and family members, follows. During the procession, a song is sung by the assembly.

The casket is positioned in the center aisle near the lit Easter candle, another symbol of the deceased person's baptism. Family members may choose to put another symbol of the Christian life (a Bible, a cross, or a Book of the Gospels) on the casket. After this has been completed, the priest prays an opening prayer.

Liturgy of the Word. This essential ingredient in the funeral celebration has the same structure as that found in other Masses. The first reading, either from the Hebrew Scriptures or the Christian Scriptures, is followed by a sung responsorial psalm. The second reading is optional. A sung Gospel acclamation precedes the Gospel reading and the homily. The *Order* clearly states that the homily should "dwell on God's compassionate love and on the paschal mystery of the Lord as proclaimed in the Scripture readings" rather than be a eulogy. In the general intercessions, the community prays for the deceased and his or her family members, as well as the needs of the entire community.

Liturgy of the Eucharist. Members of the family are encouraged to bring the gifts to the altar while a presentation song is sung. The structure of this part of the Mass remains unchanged, with the exception that the priest may incense the gifts and altar, and family members may speak in remembrance of the deceased after communion.

---

10. *Order of Christian Funerals*, #131.

Final Commendation and Farewell. This part of the liturgy is both an acknowledgement of separation from the deceased and an affirmation that all will be reunited at the resurrection on the last day. The priest invites everyone to pray in silence. Then he incenses the casket and sprinkles it with holy water (if this was not done at the beginning of Mass). After a song of farewell is sung, the priest says a prayer of commendation, such as:

> *Into your hands, Father of mercies,*
> *we commend our brother/sister N.*
> *in the sure and certain hope*
> *that, together with all who have died in Christ*
> *he/she will rise with him on the last day.*
> *Merciful Lord, turn toward us and listen to our prayers:*
> *open the gates of paradise to your servant*
> *and help us who remain*
> *to comfort one another with assurances of faith,*
> *until we all meet in Christ*
> *and are with you and with our brother/sister for ever.*
> *We ask this through Christ our Lord.*
> *Amen.*[11]

The priest and servers, casket and pallbearers, and family members then process out of church in the same order as before. At this time, a closing song is sung by the assembly.

Rite of committal

This part of the funeral liturgy may be celebrated at the grave, mausoleum, crematorium, or at sea (in the case of water burial). The *Order* provides two forms for this rite. The rite of committal is used when the final commendation was already included in the funeral liturgy. The rite of committal with final commendation is used when there was no funeral liturgy or no commendation during the funeral liturgy.

The structure of both forms is simple. Both begin with an invitation to prayer, a Scripture verse, and a prayer over the place of committal. The prayer has several options, depending on whether the body will be entombed, cremated, or buried at sea.

---

11. *Order of Christian Funerals*, "Prayer of Commendation A" from the Funeral Mass.

The words of committal express the community's beliefs regarding death. "Through this act the community of faith proclaims that the grave or place of interment, once a sign of futility and despair, has been transformed by means of Christ's own death and resurrection into a sign of hope and promise."[12]

After the committal, the people are invited to join in the intercessory prayers and the Lord's Prayer. Following the concluding prayer, the priest says a prayer over the people and blesses them. During the closing song, people may place flowers or soil on the casket.

The Rite of Baptism

The Church's liturgies of Easter and Christian funerals reflect an earlier celebration: that of baptism. In his letter to the Romans, St. Paul explains the importance of baptism and its connection to death and resurrection:

Are you unaware that we who were baptized into Christ Jesus were baptized into his death? We were indeed buried with him though baptism into death, so that, just as Christ was raised from the dead by the glory of the Father, we too might live in newness of life.

—*Romans 6:3–4*

Currently the Church has two concurrent practices regarding the reception of new members: the Baptism of Infants and Children, and the Rite of Christian Initiation of Adults (RCIA). Both rites celebrate death and rising to new life—dying to sin and rising to new life with Christ.

Regardless of which rite is followed, the following parts are included at some point: liturgy of the word, prayers of intercession, prayer of exorcism, blessing of water, renunciation of sin and profession of faith, baptism with water, anointing with chrism, clothing with white garment, receiving the lighted candle, prayer over ears and mouth, and a conclusion. Here is a brief look at what happens in each part, as well as its meaning.

Liturgy of the Word. Because God's word gives us life and is essential to Christian living, the Church recommends that baptisms take place during Mass. If not, a liturgy of the word should be part of the baptismal rite. This liturgy includes one or two Scripture readings, especially a reading from the Gospels. This is followed by a short homily, prayers of intercession, and the Litany of the Saints.

---

12. *Order of Christian Funerals*, #209.

Exorcism. In this prayer the community prays that the person will be delivered from Original Sin and all personal sins. (In the RCIA, rites of exorcism take place during Lent.) This is followed by an anointing with the Oil of Catechumens, either on the breast or the hands. The oil is a symbol of the wisdom, strength, and protection that Christ brings to the baptismal candidate by the anointing.

Profession of Faith. After he blesses the water, the priest invites the candidate (or in the case of babies, the godparents and parents) to promise to reject Satan and to make a profession of faith.[13] This profession, which is based on the Apostles' Creed, states belief in the resurrection, ascension, and Second Coming of Jesus, as well as the resurrection of the body and life everlasting.

Baptism. The actual baptism may be performed in one of two ways—immersion of the whole body or of the head only, or by infusion, the pouring of water over the head of the candidate. As this action is taking place, the priest says "N., I baptize you in the name of the Father, and of the Son, and of the Holy Spirit."

Post-Baptismal Rites. Immediately after baptism, the person (who is now called a neophyte) is anointed with chrism. This holy oil, which is also used at confirmation and holy orders, is a sign that the newly baptized shares in the priesthood of Christ and is a member of the People of God. The neophyte is then given a white robe (a symbol of his or her new life in Christ) and a candle that has been lit from the Easter candle (a symbol of the light of faith).

Opening of Ears and Mouth. The word *ephphetha* means "Be opened." The priest touches the person's ears and mouth, and prays that the person will receive the grace needed to hear the word of God and to work for salvation. (This rite occurs during Lent in the RCIA.)

Conclusion. The conclusion of the rite includes the Lord's Prayer and a prayer of blessing for the new Christian.

In recent times, the Church has come to recognize a "baptism of desire" as well as the realized celebration of the Sacrament of Baptism. For this reason the Church allows catechumens and infants who die before baptism to have an ecclesiastical funeral and burial.

---

13. In order to be a godparent, three requirements must be met: (1) The person must be mature enough to undertake this responsibility; (2) The person must have received baptism, confirmation, and Eucharist; and (3) The person must be a baptized member of the Catholic Church.

Planning your funeral

Before putting this book down, take some time to choose readings for your funeral liturgy. Pray over each reading; then select one in each section that best expresses your own faith and the "message" you want to leave for the ones you love.

First Reading

____ Job 19:1, 23–27

____ Wisdom 3:1–9

____ Wisdom 3:1–6, 9

____ Wisdom 4:7–15

____ Isaiah 25:6a,7–9

____ Lamentations 3:17–26

____ Daniel 12:1–3

____ 2 Maccabees 12:43–46

Second Reading

____ Acts 10:34–43

____ Acts 10:34–36, 42–43

____ Romans 5:5–11

____ Romans 5:17–21

____ Romans 6:3–9

____ Romans 6:3–4, 8–9

____ Romans 8:14–23

____ Romans 8:31b–35, 37–39

____ Romans 14:7–9, 10b–12

____ 1 Corinthians 15:20–23, 24b–28

____ 1 Corinthians 15:20–23

____ 1 Corinthians 15:51–57

____ 2 Corinthians 4:14—5:1.

____ 2 Corinthians 5:1, 6–10

____ Philippians 3:20–21

____ 1 Thessalonians 4:13–18

____ 2 Timothy 2:8–13

____ 1 John 3:1–2

____ 1 John 3:14–16

____ Revelation 14:13

____ Revelation 20:11—21:1

____ Revelation 21:1–5a, 6b–7

Responsorial Psalm

____ Psalm 23

____ Psalm 25

____ Psalm 27

____ Psalm 42 and 43

____ Psalm 63

____ Psalm 103

____ Psalm 116

____ Psalm 122

____ Psalm 130

____ Psalm 143

Gospel Acclamation

____ Matthew 11:25

____ Matthew 25:34

____ John 3:16

____ John 6:39

____ John 6:40

____ John 6:51a

____ John 11:25–26

____ Philippians 3:20

____ 2 Timothy 2:11b–12a

____ Revelation 1:5a,6b

____ Revelation 14:13

Gospel Reading

____ Matthew 5:1–12a	____ John 5:24–29
____ Matthew 11:25–30	____ John 6:37–40
____ Matthew 25:1–13	____ John 6:51–58
____ Matthew 25:31–46	____ John 11:17–27
____ Mark 15:33–39; 16:1–6	____ John 11:21–27
____ Mark 15:33–39	____ John 11:32–45
____ Luke 7:11–17	____ John 12:23–28
____ Luke 12:35–40	____ John 12:23–26
____ Luke 23:33,39–43	____ John 14:1–6
____ Luke 23:44–46,50, 52–53; 24:1–6a	____ John 17:24–26
____ Luke 23:44–46, 50, 52–53	____ John 19:17–18, 25–30
____ Luke 24:13–35	____ Luke 24:13–35
____ Luke 24:13–16, 28–35	

Now take the time to fill in the following outline for your vigil service, funeral, and rite of committal. After writing down your choice of readings and songs, make sure to give a copy to family members and/or close friends or put a copy in your "In Case of Death" file. Planning these services now can help to console the loved ones you leave behind; your choices can also be a beautiful symbol of your life, your beliefs, and your bonds with others.

My choice of readings and songs

Vigil Service

Opening Song:

First Reading:

Responsorial Psalm:

Gospel Acclamation:

Gospel:

Closing Song:

Funeral Liturgy

Choice of Christian symbol for placing on the casket:

Entrance Song:

First Reading:

Responsorial Psalm:

Second Reading:

Gospel Acclamation:

Gospel:

Song during presentation of gifts:

Holy, Holy, Holy:

Memorial Acclamation:

Great Amen:

Lamb of God:

Communion Song:

Closing Song:

Rite of Committal

Scripture Verse (select 1 of the following):

____ Matthew 25:34   ____Philippians 3:20

____ John 6:39   ____ Revelation 1:5–6

Concluding Song:

For your journal

Take a moment to think about all that you have learned about death and new life in this book. Then write your own reflections on each of the following symbols used by Christians to celebrate the passing from death to new life: cross, water, sacrificed lamb, poured out wine, broken bread, lighted candle, white garment, spring flowers, eggs. Which symbol speaks most clearly to you? Why?

Discussion questions

1. At every Mass, we say or sing an antiphon called "The Lamb of God." Discuss the Passover imagery in ascribing this title to Jesus. How are we called to be "lambs of God" in our own lives?

2. How can Jesus' passion and death give meaning to someone who is suffering from serious sickness or a terminal condition?

3. Why do you think the Church prays for the following groups of people on Good Friday: the Jewish people? those of other religious beliefs? atheists?

4. What are the similarities between the symbols found in the funeral liturgy and those found in the Easter Vigil service?

5. What do you think incense symbolizes?

6. What are some songs that would be appropriate for a funeral Mass?

7. Do you think it is important for friends of the family to attend the vigil service, the funeral, and the rite of committal? Why or why not?

8. What are some appropriate songs to sing at the place of interment?

Acknowledgments